16.40.

CANADIANS IN RUSSIA, 1918-1919

FOR ALETHEA

ROY MAC LAREN

Canadians in Russia, 1918-1919

Macmillan of Canada
Maclean-Hunter Press

© The Macmillan Company of Canada Limited, 1976

ISBN 0-7705-1339-5

This book has been published with the help of a grant
from the Social Science Research Council of Canada,
using funds provided by the Canada Council.

Printed in Canada for
The Macmillan Company of Canada Limited
70 Bond Street
Toronto, M5B 1X3

Contents

Preface

My father, the late Wilbur MacLaren, was badly wounded at
Passchendaele during the First World War while serving in a
Prince Edward Island heavy-artillery battery. Years later he
mentioned to me that a gunner from his battery had gone with
the Canadians to northern Russia in 1918. My father's chance
recollection intrigued me, for I had never heard of Canadian
soldiers participating in the Allied intervention in the Russian
civil war. I did not inquire further into this unlikely episode until
a friend happened to remark that a squadron of Royal North
West Mounted Police had been sent to Siberia in 1918. This
struck me as a bizarre contribution for Canada to make to the
Allied intervention. I determined then to learn everything I
could about why Canada involved itself in the intervention—an
undertaking apparently remote from this country's wartime and
immediate post-war interests. The result is this book.

This is not a book about the Russian civil war, nor is it about
the Allied intervention in general. Rather, it is an attempt to
describe why and how Canada became involved. It tells how
decisions were made in London and Ottawa that resulted in
Canadian troops and government officials going to Russia
during the civil war. It also attempts to convey something of how
it must have felt to be sent to Russia at that time, whether as

a general commanding an infantry brigade in Siberia or as a frost-bitten gunner in northern Russia fighting off persistent Bolshevik attacks. So the book has a dual purpose: to explain why certain decisions were made at the centre and to describe what it was like down the line when the time came to try to implement those decisions, which were frequently rash and almost always based on inadequate information.

In my research, I have been fortunate to have had the assistance of the always courteous staff of the Public Archives of Canada, and also the help and guidance of a number of men who participated in the Canadian intervention. I am indebted to the late Dana Wilgress, Thomas Morrisey, and John Hundevad, and to Raymond Collishaw, Gordon Hopkins, Roy East, A. A. Outram, William Bradshaw, Dick Schiller, Dennis Stairs, and W. G. MacDonald for sharing with me their personal recollections of the intervention. Mrs. Erskine Ireland and the late Mrs. James McIntosh Bell kindly made their late husbands' papers available to me, and W. Thompson his father's collection of photographs. Nina Elmsley lent me a photograph of her father and Mabel Sharman one of her husband. Anne Beatty, Evelyn Jennings, and Pat Macior typed and re-typed the manuscript until they must know it better thn I do; to them I am grateful for their patience, willingness, and good humour. I also wish to record my gratitude to Tom Fairley, who was of the greatest assistance in the organization and editing of the manuscript. Finally, my wife, Alethea, and our children have been constantly encouraging and supportive.

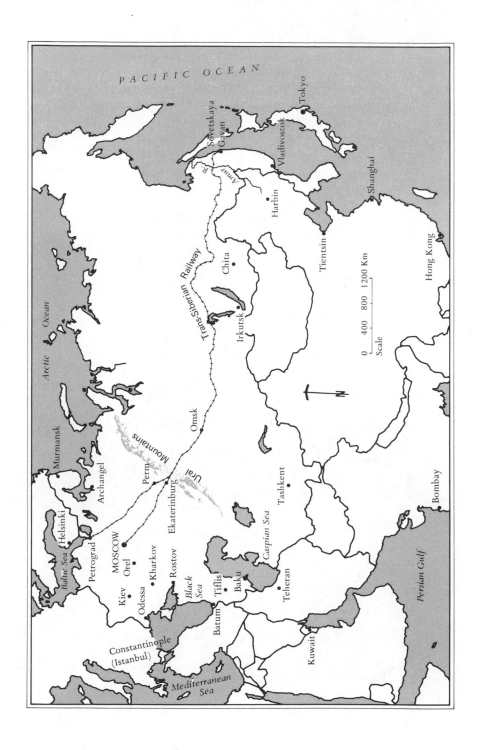

PACIFIC OCEAN

Tokyo

Sovetskaya
Gavan

Vladivostok

Shanghai

Harbin

Hong Kong

Tientsin

Chita

800 1200 Km

400

0
Scale

Irkutsk

N

Omsk

Mountains

Ural

Tashkent

Bombay

Perm

Archangel

Ekaterinburg

Caspian Sea

Murmansk

Arctic Ocean

Helsinki

MOSCOW
Orel

Kharkov

Rostov

Tiflis

Baku

Teheran

Persian Gulf

Petrograd

Baltic Sea

Kiev

Odessa

Black
Sea

Batum

Kuwait

Constantinople
(Istanbul)

Mediterranean
Sea

Trans-Siberian Railway

R. Amur

White Sea

• Archangel

Helsinki

Petrograd

• MOSCOW

Orel

Kiev

Kharkov

Ukraine

Don River

Volga River

Czaritsyn (Volgagrad)

Taganrog

Odessa

Perekop

Rostov

Sea of Azov

Crimea

Djankoi

• Ekaterinodar

Novorossiisk

Sevastopol

Simferopol

Caucasus Mountains

Turkestan

CASPIAN SEA

BLACK SEA

Batum

Georgia

Tiflis

Azerbaijan

Baku

Krasnovodsk

Aïmenia

Turkey

Kurdistan

Tabriz

Enzeli

Mosul

Kasvin •

• Teheran

• Hamadan

• Kermanshah

Persia

Baghdad

Tigris

River

Mediterranean Sea

Mesopotamia

0   200   400 Km

Scale

Basra

Kuwait •

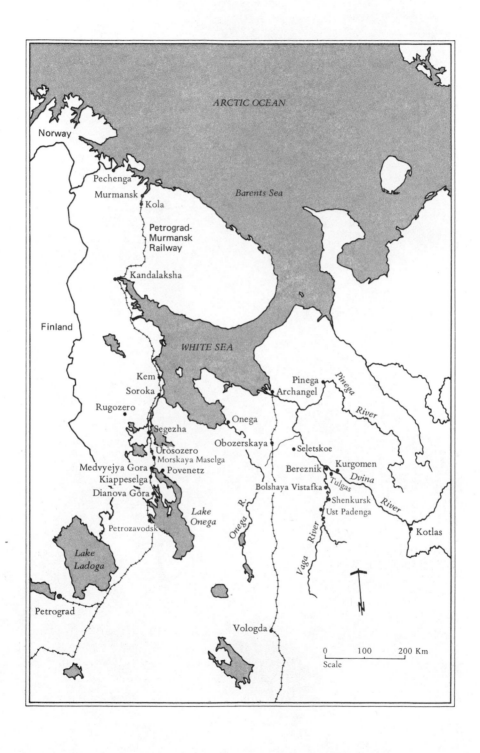

CANADIANS IN RUSSIA, 1918-1919

Introduction

Throughout the nineteenth century, the policies of Russia were of prime concern to other European nations. By 1917, the Russian Empire was the sick man of Europe. Political developments there were viewed increasingly in Britain and France as factors in their own security, perhaps even in their survival. However ineffective Russia's huge, ill-equipped armies had been in the Great War against the Central Powers, they did tie down scores of German and Austrian divisions that might otherwise have been used to tip the balance on the Western Front. There was no doubt among Allied strategists that, without the Eastern Front, victory was virtually unthinkable.

In 1917, the German submarine offensive, the Allies' lack of reinforcements, the costly failure to achieve a decisive breakthrough on the Western Front, and the delay in the arrival of the Americans combined to create a critical situation—one in which the growing shakiness of the Russian war effort was a nightmare for the Allies. No single German victory could be worse to contemplate than the disintegration of the Eastern Front, a possibility that had to be faced by the summer of 1917. In London, the Chief of the Imperial General Staff stated flatly that without the Eastern Front there could be no hope of Allied victory. The Central Powers would be able to transfer men and supplies to the Western Front in such quantities that there would be a real likelihood either of Allied defeat in 1918, or of the war dragging on into 1919, or even 1920.

After the abdication of the Tsar early in 1917, the Provisional Government of Prince Lvov attempted the impossible task of continuing the fight against the Central Powers while at the same time seeking to conciliate the increasing numbers of Russians demanding peace, political reform, and economic advance. In July, Lvov's successor, the more radical Alexander Kerensky, likewise failed to meet popular demands or to consolidate the power of his coalition government. Finally, in November, the Bolsheviks under Lenin seized power in Petrograd, determined to implement the teachings of Karl Marx and make Russia the centre of world revolution.

Their first step was to remove Russia from the war—a capitalist conflict. During the subsequent peace negotiations at Brest-Litovsk, the German demands were heavy. But Lenin, acutely conscious of the dual threat of civil war and famine that faced Russia, insisted that they had to be accepted, as the only way of gaining time for the creation of what would be the world's first socialist state. The other members of Lenin's government, faced with his threat to resign, finally agreed with him, after an all-night debate on February 23, 1918. The Eastern Front thereupon collapsed completely, and Russian soldiers, so long underfed, ill-paid, and underequipped, threw down their weapons and streamed homeward. The Germans and Austrians had already begun to move tens of thousands of men from the Eastern Front to the Western Front. In fact, forty divisions and vast amounts of *matériel* had been transferred by the time the Treaty of Brest-Litovsk was signed on March 3.

In Allied reviews of the deteriorating situation in Russia, there was another factor that received almost as much attention as the need to keep the Central Powers embroiled in the east: the need to deny them access to the enormous natural resources of Russia. Winston Churchill later wrote that "the reconstruction of an Eastern front against Germany and the withholding of Russian supplies from the Central Powers seemed even from the end of 1917 vital to win the war."[1]

At a time when the Allied naval blockade was finally damaging the German war machine, it was galling to think that the Central Powers might gain in the east the oil, food, and other resources at last denied them by the blockade. Lloyd George recalled in his *War Memoirs* that

> ... the destructive working of Bolshevism might in fact prove merely to have broken up and ploughed a field in readiness for planting with Prussianism. . . . If Germany succeeded in provisioning itself freely from these sources, the whole effect of our blockade would be lost.[2]

Further, in the northern ports of Murmansk and Archangel and in the Siberian port of Vladivostok there were vast quantities of Allied military and civil stores, including scarce raw materials, that had been provided on credit to the tsarist régime. This *matériel* could not be allowed to reach the Central Powers through the hands of the Bolsheviks who, in the minds of some British and French statesmen, were no better than gangsters in the employ of the Germans.

Another major concern of the Allies was to ensure the safe transfer of the Czech Legion to the Western Front. Czechs and Slovaks living in Russia or captured from the Austro-Hungarian army had, from the early days of the war, formed themselves into a highly effective, pro-Ally legion. They had fought bravely on the Eastern Front, their one wish being to see their homeland freed from Austrian rule. The Allied leaders, especially President Woodrow Wilson of the United States who saw the Czechs as embodying the democratic ideals of a new Europe, felt responsible for holding a way open for the Czech Legion to leave Russia so that it could resume the fight on the Western Front.

By late 1917, the thought of the Central Powers transferring division upon division from the Eastern Front to the Western Front, gaining access to the vast resources of eastern Europe, and perhaps finding a route through Russia to India, was enough to induce a feeling akin to panic in Allied leaders already beset by problems of unparalleled complexity and difficulty. It was in an atmosphere of fear and deep uncertainty that Allied statesmen

and military leaders took their decisions concerning Russia—or
failed to take them. What Sir Robert Borden, the Canadian
Prime Minister, wrote about the atmosphere in Ottawa late in
1917 was no doubt true of all of the Allied capitals:

> In all my experience I never encountered so extraordinary . . . [an]
> atmosphere as that which prevailed. . . . The varying phases of
> patriotic sentiment and fervour . . . the rumours and
> counter-rumours often finding credence although wholly absurd,
> the alternation of hesitation and distrust with frankness and
> confidence, the advances and recessions . . . the lack of balance and
> comprehension and the fluctuating moods affecting the attitude of
> outstanding figures, created a political kaleidoscope which even one
> who was in the midst of all the turmoil finds it difficult to recall in
> some of its constantly changing features.[3]

There was one ray of hope in the minds of Allied leaders
after the collapse of the Eastern Front. Certain White Russians
had signified their eagerness to reopen the front once they had
regained power in Petrograd. The Allies, without considering
either what had happened to the governments of Lvov and
Kerensky or what the great mass of Russian people themselves
might want, began to move into the Russian vortex. By supporting the White Russians, some Allied statesmen reasoned, a front
might soon be reopened in the east, relieving what could otherwise become intolerable pressure in the west. In any case, siding
with the White Russians against the Reds came naturally to
some Allied leaders. Russia, France, and Britain had been
partners in the Triple Entente before the war. Their co-operation
had deepened during the war; friendships had been made,
understandings reached, and treaties signed. Radical theories
turning the familiar institutions of Europe upside down made
no appeal to the more conservative among the Allies. For them,
co-operation with what appeared to be mendacious fanatics in
league with the Hun was unthinkable. If, by supporting a group
of Russians who were committed to the reopening of an eastern
front, they could also quarantine and eradicate the pernicious
teachings of Marx and Lenin, so much the better.

Even the more liberal leaders in the west, who had been

happy to see the end of the tsarist régime, were being alienated by what was seen as wanton excess and perfidy on the part of the communists in Petrograd. The Bolsheviks' dissolution of the popularly elected Russian national assembly was particularly shocking to western liberals. In degree, this shock was comparable to the one western capitalists and governments (especially the French) received when, in February 1918, Russia repudiated all state debts including foreign loans.

At no time did the Allies contemplate for political purposes any sort of crusade to purge Russia of communism. This idea was advocated by a few, but was never accepted by the majority in Paris or London. The impact of the Bolsheviks' behaviour in power was more subtle: had they not resorted to increasingly radical measures, the purely military arguments justifying Allied intervention would probably have been scrutinized more rigorously than they were. The fundamental point about the Allied military intervention is that it would not have occurred had the Bolsheviks' seizure of power not coincided with a crucial period of the Great War when the Allies were convinced that a reopening of the Eastern Front was essential to victory. As George Kennan has observed, "The simple fact remains: had a world war not been in progress, there would never, under any conceivable stretch of the imagination, have been an Allied intervention. . . . "[4]

The *coup d'état* of the communists in November 1917 had at once brought White forces into the field. By the time Allied military intervention began in a modest way, early in 1918, political polarization was far advanced and the reactionary White Russians were on the way to being the only major organized element in the country, besides the Bolsheviks.

But, armed though the various conservative forces were, and strongly as their leaders opposed Marxist theories, they were never effectively united. The White armies were widely dispersed and had no centre of allegiance, no common policy, no dynamic leader. Only against such a divided opposition could a small minority like the Bolsheviks have succeeded. From the beginning, it was the Bolsheviks' good fortune to find their many opponents deeply suspicious of each other. In addition to being disunited, the White forces were often poorly led, poorly co-ordinated, and poorly supplied. But they were forces of a sort, and they had arms—and, sporadically, a will to use them.

The military involvement of the Allies in the internal affairs of Russia was gradual. There is no one day on which intervention can be said to have begun. However, once under way, it gradually acquired a momentum of its own. At no time were the numbers of Allied troops in Russia significant, compared with those of the armies that had fought in France. As one historian of the intervention has noted, "They were too small to demand prolonged attention from politicians and generals with minds fatigued and sensibilities dulled by the vastly larger war . . . it was all too easy to allow matters in Russia to drift on, subject only to the most general and largely meaningless guidelines. . . ."[5]

Let outsiders who would intervene in a civil war beware. They are entering a bog, making a commitment that will grow in geometric progression. This was the hard lesson some Allied leaders had to learn after the Armistice. For one year, between the October Revolution of 1917 and the Armistice of November 1918, Allied troops were sent to Russia as part of a grand strategy for winning the war. If the Allies had been true to their stated reasons for intervening, they should on November 11, 1918, have re-embarked their troops, leaving the Russians—in a popular expression of the period—to stew in their own juice. Of course, it was not that easy. When November 11 arrived, the Allies found themselves entangled in a complex civil war, supporting White armies on several widely scattered fronts. Although Allied assistance was never of crucial importance, undertakings had been made that honourable men in London and Paris felt they could not renounce.

After the Armistice, the politicians took over from the generals in determining the course of Allied intervention. Strategic considerations no longer played a role. But the purposes of the politicians were even less clear than those of the generals had been. Two contradictory pressures were prevalent among the electorates in western Europe and North America. Both the theories and the excesses of communism made the Bolshevik régime hateful to some; for others, communist Russia was regarded as the first light of a new day in man's liberation. Churchill was by no means the only Allied statesman who urged the continuation of intervention so as to give the anti-Bolsheviks time to reorganize and to recruit new forces with which to eliminate what he later called the "foul baboonery of Bolshevism". But there was never, before or after the Armistice, any agreement among British, French, Americans, or Japanese on a crusade such as Churchill advocated. There was, in fact, widespread recognition that, after an exhausting war, there would be no popular support for an anti-communist crusade. Allied military intervention in Russia was a classic case of blundering into something far more complex than anyone anticipated and doing so without the will or the resources to make a decisive contribution.

During 1918-19, various explanations were offered by Allied governments, including the Canadian, first for the introduction of their troops into Russia and, after the Armistice, for their continued presence there. The British War Office's rationale for Allied military intervention in Russia had been explained to Sir Robert Borden, who accepted the basic strategic argument that an eastern front had to be reopened to relieve pressure on the Western Front. Accordingly, Borden approved the assignment of Canadian soldiers to the Caspian Sea theatre and to the White Sea theatre, and he personally pledged Canadian troops for the ill-defined Siberian venture and induced his sceptical colleagues to rubber-stamp his decision.*

Why Canadians went to Russia, their adventures there, and the reasons for their withdrawal must, perforce, be like details from a much wider canvas. The Canadians always formed elements of larger Allied forces embroiled in the civil war, but in northern Russia and in Siberia the Canadian role was of major significance.

* Canadian airmen, led by Raymond Collishaw, an "ace" of the Western Front, played a significant part in the British intervention in southern Russia, but they were never under the orders, directly or indirectly, of Ottawa. They were members of the Royal Air Force, not of Canadian units. For a description of their adventures, see Appendix "A".

Borden was never a man to avoid responsibility and, as prime minister, he involved himself deeply in the Allied military intervention in the Russian civil war. For him, the need to relieve pressure on the Western Front by reopening an eastern front was compelling. As late as August 15, 1918 (less than three months before the Armistice), the Committee of Prime Ministers of the British Empire—of which Borden was an active member—found that "the final decision as to whether the decisive moment for an attack on the Western front can be reached in 1919 will depend largely on the measure of success which attends the efforts now being made to recreate an Eastern front, and every possible stimulus should be given to these efforts."[6] "Every possible stimulus" was seen by Borden, as it was by most other Allied statesmen, to include military assistance to the White Russians.

However, as we shall see, Borden's interest in the Russian question was not restricted to military intervention. He took two important peaceful initiatives towards Russia during 1918 and 1919, both well-intentioned, if unrealistic in the chaos of the civil war. Although he was committed to the belief that government should interfere as little as possible in business affairs, Borden sought new markets in Siberia for the products of Canadian factories, greatly expanded to meet wartime demands. Borden's second peaceful initiative was at the Paris Conference, where he urged the convening of an all-Russian conference to negotiate an end of the civil war.

In all of these initiatives—both military and civil—Borden was working from the particular to the general, giving expression to a new awareness of Canadian nationality. Canada would no longer have external policies decided for her by Britain; she would herself enter into the making of those policies and join in their implementation by her own free consent.

PART ONE

The Caspian Sea Sector

A "very secret" request for volunteers to serve in an unnamed theatre of operations was sent early in January 1918 to forces of the British Empire serving on the Western Front. In the case of the Canadian Corps, the appeal of January 5 from the General Officer Commanding the British First Army was cryptic:

> A number of officers are required . . . for a hazardous enterprise in a foreign theatre of war. These officers must have the following qualifications: the spirit of adventure, undoubted courage, and ability to quickly estimate difficult situations. They must be of strong character, adventurous spirit, especially good stamina, capable of organizing, training and eventually leading, irregular troops.[1]

A message from Canadian Corps Headquarters to brigade commanders asked that the names of officers who volunteered be sent immediately to Lieutenant-General Sir Arthur Currie. At Canadian Corps Headquarters on the afternoon of January 10, fifteen Canadian officers paraded. Several were former non-commissioned officers. All were veterans of long service in France. Each volunteer was interviewed and invited to suggest the names of NCOs who might work well in an irregular force. But the volunteers were told nothing of their destination, simply that they would leave for London within a week.

9

The response to this unexpected opportunity to escape from the prolonged miseries of trench warfare was far greater than had been anticipated. As was later the case with the volunteers for northern Russia, few officers were deterred by the hazards vaguely hinted at. No "hazardous enterprise" in an unnamed "foreign theatre" could be worse than another winter in freezing rain, mud, bombardment, murderous attack and counterattack.

From the nominations made by the officers and through other channels, twenty-six self-reliant and able NCOs were also selected for what was becoming known among the officers as the "hush-hush army". They were directed to report by January 14 to Argyll House, Regent Street, London, the headquarters of the Overseas Military Forces of Canada.* The NCOs were even more mystified than the officers. They had not been told that they were destined for a "hazardous enterprise in a foreign theatre of war". "They were simply told to report to the Battalion Orderly Room where they received transportation to London. They were sent to the Divisional Baths, issued with clean underwear, and given a little money."

On the morning of January 14, the officers and NCOs reported to Argyll House and were ordered to present themselves at the Tower of London. There, they were medically examined—the medical officer seemed especially interested in their reactions to high altitudes—and one officer and five other ranks were found unfit. An officer and two NCOs from Canadian regimental depots in England replaced them. All officers under the rank of captain were made acting captains and all NCOs were made sergeants. The officers were given a long list of winter and summer kit to purchase and £25 each to help them do so. Five days' leave was granted to all officers. The sergeants, living in the Tower, were free each day.

By January 25, when the Canadian officers reported back to the Tower, they found that forty Australian and smaller numbers of New Zealand and South African officers and NCOs

* *Like the officers, the NCOs were all seasoned veterans of the fighting on the Western Front. Ten of the fifteen officers and eight of the twenty-six NCOs had been wounded in action.*

had joined the British officers already gathered there. The addition of fifteen officers of the Imperial Russian Army and one Persian who had lived in Manchester suggested a possible destination, but still no official indication was given of where the force might be headed. The Chief of the Imperial General Staff, General Sir William Robertson, inspected the men in the Tower, but when he departed they were no wiser.

The historic Tower now housed over 300 officers and non-commissioned officers. All armed forces are notorious for their ability to produce the most extraordinary rumours on any occasion. The unit in the Tower was no exception. Until the destination of the force was finally stated, hearsay had it destined for service anywhere from China to the North Cape of Norway. Among the sergeants, the guesses were even wilder than among the officers. Sergeant David F. McWhirter of Shoal Lake, Manitoba, later recalled that, on the basis of rumour that they were being sent to China, Sergeant "Jimmy Murray began teaching us the Chink lingo that he'd picked up in a chop suey joint in Calgary." In view of the recent rout of the Italians at Caporetto, other rumours had the force destined to bolster them against the Austrians. This led another of the Canadian sergeants to inquire anxiously whether "the mademoiselles in Italy were as nifty as the Frenchies".[2]

On January 28, all was at last made clear. A staff officer from the War Office explained—according to the recollection of a Canadian officer—that

> the capture of Bagdad by the British in March, 1917, had been
> offset by the Bolshevik Revolution. The Russian Front which had
> extended southward through the Caucasus Mountains, across the
> southern end of the Caspian Sea, and down into Persia, where it
> linked up with the British Mesopotamian Force . . . had now
> collapsed. The Russians were crowding back home, totally
> demoralized, leaving a wide-open door to the eastward advance of
> the Turks and the Germans. The age-old necessity of protecting
> India demanded some sort of a barrier to replace the defecting
> Muscovites. But the British were expecting a German offensive in
> France . . . the Mesopotamian Army had no troops to spare.

The situation was menacing. When things were at their blackest, however, a War Office visionary had a brainstorm. Somewhere in the mountains of Kurdistan, Circassia, Armenia and Georgia there were thousands of enthusiastic warriors who would snap at the chance of squaring off their own private grudges against the Turk, if only they could be entered on the British pay-roll and given good leadership. That was the proposition—to penetrate into the Caucasus Mountains, raise an army, and use that army, against the Turks.[3]

There could be little doubt that an advance on Baku by the Turks would soon be under way. It was clear that their ambitions went beyond the territory on the Black Sea that the Bolsheviks had ceded to them under the terms of the recent Treaty of Brest-Litovsk. An invasion of the Caucasus by Turkey was only cast in doubt by the desire of that country's own ally, Germany, to gain exclusive control of the rich oilfields of Baku.*

The appeal for volunteers had first been cleared by the War Office with Sir Edward Kemp, the Minister of Overseas Military Forces of Canada, who was based in London. Almost two months later, on February 24, Kemp routinely reported his concurrence to Sir Robert Borden:

> The Imperial authorities were confronted with a difficult and hazardous situation owing to the demoralization and retirement of the Russian Army in the Caucasus which was operating on the Eastern or right flank of the British Army in Mesopotamia. ... I was asked to furnish ... 15 level headed officers and 26 Non-commissioned Officers, to co-operate with the British Officers and Officers from other Dominions in organizing a somewhat mixed and irregular army of different tribes and nationalities which inhabit the territory to the North and East of the British Army.[4]

Kemp's almost casual approval of the British request was no more than he had provided on other occasions when the War

---

* The British were later to learn of secret negotiations between the Germans and Transcaucasian representatives for the sale to Germany of cotton, manganese, and oil—negotiations that clearly ignored Turkish interests. General Erich Ludendorff, the German First Quartermaster-General, declared flatly on June 9, 1918, that any attempt by the Turks to occupy Baku would be regarded by Germany as an act of hostility.

Office had sought the assistance of small numbers of Canadians for special assignment. There proved, however, to be a significance to Kemp's decision of which, at the time, he was evidently unaware.

The Canadian volunteers for service in the Caspian area were not destined to clash with the Bolsheviks in the type of bloody and decisive encounter that marked the service of Canadians in northern Russia. Nor did they go to the Caspian as part of any grand strategy to support White Russian forces in the re-opening of an eastern front, as did the many more Canadians who were later sent to Siberia. They went as part of a British force; there was no effort by the Canadian government to assert authority over them, any more than there was in the case of the Canadian airmen who later flew with R.A.F. units across the steppes north of the Black Sea.* Nevertheless, aside from its intrinsically bizarre character, their service holds interest as the first brush between Canadian troops and Bolsheviks.

Political problems did not mean much to the Canadian volunteers. High strategy, either German or British, was beyond their immediate concern. Their long service in France had made them both tough and, on the surface, light-hearted. The day after they were finally informed of their destination, they were on their way, their sojourn in London having been brought to an abrupt end to ensure that no news of their final destination could inadvertently leak out.

The 210 volunteers left London during the morning of January 29, 1918, travelling from Southampton to Cherbourg and then across France and Italy by train, stopping briefly at military rest camps along the way. A P&O steamship, the *Malwa*, escorted by three Japanese destroyers, carried them in four days from Taranto in southern Italy to Alexandria, on a voyage enlivened by the presence of forty Irish nurses headed for East Africa. Alexandria to Port Said was an overnight train trip. A filthy and decrepit transport, the *Nile*, carried them, in a fortnight, through the furnace of the Red Sea to Kuwait. There, they embarked for

* *See Appendix "A".*

Basra at the head of the Persian Gulf, where they arrived on March 2, almost two months after leaving the rain and mud of the Western Front.

The river trip in the spring sunshine from Basra to Baghdad was both agreeable and interesting for men who had recently known little but danger and profound weariness in the foul, wet trenches of France. It was especially interesting for the Canadians who met, along the way, a number of their fellow countrymen from British Columbia who were serving as members of the Royal Engineers' Inland Water Transport Service on the River Tigris.* The river was an admirable, if sometimes hazardous, natural route in a country not overly endowed with man-made ones.

To increase the numbers of transport craft on the river, the British army had gathered river boats from various sources, including the London County Council. It was on former Thames excursion steamers, manned in part by rivermen from British Columbia, that some of the Canadians travelled for much of the way to Baghdad.

At a camp seven miles south of Baghdad, the volunteers from the Western Front were joined by others from Salonika and Palestine. There, they spent six unrewarding weeks during late March and April of 1918, learning a little Persian and some sword drill. In the former they never gained much proficiency, and why they were taught the latter was never made clear. Lessons in handling camels were also of no apparent use, since they would be serving in mountainous areas. Their "training" seemed to be inspired more by the idea of filling time than providing worthwhile instruction.

The "hush-hush army" that the Canadian volunteers were about to join had by now received the official designation of Dunster-

---

* In September 1916, five officers and twenty-three other ranks from the Canadian Pioneer Training Depot in England who were experienced in work on the inland waterways of British Columbia had been sent to the Mesopotamian Expeditionary Force, where most of them remained until 1920. The men had been recruited in British Columbia where they joined the First Overseas Canadian Pioneer Details.

force. Its Russian-speaking commanding officer, Major-General Lionel C. Dunsterville, had spent most of his life in the Indian Army. Rudyard Kipling had known him well at school and had later taken him as the model for the hero in his book of public school tales, *Stalky and Co.* An impetuous officer, Dunsterville never lacked courage and initiative. He had a strong sense of humour and an ability to inspire confidence.

The orders the War Office sent to Dunsterville as the "Chief of the British Mission to the Caucasus and Representative at Tiflis" were vague. No sizeable numbers of soldiers could be spared either from the Western Front or from Mesopotamia. With only a handful of troops, Dunsterville was to encourage the formation of local units dedicated to the dual task of denying to the Germans and Turks the oil of Baku and the route to India. That the Germans might be able to threaten the route and foment a Moslem uprising was a recurring nightmare for the British in India. After the war, their fears were shown to have been unwarranted. But, "at a time when the soldiers were predicting that German troops would over-run Siberia, it was perhaps no more unreasonable to imagine Turks and Germans reaching the frontiers of India."[5]

Dunsterville was to establish his headquarters in Tiflis and to direct his irregular forces from there. As he later recorded:

> The only possible plan . . . was to send a British mission to Tiflis. This mission, on reaching its destination, would set to work to reorganize the broken units of Russian, Georgian and Armenian soldiery, and restore the battle-line against the Turkish invasion . . . it entirely failed to achieve its original object, and never even reached Tiflis! But . . . its endeavours to reach that spot . . . were of great value to the Allied cause.[6]

Soon after his arrival in Baghdad from India on January 18, and without awaiting the arrival of the main body of troops assigned to him, Dunsterville set out for Tiflis with a small force transported in forty-one light Ford vans—flimsy, canvas-covered vehicles. His route was through Hamadan (the ancient Ecbatana) in northern Persia, across the mountains to the Caspian port of Enzeli (now Pavlavi), and, on whatever shipping he could find, from there to Baku and on to Tiflis. The route was not an easy one. Aside from the physical barriers, there were no local services he could draw on, Persia being more of a geographic term than a unified state capable of providing dependable transport or supply services.

While the Canadians and other reinforcements were on their way from London to join him, Dunsterville cajoled his Ford vans through the snow of the high mountains, only to find Enzeli in the hostile hands of Bolsheviks, who wanted no further part in the war and shared the view of the Jangali, a Persian nationalist reform movement led by Kuchik Khan, that the best thing Dunsterville could do would be to return to wherever he had come from.

> ... a combined Committee of Bolsheviks and Jangalis run the port of Enzeli, united in the common desire to thwart the British: the Bolsheviks chiefly because they imagine that the British are out to prolong the war, the Jangali because, having at last thrown off the Russian burden, they fear lest the British take their place and lest their conception of "Persia for the Persians" be once more indefinitely deferred; and both of them because they are the victims (mostly unknowingly) of subtle [German] propaganda.[7]

Dunsterville rejected the idea of attempting to seize a steamer and make a dash for Baku. He had learned that Baku, like Enzeli, was now largely in Bolshevik hands. The Soviet of Baku would be no more impressed by his small force than the communists in Enzeli had been. An even more immediate and practical deterrent was the fact that the Enzeli Soviet had 3,000 men under arms and a gunboat blocking the mouth of the harbour. There could be little or no hope of eluding the gunboat, even if the guards in the port could somehow be evaded.

Dunsterville was now in a box. He could not go forward. And to go back to Hamadan meant again risking a clash with the hostile Jangali in the mountains. But it was equally clear that his force could not stay where it was. Dunsterville's prudent decision to withdraw from Enzeli was based on a growing conviction that a return to Hamadan would allow him to *reculer pour mieux sauter*. Additional officers and NCOs were now on their way from Baghdad to Hamadan. While he was fully aware that he would never have enough troops to conduct a major offensive, he would, once reinforced, have enough to ensure that any Bolshevik, Jangali, or other hostile force of irregulars would think twice before attacking his troops. He might then be able to reach his distant destination of Tiflis via Baku and carry out his original orders to organize whatever local forces he could raise to continue the war against Turkey and Germany. A return to Hamadan therefore seemed the less unsatisfactory of two unattractive alternatives.

Dunsterville successfully made his way back across the mountains from Enzeli. Disbanded Russian troops, passing through northern Persia on their way home from the Turkish front, remained sufficiently loyal to their erstwhile ally that they refused to give any guarantee of non-interference if the Jangali began fighting with the British. On the evening of February 25, 1918, the long line of now-battered Ford vans re-entered the town of Hamadan, eighteen days after leaving it. Dunsterforce learned to know Hamadan well, for there it remained during the next three months, "the original plan having for the time being quite broken down".[8]

As days of snow gradually gave way to days of sunshine and frozen roads turned to mud, all that Dunsterforce could do was to await the promised reinforcements that would permit it to move north again, this time with greater confidence. Gradually, small groups arrived. A few Russian regular officers in the area volunteered to serve and, early in April, seventy-five British officers and NCOs reached Hamadan. Nevertheless, although several hundred reinforcements were now in Mesopotamia, Dunsterville had no more than 150 men under his immediate command.

More officers and NCOs, including the Canadians, had been assigned to Dunsterforce, but there was no point in sending them to Hamadan during the spring of 1918. Exactly what their tasks in northern Persia and southern Russia would be could only be determined once Dunsterville was ready to make a second attempt to reach Baku. It was better to leave the Australians, British, South Africans, Canadians, and New Zealanders where they were, near Baghdad, until the early summer, by which time it was hoped the circumstances would be more favourable for Dunsterforce's second effort to reach the Caucasus.

The volunteers from the armies of the Empire had been hurried from the Western Front to London. From there they had been dispatched with haste to Baghdad. But, as is often the case with military movements, the initial rush was followed by a long period of waiting. There was little in Baghdad of lasting interest to the Canadians, and boredom soon set in. So it was with considerable satisfaction that they learned late in April that they were finally to be transferred to a smaller camp in the foothills of the mountain range separating Mesopotamia and Persia. Although they had never been told much about the purposes of the force for which they had volunteered, at least it now seemed that they might move closer to whatever action there was.

Divided into two groups, the 67 officers and 204 NCO reinforcements for Dunsterforce (of whom 41 were Canadians) left their camp near Baghdad on May 1 and May 6. Led partly by two officers from Vancouver, Lieutenant-Colonel John Weightman Warden* and Captain Cecil John Lewis (Adjutant), they travelled the first seventy miles by rail. The remaining 230 miles they walked. At first, they moved only at night so as to escape the intense heat and dust of the day. While Dunsterville was embarking upon a second move towards Enzeli, the reinforcements spent June 7 and 8 resting at Kermanshah before marching a further 103 miles to Hamadan. During their 230-mile march, they followed an ancient caravan trail for more than 200 miles through valleys and gorges. Along it, centuries before, had passed the armies of Darius, Xerxes, Genghis Khan, and Tamburlaine.

In their homelands throughout the British Empire, many of the volunteers were familiar with similar mountain gorges and rough trails, but none of them had ever before seen a famine.

* Warden (1871-1942) had served in the South African Constabulary in 1904 and had commanded the 102nd Battalion (Northern British Columbia) on the Western Front until January 11, 1918.

By the spring of 1918, crops had been neglected and trade had come to a standstill in northern Persia, as a result of the disruptions of war, the ravages of Turk and Russian, and the feudal system of land tenure. A selfish upper class aggravated the problems of poverty and hunger by refusing to sell grain until it had reached fantastic prices. Starvation was widespread among the peasants the troops encountered on the march northward. Corpses were occasionally seen by the roadside and funeral processions were frequent. Two demented women had been stoned to death for eating their own children.

The sort of charity that was shown by the Dunsterforce reinforcements, who gave all they could of their own food, was seldom practised either by the rich Persians who had grain or by the officials, who were sometimes in the pay of grain dealers. In one village, the Canadians met a fellow countryman who was attempting to do what she could to alleviate the suffering. The wife of an American missionary, Mrs. John Stead had opened an orphanage in the village. But she, like the other missionaries, received no encouragement in her humanitarian efforts from the local Persian authorities, who appeared to be as amused by her efforts as they were by those of the Dunsterforce men when they undertook such relief as their limited supplies would permit.

General Dunsterville was also doing what he could from Hamadan to relieve the starvation prevailing throughout northern Persia, partly by initiating and supporting local works projects. Aside from his humanitarian instincts, there was a strategic reason behind Dunsterville's charity. If his force was to be free to move northward in reasonable safety, its single and exposed line of communication with Baghdad would have to be made as secure as possible. A people wracked by disease and famine are not reliable inhabitants on any line of communication, and Dunsterforce's line was dangerously long.

By early May, Dunsterforce was well established in Hamadan and its line of communication with Baghdad was as secure as the limited resources available could render it. With the arrival of twenty additional officers and NCOs in April, Dunsterville had begun to implement his plans for making his way a second time to the Caspian port of Enzeli, without waiting for the reinforcements of which the Canadians were a part. The War Office had ordered the seizure of Enzeli, primarily to help secure the northern borders of Persia and to gain control of Caspian shipping. Dunsterville still had only a few troops that he could take with him. Many had to be left in Persia, keeping the communications open, administering towns, training levies, and collecting intelligence and supplies.

To the town of Kasvin, Dunsterville first sent a small advance party to help hold the way northward open for the main body of his force. Fortunately, the town was already in the hands of Russian Cossack "Partiskanski", remnants of former Imperial Russian units in northern Persia. They had sworn personal allegiance to their colonel, a tough old soldier named Lazar Bicherakov, and were evidently prepared to follow him on any venture. They were brave and, for Cossacks, disciplined. They were, therefore, one of the very few stable forces in the chaos of northern Persia. Like the other Russian troops scattered through northern Persia, they were on their way home. But, unlike the disbanded Russian soldiers along the route northward, Bicherakov's 1,200 men were still an effective fighting unit and not a demoralized rabble. For a price, they would assist the British, if that was the wish of their colonel. Dunsterville resolved to seize this opportunity. On June 1 he decided to transfer his headquarters from Hamadan to Kasvin. From there he would push small advance parties forward into Enzeli, on Bicherakov's heels. Major Harold Menzie Newcombe of Winnipeg was sent on ahead of the main body of Dunsterforce to join the Cossacks in Enzeli as "financial adviser" to Bicherakov (the War Office having authorized the funds necessary to engage his services).

The Cossacks, with some British assistance, duly cleared a way through Kuchik Khan's Jangalis. By June 15 the advance party of Dunsterforce was firmly established in Enzeli. Soon after Enzeli was entered, the Canadians and their imperial comrades finally caught up to the main body of Dunsterforce in Kasvin, almost six months after leaving the Western Front. But, much farther north, Tiflis, the final destination of Dunsterforce, had passed in May into the hands of a small German expeditionary force. The long-term outlook was not promising, even though Enzeli was now secure.

Dunsterville entered Enzeli for the second time on June 27. He found the situation in the town somewhat more encouraging than it had been four months earlier. Then, the port was controlled by a large and belligerent committee of Bolsheviks. Now it was in the hands of three half-hearted revolutionaries who had only a few armed men to support them, instead of the 3,000 who had been under the orders of the Soviet in February. Revolutionary ardour had waned, and the arrival of the Cossacks had reduced it still further. A few days after his arrival, Dunsterville quietly deported the three members of the Soviet from the town. The port remained thereafter in the hands of his force.

Control of Enzeli was essential if the policy of intervention in the Caucasus, recently reaffirmed by the Eastern Committee of the British War Cabinet, was to be implemented. A telegram of June 28 from the War Office to the General Officer Commanding in Mesopotamia ended speculation about a possible change of policy in the face of the hostility Dunsterforce had encountered. Dunsterville was to be given full support in his efforts to reach Baku and, if possible, Tiflis.* However, the War Office added that "a permanent occupation of Baku is not in question. . . . If we can get complete control of Caspian shipping, destroy the Baku pumping plant, pipe line and oil reservoirs, we shall have attained our present objective."

Later, on July 25, 1918, in a long memorandum prepared for the Imperial War Cabinet, General Sir Henry Wilson, who on February 16, 1918, had succeeded General Robertson as Chief of the Imperial General Staff, endorsed in a vague way the belief that a friendly Transcaucasus was very important for British strategy. "The despatch of a small force to Baku has been

---

* Discussions of the various factors that influenced British thinking about the role of Dunsterforce as it moved northward are in Operations in Persia, 1914-1919 (London: HMSO), and The Campaign in Mesopotamia 1914-1918, Vol. IV (London: HMSO).

sanctioned, admittedly as a gamble, but the stakes involved are so valuable as to make the hazard justifiable."[9] General Wilson did not, however, attempt to explain to the cabinet what, precisely, these "valuable stakes" were. Nevertheless, the cabinet approved the War Office proposal to strengthen Dunsterforce. The 39th Brigade, composed of battalions from the Worcestershire, Warwick, Gloucester, and North Staffordshire regiments, was accordingly ordered from Mesopotamia to Enzeli.

It was typical of the confused situation that, at the moment when Dunsterville was congratulating himself on the abolition of the uncooperative communist authority in Enzeli, his ally, Bicherakov, was deciding whether he should announce his conversion to communism. The Baku Soviet had sent a message to Bicherakov, appealing for the help of his men in saving the city from the encircling Turks. To Bicherakov, such co-operation was the only safe way of re-establishing himself and his Cossacks in their Caucasian homeland. Upon receiving his pledge of support, Bicherakov was promptly hailed by the Soviet in Baku as their generalissimo, although some Bolsheviks retained suspicions about him.

Dunsterville had agreed in advance with this devious plan. He had the Cossack colonel's word that he would continue to assist the British. Accordingly, on July 3, the Cossacks, with a small British staff and four armoured cars, embarked for a minor Caspian port thirty-five miles southwest of Baku from where it could co-operate with Red forces in Baku and yet not be within their grasp. Upon landing, Bicherakov soon found that he could do little to help stop the large Turkish army advancing on Baku. The Red Army force defending the city was little more than an armed rabble drawn from the unemployed and disbanded soldiers. It crumbled wherever the Turks pressed. It was clear to Bicherakov that he could rely only upon his own Cossacks, but they were not numerous enough to offer any real resistance to the much larger Turkish forces. During the first weeks of July, the Red Army was driven steadily back on Baku. By the end of the month, the Turks were within two miles of the harbour.

For some reason, the Turkish army then stopped. Nothing was preventing it from taking the city, yet it did not do so. Perhaps wary of imagined British or Russian cavalry in their rear, the Turks withdrew to a line farther back from the city, but still surrounding it. Unfortunately for the British, however, Bicherakov chose this same moment to withdraw his Cossacks northward from Baku towards the White Russian forces. Suspicions about the sincerity of his recent conversion to communism had reached such a point among the Baku Bolsheviks that any further co-operation between them was fast becoming impossible. With Bicherakov's departure, there was no nucleus around which a determined defence might be organized.

Another event, however, encouraged Dunsterville to continue with his plans for moving his small force to Baku. On July 25, the Baku Soviet had voted 259 to 236 to seek British help against the Turks, resulting in the resignation of the Bolshevik–Left Socialist coalition, which was under strict instructions from Moscow not to co-operate with the British. It was replaced by a new revolutionary government calling itself the Centro-Caspian Dictatorship. With the assistance of the British vice-consul in Baku, Dunsterville had encouraged the "Dictators" (a heterogeneous collection of social revolutionaries, Armenians, and various right-wing elements) in their plans to oust the dominant Bolsheviks. In aiding them, Dunsterville was carrying out the orders of London; on August 12 the War Office had instructed him to dispose of any remaining Bolshevik influence in Baku, by force if necessary. As had been previously arranged with Dunsterville, one of the first acts of the Dictatorship was to wire urgently for military help against the encircling Turkish forces. The forty-four troops (drawn from the 7th North Staffordshires) that Dunsterville was able to send on August 4 were few in number, but they were an immediate and tangible pledge of more assistance to come. But at no time could Dunsterville send many British soldiers, for the simple reason that he never had many at his disposal. Dunsterville had made this plain to the Dictators from the beginning of his covert contacts with them. The successful defence of the city, he kept repeating, would depend ultimately on the determination of its own inhabitants.

Dunsterforce was never, during its five weeks in Baku, in a

secure position. The Dictatorship, an uneasy and incoherent coalition at best, alternated between gratitude for the presence of even the limited number of British troops, and suspicions about why they had come. Within the city, racial tensions among the Armenians, Tatars, and Russians were mounting, food shortages were becoming serious, and labour unrest was endemic. "Baku was the victim of its own geography, its ethnic diversity, and the class divisions and hatreds bequeathed to the city in the decades of capitalist industrialization."[10] In the harbour, gunboats were manned by revolutionary sailors sharing the ambivalent attitude of the Dictatorship towards the small British force. As long as that force pursued policies more or less in accord with the Dictators' own confused ideas, all was well. But when disagreements arose, as they did increasingly after the arrival of the main body of his force, Dunsterville took care to ensure that he always had ready a 2,100-ton steamer (with the ominous name of *President Krüger*) which he had seized in the harbour of Enzeli. He also retained control of two other ships, the *Kursk* and the *Abo*, which his advance party to Baku had managed to secure.

In Enzeli, units from the 1/4th North Hampshire Regiment and detached officers continued to arrive in small groups. Dunsterville embarked most of these at once on the 300-mile voyage to Baku. By late August, he had shipped more than 1,200 troops to Baku: the 7th North Staffordshire, 1/4th North Hampshire, 9th Royal Warwickshire, and 9th Worcestershire battalions, their support services, and detached officers and NCOs from Australia, New Zealand, South Africa, and Canada, as well as Britain.

Comprising the initial Canadian contingent in Baku were five officers: Colonel Warden and Captain Lewis, both of Vancouver; Captain John William Henry Gerritt Hopman Van Den Berg, born in Amsterdam and previously machine-gun officer of the Princess Patricia's Canadian Light Infantry; Captain Robert Harrison of Minnedosa, Manitoba; and Captain Gordon Scott Hopkins of Hopkins' Landing, British Columbia. Several sergeants later joined them. A sixth officer, Major Adam H.

Gilmour of Winnipeg, was sent by Dunsterville to Kransno-vodsk, a small port across the Caspian Sea opposite Baku, where moderate Social-Revolutionaries were holding off intermittent attacks from irregular Bolshevik forces directed from Tashkent. In Krasnovodsk, Gilmour served as a liaison officer with the Social-Revolutionaries in much the same way that Major Newcombe had served with Bicherakov's Cossacks.

The first two Canadians in Baku, Harrison and Hopkins, disembarked from the *Tamude* on August 17, the day Dunster-ville arrived (and a day when, on the Western Front, the Cana-dian Corps was helping to bring the Battle of Amiens to a successful conclusion). The following day, Newcombe arrived in Baku, bringing Dunsterville dispatches from Bicherakov. A few days later, Warden and Van Den Berg sailed into the port. All of them were astonished by the appearance of Baku. During their long trek through Persia they had become accustomed to filthy, crowded towns of mud walls, squalid alleys, and open sewers. But, as their steamers entered the harbour of Baku, the Canadians saw a different type of town, a town with broad, tree-lined streets, Western-style shops and hotels, pretentious residences of the mainly Russian bourgeoisie, and a brightly lighted lake-front that was thronged each night despite the approach of the Turks. Near the city, to the south, more than a thousand oil derricks, built of wood and looking like a burnt forest, were tangible evidence of the cause of the city's prosper-ity.*

Only two of the Canadian officers remained in the city itself: Hopkins was appointed assistant landing officer and Newcombe was made a pay officer. Warden became Inspector of Infantry, a job that took him on constant tours of the twelve-mile defen-sive line around the city. Van Den Berg, the former machine-gun

* Formerly Persian, Baku had become part of the Russian Empire in 1806. With the discovery of the rich oilfields in the second half of the nineteenth century, the little market town had rapidly become a flourishing city of almost 300,000 inhabitants. During the abortive revolution of 1905, the oilfields had been destroyed, but they had soon been rebuilt and the prosperity of the social élite restored. Baku was, however, never a tranquil city, given the racial and economic tensions that had accompanied its development.

officer, supervised all machine-gun emplacements. Harrison was appointed adviser to the commanding officer of the 24th Armenian Battalion (which, to all intents and purposes, he thereafter commanded).

> Behind them, in Persia, they had left about 40 other Canadians—officers and sergeants—all engaged in the onerous duties of raising and drilling native levies, administering cities that were already ancient when Alexander the Great was performing much the same task over 2,000 years ago, preserving order in an environment of treachery and open hostility, battling against brigands in the mountains of Kurdistan, and relieving victims of a famine that was ravaging the country.[11]

The five Canadian officers in Baku were as shocked by what they saw of the defences of the city as they were surprised by its modernity. Most of the 6,000 defending troops, largely Armenian, were untrained, undisciplined, and without much idea of what to do if the enemy attacked. Dunsterville felt a mixture of contempt and pity for such soldiers:

> Had we been able to instil the least spirit into the local troops we might even without outside aid have won the day, but cowardice and disobedience of orders were rampant. . . . I do not blame the Armenian soldier of Baku for his cowardice. . . . He was not a soldier by instinct or training, but just an ill-fed, undersized factory hand.[12]

There was no lack of equipment. At several points in the city there were large military stores, including new guns and ammunition sent by the Allies to help the Russians against the Germans. Dunsterville collected all the *matériel* he could find and sent it to be refurbished and assembled at workshops that he set up near the docks.[13] But the abundance of equipment proved to be no real advantage when there was no will to use it. When Harrison arrived at his Armenian battalion, he found it in a vulnerable position,

> . . . the flanks being left to look after themselves. No digging had been done. We had no supports or reserves.
> The Armenian commander could give me little or no information as to his numbers, organization or intention, nor had he ascertained

the enemy's position. He was chiefly concerned in carting away fodder and grain to sell at the expense of our own horses which were being starved. He put on a kind of command performance when I went round to his line at night, for I found no one in it at all the following night, when I went round without him. . . . After some difficulty I moved the position three-quarters of a mile forward, had some lunettes dug and made some system of cavalry patrols. Old men, children and one woman picked up by the patrols and brought in to me for examination I discovered subsequently were not sent back according to my orders, but were murdered by my own men.[14]

A British intelligence officer later recorded his recollections of Warden and what he thought of the situation:

. . . a blunt, straight-spoken Canadian, and a very keen and efficient infantry soldier whose permanent telegraphic address in Flanders had been "Vimy Ridge". Warden was generally an optimist, but the Baku problem was responsible for his passing sleepless, unhappy nights; and finally he gave up attempting to instil martial ardour into the non-receptive mind of the Baku soldier. In his own racy speech, redolent of his native prairie, he summed up his efforts in this direction as being as futile as trying to flog a dead horse back to life.[15]

Warden had formed a favourable opinion of Dunsterville on first meeting him in Kasvin: "a genial old soul, I think I shall like him very much". Soon, however, Warden began to complain vigorously about the lack of organization in Dunster-force, the bad staff work, and the lack of co-ordination and support from headquarters in Baghdad. By August 1, when Warden was Town Commandant of Kasvin, his opinion of Dunsterforce had markedly deteriorated.

This is the most disorganized show I have ever been on. Gen. Dunsterville has not the vaguest idea of organization, and most of his staff is worse. . . . I am getting very worried. I do not mind fighting if I have a chance, but I object to being forced into committing suicide. This is the biggest game of bluff I ever saw played.[16]

Enemy agents and sympathizers were everywhere. It was soon

obvious that the political situation in the town was no better than the military. Crude ideas of communism were still prevalent, even though the Bolshevik leaders had been expelled. Such ideas, when combined with an utter absence of discipline, led only to chaos. The apparatus of a communist state persisted long after any understanding of its real purpose had disappeared.

> In Baku the Central Caspian Dictatorship . . . held meetings lasting days on end; resolutions were passed by the truck-load. All men being equal, all men therefore felt free to give orders, to interfere in the execution of same, and to obey or disobey as they pleased. Inasmuch as obedience is the stamp of serfdom and disobedience the defiant expression of independence, freedom and liberty, no one paid the slightest heed to either the orders or the resolutions. But everybody talked. The dictators, of whom there were five, began to suspect Dunsterforce of being "counter-revolutionary". Their invariable action—whenever they really acted—was merely to oppose Dunsterville's every suggestion, to block all defence works, and to open his eyes to the fact that, British troops now having arrived, they would be expected to do all the fighting.[17]

In the event, they did. Dunsterville reiterated that his few troops could not defend Baku alone. The fate of the city rested with its inhabitants. Yet on August 26 and again on August 30 and 31, many of the Baku troops faded away at the first sign of an enemy advance, leaving the few British troops to try to hold a line of twelve miles—impossibly long for so few troops. On August 31, in fighting ten miles north of Baku, the only Canadian casualty, Sergeant Ambrose J. Mahar, was wounded in the shoulder and evacuated to a hospital near Enzeli.

By the evening of September 1, it was clear to Dunsterville that the fall of Baku had to be considered a probability. The only question was how long the fall could be postponed. That day, the Turks, who numbered more than 14,000, mounted a determined offensive all along the line. Everywhere they pushed it in. The Armenians fled in wild disorder down the suddenly crowded roads into Baku, leaving the British to attempt an orderly retreat.

Here and there little knots of Dunsterforce officers and sergeants established machine gun posts, offering themselves as sacrifices against the Turks. Australians, New Zealanders, South Africans, Imperials—officers and sergeants—sought to defend isolated positions, as the terror-stricken droves of Armenians panted through them. By nightfall all that remained of the 24th Battalion in the front line were Harrison, Sergeant Stokes, and the Canadian's batman, Pte. Long. All the other "troops" had scuttled into Baku.

Everywhere along the line surrounding the city the story was the same—only a few Russians, the remnant of the Worcesters, the Warwicks, the North Hants and the Staffords were left to conduct the defence. Casualties had been heavy, and the total of the Dunsterforce now available to ward off a further offensive by the Turkish army did not exceed 800 men. The job was impossible. Nothing could save Baku, unless the citizens were willing to fight. And that was the one thing they were unwilling to do.[18]

It was an impossible situation. The defensive line facing the Turks now consisted almost entirely of the survivors of Dunsterforce. For the second time in six months, Dunsterforce was in a box. Six thousand regular and 8,000 irregular Turkish troops enclosed it in the city. The Caspian Sea offered the only possible route of escape. But now the Dictators began to take steps to prevent the departure of the British soldiers, the last unit standing between them and their capture by the Turks. They were quick to let Dunsterville know that the gunboat anchored at the harbour's mouth "would not look with favour" upon any attempt by him to leave Baku.

Two pieces of news made it even more imperative that Dunsterforce quit Baku without delay. Another Turkish army had begun to advance southward towards Hamadan, thus threatening Dunsterforce's already precarious line of communication.

Stretching for 600 miles back from Enzeli to Baghdad there were only a few score of Dunsterforce officers and sergeants, in charge of some Persian levies. The largest group of Canadians—Chambers, Lewis, Burbidge, Roberts, Murray, Petrie, MacLean, Hodgson, Fisher and the sergeants, Gattey, McWhirter, Casey, Brophy and the 20-odd others—were still scattered somewhere athwart that 600-mile road. Some were on outpost duty in the Kurdish mountains, endeavouring to put up some sort of showing against the tribesmen and the Turks. But the expected happened . . . the Turks launched an offensive from Tabriz, and against it the meagre outposts were quite inadequate. The Moslems advanced towards Hamadan and Kasvin, practically cutting Dunsterforce off altogether.[19]

The second piece of news was even worse: there was good reason to believe that some of the Dictators were seriously considering surrendering the city with Dunsterforce still in it, hoping thereby to obtain better terms for themselves.

Nevertheless, after having bluntly stated the great peril in which the city lay unless its people joined actively and energetically in its defence, Dunsterville agreed with the "Committee of Workers, Soldiers, and Sailors" to attempt yet another stand against the Turks swarming towards the city. He did so on the understanding that the Armenians would return to the line and that the Russians would help to see that they stayed there. Harrison, the erstwhile commander of the now-vanished 24th Battalion, again served in the line, until he was relieved on September 10 by an Australian and took up the work of cypher officer. Warden, Inspector of Infantry, and Van Den Berg, in charge of machine guns, made whatever improvements the obstinacy and ignorance of the Armenians would allow. Hopkins and his fellow officers in the commissariat did all they could to help feed the miserable local troops. They had travelled up and down the Caspian in a chartered vessel, buying at exorbitant prices the few supplies available: grain, sheep, watermelons, and caviar (the British troops were not much pleased with their "herring paste"). To pay for these and other purchases, Newcombe had struggled with the chaotic monetary situation in the town, trying to keep currency in circulation and eventually printing his own in the face of the general hoarding and reluctance to spend that anticipated a debacle.*

During the first half of September, the exertions of the Dunsterforce appeared to make some small impression on the

_____

* A long extract from Newcombe's final report on his imaginative financial transactions is in Dunsterville's book Dunsterforce, pp. 241-3.

Armenians. But there was not much time for improvement. On the night of September 12, an Arab defector from the Turkish army divulged that a large-scale attack was being planned, probably for September 14. Warden, Van Den Berg, and the other advisers from Dunsterforce, drawing on their long experience on the Western Front, redoubled their efforts to ensure that machine guns were sited with intersecting lines of fire, that trenches were well placed and wired, and that ammunition was ready. Hopkins was given a rather different assignment. He was charged with helping to work out the final details of Dunsterville's plan for a rapid embarkation in an emergency. Hopkins and several others supervised the placing of the wounded on one of the steamers.

At four o'clock in the morning on September 14, the anticipated Turkish offensive began. Within the first few minutes, it became obvious that the Armenians would no more stand against the attack that day than they had on any past occasion. The battle was over almost before it began. The Turks soon drove the Armenians from one of the strongest points in their line. The whole front then crumbled, except for isolated pockets of British troops who fought desperately to extricate themselves.

There was now no possibility whatever of stopping the Turks. There remained nothing for Dunsterforce to do but to leave Baku as quickly as possible.

The confusion in the city itself matched the confusion at the fast-disintegrating front. As the survivors of Dunsterforce made their way in small groups into the port, they found the streets filled with Christian Armenians terrified by the shelling and the imminent entry of the Moslem Turks, especially the Tatars (or Azerbaijanis), their traditional foe.* Against just such a contingency, all of the members of Dunsterforce had been

---

* *Ernest Raymond, who became a popular novelist in post-war England, included a semi-fictional account of the fall of Baku in his novel,* The Old Tree Blossomed, A Realistic Romance *(London: Cassell, 1928); his recollections of Dunsterforce (in which he served as chaplain) are included in* The Story of My Days: An Autobiography 1888-1922 *(London: Cassell, 1968).*

carefully instructed in advance where to congregate at the docks. There, Warden joined Harrison in directing the troops aboard the steamers, as they arrived from the fighting. Hopkins was ordered to bring away a squad of the Warwicks who were still stubbornly holding out in a girls' school on the outskirts of the city. In the midst of a Turkish machine-gun barrage, the squad formed up in the street and, in front of Hopkins' admiring eyes, calmly marched off to the docks as if on parade.

> It was now dusk. In squads and platoons the survivors of the North Staffords, the Worcesters, the North Hants and the Warwicks were trudging in from the battle-front. For fourteen hours they had had to bear the brunt of the fighting almost alone, and that fighting had been continuous. The men were dog-tired. Casualties had been heavy, for they had offered the most determined resistance against resolute Turkish attacks, the while the Baku troops had been running the other way. Angry at having sacrificed so many valiant comrades in such a discouraging cause and sick at heart, they dragged themselves aboard the ships. Crowding into whatever space could be found, they lay down and slept, dismissing Baku and all its miseries. What happened to the town was none of their business: they were fed up.[20]

On the docks, the gunners of the 8th Battery, Royal Field Artillery, turned loose the mules that had dragged their guns all the way from Baghdad to Enzeli. Armoured cars and trucks for which there was no room aboard were demolished and the last of the British wounded were carried aboard the *President Krüger*, the *Kursk*, and the *Abo*. By nightfall, all was as ready as it ever would be. The gunboat still lay at the harbour's mouth but, as far as Dunsterville knew, no communication had yet passed between the enraged Dictators, furious over the withdrawal of the British, and the crew of the gunboat (who had no wireless). But, whether the gunboat was alerted in advance or not, there was still an enormous risk in attempting to run past it to reach the sea. But there was no other way out. When it was completely dark, Hopkins and an Australian officer, among the last members of Dunsterforce still ashore, clambered aboard the *Krüger*. The prospects of escape seemed slight, but the men were encouraged by the fact that the *Kursk* and the *Abo* had successfully slipped out unnoticed shortly after sunset, carrying most of the sick and wounded.

At midnight on September 14, the *Krüger* sailed. With 870 officers and men crowded aboard, a few well-placed shells from the guardship would have brought an abrupt and bloody end to Dunsterforce. The guardship was inattentive. It was only when the *Krüger*, steaming slowly and quietly out of the dark harbour, was about 500 yards abeam of her that the guardship finally realized that a ship was sailing without permission. Shells soon began to fall around the *Krüger*, but she had the advantage of being already under way. Full speed soon took her out of the range of the armament of the anchored gunboat. The next morning, the day when Baku fell to the Turks, and when a massacre of Armenians commenced, Dunsterforce arrived safely in Enzeli, leaving behind in Baku 125 dead or missing. The following day, the *Armenian*, carrying guns and high explosives, also arrived safely after a remarkable escape from a pursuing Bolshevik gunboat.

The return of Dunsterforce to northern Persia had one salutary effect: the Turkish army terminated its advance into Persia and restricted itself to Baku and the Caucasus.* But the return of Dunsterforce to Enzeli also led to its abolition. The War Office abruptly disbanded it on September 22, 1918. The armistice with Germany was less than eight weeks away. There was no longer any need for Dunsterforce. Colonel Warden was not sorry to see it go. His epitaph for the force was reflected in his final diary comment about Dunsterville: "Major Gen. Dunsterville should be made a full Gen. and knighted and kicked out as they do everyone who makes a mess of his job."[21] Warden wrote his sour farewell to what he was calling "Dunsterfarce" on the night of its evacuation from Baku. He was weary and disillusioned, and his bitterness is understandable, if unfair to Dunsterville personally. It would have been better directed at

---

* *Baku remained in Turkish hands for only a month. A fortnight after their capture of Baku, the Turks signed an armistice with the Allies that included provision for their evacuation of the city. A small British and Indian army contingent (from Major-General W.M. Thomson's North Persian or "Norper" Force) entered Baku on November 17, a month after Dunsterforce had left it.*

those in the British headquarters in Mesopotamia who had failed to provide the force with essential support and at the "native levies" who had broken and run. Dunsterville was at least as conscious as Warden of the shortcomings of the material he had been assigned and of the complexity of his orders.

Arrangements were made for the members of Dunsterforce to return to Britain, or if they preferred, to serve in Mesopotamia, northern Persia, or Siberia. Van Den Berg, Harrison, and Hopkins were reunited with the Canadians who had served in Persia. Most were soon on their way back to Britain, where they arrived after the Armistice. Captains Peter S. Murray and Guy B. Roberts and Sergeants David F. McWhirter and Alfred P. Gattey volunteered to join the 1st Battalion, "McCarthy's Irregulars", in northern Persia. Newcombe (now a lieutenant-colonel and soon to become an acting brigadier-general), Captain Gilmour, and Sergeants Lorne F. Weidmark and Samuel Hamilton joined other sections of the North Persian Force. Warden and Captain Lewis, and Sergeants Ambrose J. Mahar, John Lawrence, and Alexander M. Ramsay sought further adventure by volunteering for service with the British Military Mission to Siberia.* Major Gilmour, whom Dunsterville had sent across the Caspian Sea to Krasnovodsk, was the last Canadian to leave the region. More than 100 miles into Turkestan, Gilmour had served with a small British detachment sent to encourage social revolutionaries who were holding off Bolsheviks pressing westward from Tashkent. Gilmour left Krasnovodsk only in late September, after the fall of Baku (other members of the British mission remained there until early November when the Bolsheviks won control of the eastern shore of the Caspian). One Canadian of Dunsterforce did not return. Sergeant D.J. MacDonald, who had been evacuated to Bombay with smallpox, died there on December 5, 1918.

* *Major-General Alfred Knox (1870-1964), the head of the British Military Mission in Siberia, had asked for volunteers from Dunsterforce, since he believed that their experience with irregular forces on the borders of Russia might prove valuable in Siberia. Warden served briefly in Krasnovodsk and Askhabad on the eastern side of the Caspian Sea before his departure for Baghdad, India, Japan, and Vladivostok.*

Dunsterforce made no significant contribution to the Allied victory over the Central Powers. Events on the Western Front were to determine that its contribution was too late to be of any marked assistance to the total Allied effort. The failure of the German offensive during the spring of 1918 and the inability of the Central Powers to wage further war meant that, by the time Dunsterforce finally reached Baku, there was in fact no strategic need for its attempt to help re-create an eastern front or bar the way to Bolsheviks intent upon fomenting revolution in Mesopotamia or India. There was by then no further cause to worry about the oil of Baku falling into the hands of the Central Powers, or about a threat to the Indian Empire through Afghanistan.

There was a growing realization that perhaps Britian was involved in too many areas for her post-war army to oversee effectively. The limits of British influence in the Middle East would have to be set well south of Baku. Yet, if German resistance had not collapsed in the summer of 1918, if the war had dragged on into 1919, as some thought it would, no doubt the little campaign of Dunsterforce would now be recalled in the annals of the Allied forces as a minor but useful enterprise that delayed the Central Powers in their attempt to exploit the resources of southern Russia.

And the Turks had been compelled to keep an army in Kurdistan, instead of attempting an advance on Baghdad. An officer in the armoured car unit later wrote:

> We had no cause to reproach ourselves. . . . Playing a lone hand, let down by all who should have helped us, fighting alongside troops who, we knew, were utterly unreliable, hemmed in by intrigue more dangerous than enemy attacks, we kept at bay for a period of six weeks almost ten times our numbers.
>
> Baku was merely a side-show, and no doubt is already forgotten, but even side-shows must needs have their rows of wooden crosses, their wards of maimed men.[22]

Almost incidentally, the adventures of Dunsterforce brought it into contact with communists. Whenever they declined to co-operate in the continued struggle against the Central Powers—as at Enzeli and Baku—they were deposed. But they were deposed only as part of the effort to stop the Turkish advance, not for their radical social or economic theories. If the Bolsheviks around the Caspian Sea had co-operated in actively opposing the Turkish advance, then they would have been supported. Since they did nothing to help the Allies, they were pushed aside. There were, however, no armed confrontations between the Bolsheviks and Dunsterforce. It was in the north of Russia, not in the Caucasus, that the first violent clashes between the Bolsheviks and the Allies occurred.

PART TWO

The White Sea Sector

I Strategic Considerations

During the 350 years since Dutch traders had established the bleak White Sea port of Archangel, its fortunes had varied widely, but by 1917 it had reached its apex of importance. Both the Baltic and the Black Sea routes to Russia had been closed by the Central Powers. Other than via Vladivostok, the only route available for Allied shipments to Russia was from the north, where a rail-line ran to Petrograd and Moscow. A British officer who had served there observed later: "In the course of the war, in response to urgent appeals, we had sent munitions in great quantity to Archangel, and it was typical of the Russian administration that that was the nearest they got to the armies that needed them so sorely."[1]

Allied shipments had arrived in Archangel in such profusion that, during the summer of 1916 alone, one million tons of coal and one and one-half million tons of foodstuffs and ammunition were delivered by 600 Allied ships. By the end of 1917, the United States Embassy in Petrograd estimated that there was a backlog of 162,495 tons of supplies in Archangel, including such precious and scarce commodities as copper and lead, drawn from the depleted stocks of the Allies and sent to Russia on credit. In fact, so much *matériel* had accumulated that only a fraction could be handled by the limited port and rail facilities.

During the long northern winter, Archangel was closed by ice. Murmansk, however, though it was 400 miles to the northwest, was ice-free all year round, thanks to the Gulf Stream. Largely at the prompting of the British, the Russian government had begun the construction of a port at Murmansk in September 1915. Not only had docks, crude wooden warehouses, and a small naval base been hastily built, partly at British expense, but a single track had been laid over the 800 miles of swamp, tundra, and pine forest to join the railway line from Archangel to Petrograd. Both port and railway were largely built by ill-fed, ill-clothed, and often sick German and Austrian prisoners-of-war and by Korean and Chinese labourers. From the autumn of 1916, almost 500 Canadian railway craftsmen helped to provide the skills necessary to complete the track.* By the spring of 1917, the new port and railway, although crudely and hastily built, were opened to Allied shipments. Soon it became obvious that the limited facilities of Murmansk could no more cope with the flood than could the much older and more sophisticated port of Archangel.

In February 1918, a Bolshevik commissar was sent to Archan-

---

* *An account of some of the difficulties encountered in building the railway is given by Alfred Knox (who was British military attaché in Petrograd from 1914 to 1917) in his* With the Russian Army 1914-1917 *(London: Hutchinson, 1921, vol. II, pp. 509-11). The 500 Canadian artisans were recruited in September 1916 in response to a Russian offer of $1.50 per day for six months. They sailed for Russia on October 12, 1916. (PAC, Borden Papers, file OC 244 (1))*

In October 1917, the War Office raised with the Canadian High Commissioner in London the possibility of Canada providing seventy sapper subalterns and NCOs to assist in railway construction work in Russia. Borden and the military authorities in Ottawa were favourably disposed, but there is no further mention of the suggestion in Canadian files. Presumably the October Revolution ended any thoughts of such assistance. (PAC, Borden Papers, MG 29 H1 (C), vol. 226)

Earlier in 1917, Sir George Bury, a vice-president of the Canadian Pacific Railway Company had visited Russia—as did many other Allied experts before Russia left the war – to advise on the organization of shipping. (Documents on Canadian External Relations, 1909-1918, vol. I, Ottawa, Department of External Affairs, 1967)

gel with orders both to ensure communist control of the sparsely populated region—it was in the hands of the moderate Social-
Revolutionaries—and to seize the *matériel* in the port. By ruth-
less efficiency, within two months, not only was he in complete
control of the port, but he was sending south every week about
3,000 tons of valuable supplies that had been shipped to Russia
for use against the Central Powers. These supplies were now,
it seemed to British officials, being purloined by a quasi-
government treacherously seeking a separate peace with the
common enemy. Who could be certain that they would not
reach the Central Powers? At the very moment when the Allied
blockade of Germany was finally causing severe shortages of
essential raw materials, it was intolerable that the Bolsheviks
could convey such supplies to the Central Powers. An offer by
the British government to provide foodstuffs and other goods to
Archangel if the scarcer raw materials were left intact was
ignored by the Bolsheviks.

The Allies were also afraid that Murmansk might be seized
by the Germans and used as a submarine base. U-boats had long
been operating in northern waters, and in April 1916 the Russian
government had formally transferred responsibility for the
seaward defences of Murmansk and Archangel to the Royal
Navy. Throughout 1917, there had been stationed in Murmansk
four or five British warships to help protect Allied shipping
carrying supplies to the two ports. Early in 1918, more U-boats
began to appear in northern waters. In Petrograd, the Germans
had protested to Lenin's government about the continued
presence of the Royal Navy in Murmansk and had backed up
their protests by sinking several merchant ships off the coast
near Murmansk.

Early in February 1918, the Russian admiral commanding the
port had been first placed under constant surveillance by Bolshevik sailors and then murdered, allegedly by fanatics among
them. Rear-Admiral Thomas W. Kemp, who commanded the
Royal Navy squadron, and those in the War Office in London
who had followed the situation in Russia closely, regarded the
murder as final confirmation that Murmansk, like Archangel,
was passing into the hands of men so hostile to the Allies that

they would do little, if anything, to oppose the establishment by the German navy of bases in northern Russia.

Fortuitously, at the moment when Kemp was urging London to dispatch a garrison to Murmansk, the Bolshevik and German representatives discussing peace at Brest-Litovsk broke off their negotiations. A new German advance into Russia began. In these changed and alarming circumstances, Trotsky authorized the Murmansk Soviet to enter into an agreement with Kemp about how the area might best be governed, fed, and defended. As a result of their agreement, 130 Royal Marines from Kemp's flagship, H.M.S. *Glory*, landed unopposed on March 6, 1918. But before another fortnight had passed the situation had changed again. When Lenin forced his reluctant colleagues to accept the harsh terms of the Treaty of Brest-Litovsk, the German advance halted as suddenly as it had begun. By then, however, the Royal Marines were in Murmansk. And in the harbour lay the newly-arrived British cruiser H.M.S. *Cochrane* and the French heavy cruiser *Amiral Aube*.

At the same time that the British Admiralty was worrying about German naval designs on northern Russia, the War Office became increasingly convinced that both Murmansk and Archangel might be seized at any time by a German force from nearby Finland. There, the White Finns in their civil war against the Red Finns were supported by regular units of the German army. On April 3, a German division landed to co-operate with General Gustaf Mannerheim, a former Russian Imperial Guard officer, and his 50,000 White Finns in driving the communists from the country. By May, London convinced itself that the German troops in Finland might be tempted to seize Murmansk and Archangel, possibly to encourage the Bolshevik leaders in Petrograd to pursue a more pro-German line. In fact, there was no danger of large-scale overland attacks by the Germans on either port. There were few roads or trails in the region and, until winter came, the surrounding tundra remained little more than a swamp. The rivers were mostly swift and hazardous. Over such terrain, the movement of major formations of troops from Finland was almost an impossibility. It was nevertheless argued in London that Allied landings in the north were doubly necessary: first, to prevent the use of the two ports as U-boat depots and, second, to secure them from the Germans in Finland. It was further argued that, in any event, an Allied force in northern Russia would help to pin the Germans down in Finland and prevent them from being transferred to the Western Front. Although the Germans in Finland never in fact approached within several hundred miles of the Murmansk-Petrograd rail-line, they were an additional factor in convincing the British and French that early and total control of both northern ports was desirable.

As early as March 16, an Allied conference in London had reviewed a proposal by Major-General Alfred Knox, the former British military attaché in St. Petersburg, that a force of 5,000 should be dispatched to northern Russia to counter possible German activity. Consideration was as hurried and superficial in this case as in most Allied decisions about military intervention in Russia. Approval was promptly given and planning for a British expeditionary force went forward rapidly. As a temporary reinforcement, 370 more Royal Marines were landed in Murmansk on May 29, bringing the total ashore there to 520. Joined by White Russians and Finns, a few Poles, and a regiment of Serbs (who had made their way overland from Odessa), and backed by the guns of Kemp's few warships, the Royal Marines could hold on until the proposed expeditionary force arrived.

At the same time that the Royal Marines were quietly establishing themselves in log barracks in Murmansk, fighting broke out along hundreds of miles of the Trans-Siberian railway. The antagonists were local Bolsheviks and units of the large and determined pro-Allied Czech Legion. Almost 70,000 Czechoslovaks had joined the Legion's ranks, after serving in the Russian army or after being released from Russian prisoner-of-war camps. All were eager to make their way towards Vladivostok and from there to the Western Front, to take up the fight against the Central Powers. The Allies had led them to believe that ships would await them in Vladivostok. But somehow the belief grew in the War Office—how, exactly, it is difficult now to say—that a detachment of Czechoslovaks were on their way to Archangel, rather than to Vladivostok, or, if they were not, that those Czechoslovaks who were still in the region of the Urals could be diverted northward to embark for the Western Front.

Some Allied strategists went further. They began to hope that somehow a major part—and not just one detachment—of the Czech Legion might be induced to reverse its eastward journey and head north to Archangel. The Legion would then become the vital link in a chain binding the Allied forces in the north with Japanese forces advancing from the east—if the Japanese could be induced to advance from the east. Assuming that this grand strategy could be realized, here was one more compelling reason why the two northern ports should be firmly in pro-Allied hands. If the plan miscarried, the Czechoslovaks could always be shipped from Vladivostok to the Western Front, as originally envisaged. Lloyd George later noted:

> The Allies were of the opinion that if [the Czechoslovaks] could be encouraged to make their way to North Russia, they would be able there to join hands with our forces and assist in re-forming an anti-German Front in the East. For this purpose it was necessary to go farther with the organisation of pro-Ally forces there, and on May 17th we dispatched General Poole to Murmansk with a Military Mission of 500 officers and men, for organising the Czech troops it was hoped to rally there. . . .
>
> The scheme of effecting a connection with the Czecho-Slovaks in North Russia made it imperative to occupy Archangel.[2]

The Czechoslovaks were experienced soldiers in no need of any prolonged training to prepare them for the Western Front. Nevertheless, the War Office included in its planning for an expeditionary force for northern Russia a training unit to go on from Murmansk to Archangel to train the Czechoslovaks whenever they arrived in that port. A training unit would also be useful to prepare willing Russians in the region for the re-opening of the Eastern Front. Additionally, it would prevent the continuing removal of Allied supplies. This was the only assignment proposed for the Allied force that could be remotely described as anti-communist. Later, everything the Allies did in the north would be characterized by the Bolsheviks as part of a massive attempt to crush them. In fact, the strategy was entirely intended to contribute to the defeat of the Central Powers. In the original instructions to the commanding officers of the Murmansk and Archangel formations, no Russian political faction is even mentioned.

For these various strategic reasons, the Supreme War Council endorsed on June 3, 1918—without much discussion—the British proposal for the dispatch of a small Allied expeditionary force to Murmansk.

Major-General Frederick C. Poole was assigned the over-all command of Allied forces in northern Russia. Under him, Major-General Charles Maynard, a veteran of campaigns in Mesopotamia, was named to command the expeditionary force for Murmansk (given the code name of "Syren"), which was to consist of 600 British infantry, machine gunners, and engineers. The training mission for Archangel, designated "Elope", was to be headed by Brigadier-General R.G. Finlayson, and was to have 560 all ranks, among whom could be men unfit for general service.

The composition of the force for northern Russia was discussed at a meeting at the War Office on May 16, 1918, attended by representatives of the Dominions. In response to a War Office request made after the meeting, sixteen Canadian, nine Australian, and four New Zealand officers and NCOs were promised by their respective headquarters in London. The men were requested "for the purpose of training and leading the local forces raised in that theatre, and to assist the Imperial [British] authorities in administrative work".[3] The secondment of five Canadian officers and eleven NCOs was approved on May 27 by Sir Edward Kemp, the London-based Minister of Overseas Forces of Canada. The sixteen volunteers, all unfit for further general service on the Western Front, had been rapidly found among units in England, especially in the 18th Reserve Battalion of the Corps of Canadian Railway Troops.

There were also a number of Canadians already serving with British units who went to Murmansk. One of them, Major

George Conway Brown, wrote in the Vancouver *Province* on December 6, 1934:

> When the original expedition was organized, many Canadians serving in the Imperial forces were selected because it was thought their knowledge of conditions in Arctic regions would be of value. Consequently, there was hardly a mess in the whole area in which it was not possible to find a Canadian.*

The War Office obtained the agreement of the French to provide troops, but had less success in encouraging immediate participation by the United States. However, as a result of British urgings, the United States did dispatch the old cruiser *Olympia* to Murmansk as a tangible token of its solidarity with its Allies. It was on the *Olympia* that Poole, travelling in advance of his troops, sailed to northern Russia. On May 24 he landed in Murmansk, a few days after a German submarine had sunk several Russian ships in nearby waters. On June 8, 150 United States sailors, the first Americans to land in Russia, went ashore to reinforce the 520 Royal Marines who had landed more than a month earlier. They were deployed southward along the Murmansk-Petrograd railway.

As Dunsterforce had done five months before, the "Elope" training mission for Archangel congregated at the Tower of London. The slightly larger Syren expeditionary force for Murmansk was assigned to a camp near Colchester. On June 15, these two parts of Poole's command were confined to their quarters, preparatory to departing "overseas"; their destination

---

* *In addition to Brown himself, among the Canadians serving in the British forces in northern Russia were Brigadier-General H. Needham, who had lived in Vancouver for a number of years, Quartermaster-General in the Archangel theatre; Lieutenant-Colonel J. Guard, G.S.O.1 on the Archangel staff; Lieutenant-Colonel A.T. LeFevre and Captain Henry John Griffin of the Syren railway unit; Lieutenant-Colonel R.B.S. Burton, who commanded the Finnish Legion; Major Paul Mills, who commanded an artillery school for Russian gunners near Archangel; Captain Royce Dyer, who was assigned to the Slavo-British Legion; Majors Arthur Henry Whittington Landon, Wilfred Ormonde White, Royes Lionel Alexander Turner, and Seth Bernard Pepler; Captains Edmund Dorey Allen and Vladimir Nowitski (who was born in Odessa); and Sergeants R. Ball, A.D.P. Clark, J.A. Cowie, E. Doherty, and R. Wood.*

remained a secret. Rumours were in great supply: some pointed to Afghanistan, others to southern Russia and Dunsterforce.

At eleven o'clock in the evening on June 16, the Elope volunteers marched through the quiet streets of London to entrain for Newcastle. The next evening, June 17, they sailed for Murmansk (Archangel being in Bolshevik hands) on the *City of Marseilles*, "the nearest approach to a pig-boat it would be possible to find". The ship was unescorted. A careful watch was kept for U-boats, and machine guns were constantly manned. But the real danger on the six day voyage was from influenza, not torpedoes. The disease was rife among the Lascar crew; thirteen stokers and one British soldier were buried at sea. Volunteers to replace the dead stokers had to be found among the troops. It was not until the fourth day out that the troops were mustered on deck and told where they were going.

The *City of Marseilles* steamed into Murmansk on June 23, a fortnight after the 150 United States sailors had joined the garrison there, which consisted of Royal Marines, Serbs, and a recently arrived group of French artillerymen, who had found their way to Murmansk after serving with a French mission in Romania. A detachment made up of Royal Marines, French gunners, and Serbs now garrisoned Kandalaksha, a town on the White Sea coast 150 miles to the south, on the rail-line from Murmansk to Petrograd. There, Poole enlisted 500 Red Finns who were willing, in order to have a better chance of striking at the White Finns and the Germans, to co-operate with the Allied force. (This force was soon to clash with Red Russians, such were the anomalies of the Revolution. For the time being, however, the anomaly of Red fighting Red did not arise.) The Regional Soviet in Murmansk, believing with the Allies that the area was threatened by Germans and White Finns, and dependent in any case on Allied food supplies, decided to throw in its lot with the Allies, despite specific orders from Moscow that co-operation was now out of the question and that the Allies were to be ejected, if necessary by force. On July 6, the recalcitrant Soviet signed with Poole and the captains of the United States and French cruisers an agreement governing "the defence of the Murmansk region against the powers of the German coalition". Moscow later denounced this accord, but the door had by then been opened for the unopposed landing in Murmansk of larger numbers of Allied soldiers.

Soon after his arrival on June 23, General Maynard set about consolidating his position in and around Murmansk by constructing a system of defensive outposts and log barracks near the rail-line to the south. "Holding Murmansk meant holding the railway; and, within limits, the farther south we could hold it, the better for us," Maynard succinctly summarized the situation as he saw it.[4] Early in June he seized the line as far south as the town of Soroka. His move was timely. During the preceding week, his train, travelling southward, had encountered trainloads of Red Guards* sent by Lenin to regain control of the Murmansk region. Maynard's few troops promptly disarmed them, gave them rations, and turned them back towards Petrograd. Thereafter, the main task of the Allied soldiers was to fend off small, intermittent Bolshevik attacks along the line. The Red Army did not yet have the men or the supply organization to operate in any large numbers across swamp and tundra. The small Allied garrisons sent to Kem and Kandalaksha, both rail towns on the White Sea, were doubly secure because they could, if necessary, be supplied by ship.

Concurrently with Maynard's efforts to establish a defensive position for his Murmansk force, Poole and Finlayson undertook the more complex task of occupying Archangel, which was ruled by a small and suspicious group of Bolsheviks. Through the use of agents, Poole encouraged a pro-Allied faction, led by a reactionary Russian naval captain and assisted by a Cossack chief calling himself Prince Aristoff, to stage a *coup*, which was successfully carried out on July 31, the eve of Poole's arrival off Archangel with a force of approximately 1,500, made up of a battalion of Royal Scots, the French 21st Colonial Battalion

---

* "Red Guards" was the contemporary phrase used indiscriminately to describe Bolshevik troops. It refers to no specific unit or status and has been used throughout this chapter and elsewhere to accord with the usage in documents and other source material of the period.

(which had reached Murmansk on July 26), 100 Royal Marines, 50 United States sailors, and some Poles. Three seaplanes from H.M.S. *Nairana** and the guns of H.M.S. *Attentive* (the French heavy cruiser *Amiral Aube* having temporarily grounded) silenced the guns on the island guarding the entrance to the port. Two icebreakers, hurriedly sunk by the Bolsheviks to block the channel, were easily by-passed. The Allied troops, who landed unopposed,

> . . . were accorded a dignified and respectful welcome by the Prince, who, in presenting the Keys of the City to the Allied Staff, explained what pains he had taken to ensure the safety and comfort of the Allied and foreign representatives [in Archangel]; and, at the same time, how he had provided for the safety of all White Russian leaders. As a final stroke, he delivered over in custody to the Allies a potentially very troublesome gang of Reds. All thereupon agreed he was a fine fellow indeed and when, with fitting modesty, he accepted an invitation to join the Allied cause, satisfaction knew no bounds.[5]

The ports of Murmansk and Archangel were now firmly in Allied hands. Yet it was already evident that at least one of the original reasons used to justify their occupation was no longer valid. Once the Allies had established themselves in Murmansk, the Bolsheviks had quite naturally assumed that an advance on Archangel would soon follow. Hence, during the two months that had separated the first Allied landings in Murmansk and the Allied occupation of Archangel, the Bolsheviks had shipped south much of the *matériel* in Archangel, thereby weakening one of the original justifications for the landings.

While the seizure of the two ports had not been difficult, their retention might not be so easy unless reinforcements were sent soon. The somewhat irregular character of the Red Army in the area did not deter the Bolsheviks from early attempts to dislodge

---

* One seaplane was piloted by Captain Dugald MacDougall of Lockport, Manitoba, who later transferred to the Royal Air Force detachment in the Archangel theatre. In June 1919 he volunteered to remain behind after the departure of the detachment, to help provide air support for the relief force. MacDougall was killed on August 25, 1919, while attempting to put out a fire in an ammunition shed near Archangel.

the invaders. Three battalions of United States infantry would soon arrive from England, but they were without artillery. More troops, especially artillerymen, had to be found somewhere to help prevent any large Bolshevik forces from advancing up the rail-line or down the rivers, from the south. The War Office again looked to Canada.

Many more than a few dozen Canadians would have disembarked in Murmansk during the early summer of 1918 if the War Office had had its way. On July 12, the War Office asked Canadian headquarters in London whether a whole Canadian infantry battalion could be made available to reinforce what was coming to be known as the North Russia Expeditionary Force. It was rapidly becoming clear, as is often the case in military operations, that many more troops would be required than had originally been envisaged. Canadian troops were favoured, since it was assumed that they were "acquainted with a rigorous climate". This second request for Canadians for northern Russia came only two days after the War Office had asked Sir Robert Borden, then in London for meetings of the Imperial War Cabinet, whether Canada would provide a large number of troops for an Allied force that was being organized to intervene in Siberia. The response of Borden and his principal military advisers in London was prompt. Lieutenant-General Sir Richard Turner, the Chief of Staff of the Overseas Military Forces of Canada, recommended to Sir Edward Kemp, the Minister of Overseas Forces, that the request be refused, since all Canadian infantry reserves were required for service with the Canadian Corps on the Western Front. This recommendation was in turn passed on by Kemp for Borden's approval. The Prime Minister agreed that a battalion could not be spared, but he approved Kemp's counter-proposal that a further limited number of officers could be offered.

Consequently, on July 30, the War Office requested the assignment to Syren of eighty-eight Canadian officers and NCOs. The men were needed, the War Office explained, for a "special mobile force" that was being organized by a French-Canadian captain named Barbateau who was serving in the French army and who was already back in Canada purchasing dog-sleds and other arctic equipment. Since it was envisaged that the Canadians, along with French and Italians, would act primarily as instructors for White Russian reconnaissance troops, they "should be acquainted with the use of snow-shoes, and of sleigh transport and some should, if possible, be accustomed to driving dog teams. A knowledge of French, Italian, Russian or Serbian would be useful."[8]

After discussing this request, Kemp and Major-General S. C. Mewburn, the Canadian Minister of Militia and Defence, who was visiting London, recommended to Borden that he should agree. The following day, August 2, the War Office was informed of Borden's acquiesence. The machinery was then put in motion to find volunteers to meet the British request for instructors for the special mobile force and, as the War Office said in a phrase wonderfully redolent of the Indian Army, "for the purpose of commanding a force of native levies".

The officer appointed to select and lead this second and larger Canadian detachment for northern Russia, additional to the sixteen men originally contributed to Elope, was Lieutenant-Colonel John Edward Leckie of Vancouver, a graduate of the Royal Military College of Canada, a Boer War veteran, and a former commanding officer of the 16th Battalion (Canadian Scottish) in France. A friend of Jack Leckie's later suggested why he had been chosen for what was bound to be a difficult assignment:

> Stocky and powerfully built, well read, breezy, with twinkling little
> eyes, ruddy complexion, and possessing a keen sense of
> humour—which could upon occasion become Rabelaisian—
> generous, lacking in business acumen, it was impossible
> to spend any time, however brief, with him without finding
> oneself entertained and interested . . . he was, before all else, a
> first-class soldier.*

---

* From an obituary by Noel Robinson in the Vancouver Province and the Ottawa Journal of August 24, 1950. Leckie was born in Acton Vale, Quebec, in 1872 and died in Port Hope, Ontario, in 1950. As a young man he served in the Boer War in Lord Strathcona's Horse and the 2nd Canadian Mounted Rifles, participated in revolutions in Mexico and Venezuela, and worked as a mining engineer.

Leckie's second-in-command was Major Lawrence Howard Mackenzie of Gairloch, Nova Scotia. Together they conducted interviews in London and visited Canadian reserve camps in southern England to choose their men from among 900 volunteers for "a special mission to an unknown destination abroad". Most of the eighteen officers and seventy-five NCOs finally selected were unmarried, all were veterans of the Western Front, and most were knowledgeable about life in the north. Many were eager to continue, in an entirely new theatre, the military life that had become so familiar to them. They assembled by August 28 at Witley Camp in Surrey, where they found that Captain Calvin Proctor Fee of Millbrook, Ontario, had been appointed their quartermaster and Captain Eustace Herbert Cope of Saskatchewan, their adjutant. Their "unknown destination" became less of a mystery when they were issued with arctic clothing (designed by Sir Ernest Shackleton, who had volunteered to accompany the North Russian Expeditionary Force as an "expert consultant").* Further evidence of where the volunteers were going was provided when the NCOs were trained in the use of long Russian rifles with fixed bayonets. (The rifles, manufactured mainly in the United States for the Tsarist army, were issued to some Allied troops in the erroneous belief that warehouses at Archangel still contained large quantities of suitable ammunition.)

At Witley on September 9, the Duke of Connaught, recently Governor General of Canada, inspected the ninety-three volunteers bound for Murmansk. They were inspected again five days

---

* The troops were, later, unanimous in their praise for the winter clothing and equally unanimous in their condemnation of the boots Shackleton had recommended. He was soon aware of his error. Myriad anecdotes about the ill-chosen boots (which were available in large sizes only) circulated. "Snow boots, ankled in canvas with leather soles, had been issued. These were of the skiing type, but the leather soles had been polished instead of the rough surface outside with the result that the men slipped and fell on the icy trails. Seeing a man walking on the trail wearing ordinary ammunition boots, Sir Ernest stopped him and asked, 'Why are you not wearing your snow boots, my man?' 'You see, sir,' he replied, 'they are all very well as drawing room slippers but they're no bloody good outside.' Shackleton used to tell this story against himself with great relish." (Evans, Campaigning in Arctic Russia, p. 296)

later, this time by General Turner who, despite a multitude of other pressing demands on his time, was to take a close personal interest in their welfare throughout their service in northern Russia.

Leckie and his men went by train to Leith where, on September 18, they embarked on the *Leicestershire*, which also carried British and French reinforcements for Murmansk. Their crowded transport entered Murmansk harbour on September 27, just over three months after the arrival there of the first troops for Syren and Elope.

On August 3, three weeks after the rejection of the War Office request for an infantry battalion, Sir Edward Kemp had received a further request, this time for a field artillery brigade for the Archangel front—the fourth proposal in two months for Canadian troops to serve in Russia. Gunners were in somewhat greater supply than infantry and Kemp suggested that a new artillery brigade be formed from volunteers, a proposal Borden concurred in without comment on August 9. Formation of the 16th Brigade, Canadian Field Artillery, was thereupon authorized.

During the evening of September 19, less than eight weeks before the Armistice on the Western Front (and, incidentally, five days after the hazardous withdrawal of Dunsterforce from Baku), the 16th Brigade's 497 soldiers boarded four trains at King's Cross Station in London for Dundee.

The brigade was only three weeks old, having been officially designated on August 21. However, its men required no training.

> Few of the men were keen on returning to France, but they were weary of the ennui and routine of camp life in England, and saw in the Russian expedition an opportunity to vary their military careers. . . . All the combatant officers, with one exception, as well as the gunners and a number of signallers and drivers, had seen active service in France.[7]

A thirty-seven-year-old lieutenant-colonel of outstanding ability had been appointed to command them. Charles Henry Ludovic Sharman had been born in England, but as a young man emigrated to Canada to realize a boyhood ambition to join the Royal North West Mounted Police. A veteran of service with the Mounties on the Prairies and in the Klondike Gold Rush, he served in the Boer War with the 5th Canadian Mounted Rifles. Commissioned in the Canadian Militia in 1905, he commanded batteries on the Western Front from September 1915 to January 1917. After recovering from wounds received during the second battle of Ypres, he was appointed chief instructor of the Canadian Reserve Artillery at Witley. A tall, well-built man, Sharman had a quick and sceptical turn of mind and an ability to inspire great confidence in his men.

The 16th Brigade was composed of two six-gun batteries: the 67th, commanded by Major F. F. Arnoldi of Toronto, and the 68th, commanded by Major Walter C. Hyde of Beaconsfield, Quebec. "Bay" Arnoldi had been educated at Upper Canada College and the Royal Military College of Canada. Hyde was a 1915 graduate in architecture of McGill University. Both had served with distinction in France. Signals, medical, pay, dental, and veterinary officers were added to the normal artillery brigade establishment so as to make the 16th as self-sufficient as possible in the isolated conditions of northern Russia. A reinforcement party of five officers and fifty men was also sent, since there would be no ready replacements for casualties or for the sick.

Sharman selected from among the many volunteers for service in his brigade a group of men who had among them a formidable array of military experience.

> The actual gun crews were all men of long service, as also half the drivers and a proportion of signallers but it was not considered fair to drain the Reserve Artillery too much of its seasoned personnel. ... The men without previous experience did excellent work and very soon settled down to the task of maintaining the very high standard set. ... The only outstanding point of difference between the two types of men was that while the young drivers had been well trained and were good men, the old and seasoned drivers' experience of numerous tight corners in France proved invaluable on numerous occasions and made all the difference in the style of fighting in which we were engaged. Their knowledge of how to

look after their teams under extremely adverse conditions, their faculty of [sic] making shelters for themselves and their horses, and their general sense of "accustomedness" in frequent spells of hard and heavy work, changing position over impossible trails etc., was a source of admiration to us all.[8]

One of the warmest admirers of the Canadian gunners was to be a British gunner going to Archangel as General Poole's chief of staff. On the platform at King's Cross, some of the Canadians recognized the tall, formidable young brigadier-general. With the appropriate surname of Ironside, this massive officer of thirty-eight had already earned renown in the British army. He stood six feet, four inches tall, and weighed proportionately. With varying degrees of proficiency, he spoke six languages. He had been noted for his bravery during the Boer War. Since then he had proved himself, both in India and at home, to be a most able staff officer. His abilities were such that while he was still only a thirty-seven-year-old major in the Royal Artillery, "Tinribs" or "Tiny" had been appointed a temporary brigadier-general. Destined to become the Chief of the Imperial General Staff and a field marshal at the beginning of the Second World War, he had been taken by a popular author as the model for a larger-than-life hero of his adventure novels. In somewhat the same way that Rudyard Kipling had based "Stalky" on Dunsterville, John Buchan, impressed by the outstanding abilities and valour of Ironside, had modelled Richard Hannay on him. Like Dunsterville, Ironside later wrote an account of his adventures in Russia, making a lively complement to the more factual official records.[9]

Some of the Canadian gunners recognized Ironside as a staff officer who had played a leading role in the successful handling of the 4th Canadian Division on the Western Front. They were pleased to see him again, and he no less to see them.

There were bearded Russian officers in khaki jackets and baggy light-blue breeches with broad red stripes down their sides. . . . There were several officers of the French Colonial infantry and a large detachment of their men, in sky blue; a battery of French 75's, their men in khaki with blue képis; there was even a Japanese colonel in a blue braided jacket, trailing a long sword alongside his small figure. And at the end of the platform I discovered the men of the two Canadian batteries. They gave me a cheer as I came up, and there in the front rank was Piskoff with his usual welcoming smile. I had to stop and shake him by the hand. Another welcome sight was my old G2 of the 4th Canadian Division, Colonel Morgan-Grenville.[10]

Piskoff had been employed as a groom by Ironside when he was with the 4th Canadian Division. At the time of the October Revolution, many soldiers of Russian birth serving with Canadian combat units were withdrawn to England. It was widely believed that Russia under the Bolsheviks was rapidly becoming pro-German. Even Russian-born Canadians were not, in the fever of wartime suspicion, to be trusted.* Piskoff, along with 313 other Russo-Canadians, was employed with the Canadian Forestry Corps in Scotland when he learned of Ironside's new appointment. Eager to leave forestry work and see his native Russia again, he immediately wrote to Ironside volunteering his services.

For Leckie and the other Canadians assigned to Syren, the voyage on the *Leicestershire* to Murmansk was comparatively easy. But for Ironside and the men of the 16th Field Brigade, and especially for some of the other reinforcements being sent to Archangel, the voyage a few days later on the *Stephen* was long and difficult: "Some thirteen hundred Canadian, British and French troops were packed in . . . accommodation for about two hundred. Consequently, the nine days' voyage was extremely hard on officers and men alike."† The rough northern seas, through which the *Stephen* and another overcrowded transport, the *Porto*, constantly zig-zagged, caused much sea-sickness.

---

* *Many Canadians of Russian background had, in fact, served with distinction. A former bayonet instructor in the Russian Imperial Army, Corporal Filip Konowal of the 47th Battalion, had won the Victoria Cross "for most conspicuous bravery and leadership" in the bitter fighting near Lens in August 1917.*

† *Donnell, "The Campaign in North Russia", p. 223. Among the officers aboard the* Stephen *were pilots and observers of "the R.A.F. Elope Expedition".*

Worse, influenza and pneumonia, beginning among the French troops, spread quickly through the *Stephen*. Two French gunners were buried at sea. The Canadians undertook daily physical drill even on the rolling decks and arrived in Archangel free of illness. The two transports, after entering the mouth of the Dvina River (where the silent sawmills attested to the pervasive economic disruption of Russia), reached Archangel harbour in the evening on September 30, nine days out of Dundee and three days after the arrival of the *Leicestershire* in Murmansk.

By the end of September, the last great battles of the Western Front were underlining the imminence of a general German collapse. The need to reopen a front in the east, the basic reason for Allied intervention in Russia, was now rapidly disappearing. Furthermore, only a week after the Allied seizure of Archangel, the British consul in Helsinki reported that German troops in Finland were being embarked to help stop the Allied offensive on the Western Front. And it was now clear that there was no hope of any Czechoslovaks reaching Archangel. Along much of the Trans-Siberian railway, the Czech Legion had become embroiled in conflicts with local Bolsheviks. As early as August 10, when it sent Poole new orders, if anything vaguer than his original orders, the War Office implicitly recognized that the primary reason for Syren and Elope was vanishing. But Poole was still assigned the nebulous tasks of co-operating "in restoring Russia with the object of resisting German influence and penetration" and helping the Russians to "take the field side by side with their Allies".

The increasing flow of Allied troops and supplies into Murmansk and Archangel in the second half of 1918 was like a large machine slowly gathering momentum, and not easy to stop. Of all men, professional soldiers sometimes seem especially helpless to alter a major undertaking that they themselves have initiated. The Allied intervention in northern Russia was no exception. The original reasons quickly disappeared with the approach of the Armistice on the Western Front. But, in the absence of any contrary orders from the Allied leaders, soldiers and supplies continued to arrive. As we shall see, their presence in northern Russia had then to be rationalized in terms related to the Russian civil war.

But for the troops on the spot all such rationalizations were less important than the simple fact that, during November, Archangel became icebound. Whatever the justifications of Allied strategists for the continuation of their operations in northern Russia, the Italians, Poles, Americans, French, British, Finns, Serbs, and Canadians could not be withdrawn during the winter without great danger and difficulty, if at all. Allied troops that were in northern Russia in the autumn of 1918 were going to be there until the spring of 1919, however strongly sceptical Allied statesmen or hostile Russians might wish otherwise.

II *Archangel: Operation Elope*

The Canadian gunners on board the *Stephen* were not landed until the morning of October 3, four days after the ship's arrival at Archangel. Eager as they were to disembark and welcoming though the greeting from the ships in the harbour and the people on the quays had been, Archangel was not inviting. About all that could be said for it was that it was more developed than Murmansk, which Colonel Leckie and his men were discovering was no better than a drab frontier town. According to a White Russian who served there, Archangel was

> ... a small provincial town, mostly of frame and log buildings stretching along a single paved street which ran for some five miles ... with sidewalks of wooden planks. A trolley ran the length of that street. All the side streets were unpaved, and in autumn and spring presented a mire of mud which became the nemesis of many an uncautious military staff car. ... The few brick buildings, plaster-ed and painted either white or yellow, were government offices and the residence of former governors of the province. The town was dominated by an imposing cathedral painted white and surmounted by five green domes dotted with golden stars, which stood near the waterfront. Painted above its broad entrance doors was a huge fresco depicting in sombre colours the scene of the Last Judgment, serving as a constant reminder of the ultimate end of man. It must

surely have conveyed its meaning to the Canadians as they disembarked on that bleak October morning.[11]

General Poole had been heavy-handed in administering Archangel and dealing with its socialist government. As a result, he was recalled to London for "consultations" as soon as General Ironside, his new Chief of Staff, arrived. Poole never returned to northern Russia (he was, however, sent in November 1918 as head of a British mission to General Anton Denikin in southern Russia). Ironside was promoted to the temporary rank of major-general on November 19 and formally assigned to command the Elope force. Not many weeks before, he had been commanding an infantry brigade on the Western Front. He knew little about the confused situation in revolutionary Russia, but he did speak Russian. And he possessed great energy, confidence, and optimism—qualities that would be sorely needed over the coming winter.

Archangel aroused no enthusiasm in the Canadians or in any of the Allied troops. Their erstwhile ally aroused even less. A young British signals officer later recorded the incomprehension with which the newly landed forces viewed the Russians whom they had been sent to support.

We, fresh from England, felt an alien atmosphere, and sometimes remarked with surprise that our new friends behaved like characters in a Russian novel, without considering how much more surprising it would have been if they had not. They were highly intelligent, but cursed with a strange fecklessness, baffling and frustrating. When we looked at them we often wondered, not that there had been a revolution but that it had been so long postponed. The idea of their standing up to the Germans in the field seemed fantastic. They found us equally trying, indeed incomprehensible. We had to get on with them, but they made heavy drafts on my slender reserves of charity. I found relief by letting off steam in letters home, and the following, written in November after half a year's experience, is an example. "I have not met the peasants as a class, but the officials and town birds and ex-officers, etc., are simply decayed, morally and physically. They are almost impossible to help because they are so suspicious of one another (quite rightly) and of everyone else (from force of habit) and almost incredibly indolent, and crooked and shamelessly on the make, and very, very touchy in punctilio. And they all live in the most stifling fugs and have white, squdgy faces, and smell. It's very hard not to be a little insular and unsympathetic."[12]

Ironside was no more impressed with the majority of White Russian officers than were his men with their counterparts. He found many of the White Russians either lazy, or reactionary monarchists, or both. Worse, perhaps, was the fact that some British officers were not of exemplary character. Most first-rate officers had been retained for service on the Western Front. In a number of his officers, Ironside discovered both drunkenness and a tendency to intrigue with White Russian reactionaries.

Some offenders he promptly sent back to England. Others he assigned to tasks where they could do no harm. There was, however, little that he himself could do to counter another factor affecting morale: the Bolshevik propaganda that flowed continuously into Archangel. The polygot nature of the command he had inherited from Poole did not make his life any easier, but his most pressing problem was the absence of any organized supply system for the units moving inland. Only six weeks remained before the rivers would freeze. Then all supplies from Archangel would have to be transported from the nearest point on the rail-line to the forward outposts by an improvised system of pony-drawn sleighs.

On September 4, one month before Ironside and the 16th Brigade, Canadian Field Artillery, arrived in Archangel, three British transports had landed 4,500 United States troops (mainly men of the 339th Infantry Regiment from Michigan and Wisconsin, the 337th Field Hospital Company, and the 310th Engineers) to join the French 21st Colonial Battalion and the 10th Battalion, Royal Scots. A battalion of the Durham Light Infantry, a company of the Liverpool Regiment, and a battery of the Royal Field Artillery, along with various support services, brought the total of Allied troops in Archangel by the end of 1918 to 13,000. Under Ironside's command were Serbs, Finns, Canadians, Americans, Poles, Australians, French, British, Italians, and even Chinese (organized into a paramilitary force).

Gradually, these troops were spread over a wide front that had its centre at Archangel. The natural difficulties of holding such an area during a severe winter were increased by the fact that the front was really five fronts, or columns, stretching southward like the five fingers of a hand. From east to west, these five fingers touched the town of Pinega on the River Pinega; Tulgas on the River Dvina; Shenkursk on the River Vaga; Obozerskaya on the rail-line to Vologda and Petrograd; and Onega on the White Sea. Each of these five columns was on a river, or on the railway, or on the White Sea—the only available supply routes. The Dvina was the main north-south artery. Here operated the largest units of Red Guards attempting to deny the Allies the use of the river. There was no regular contact between these five fingers of Ironside's extended force. Separating each one from the next was an ill-defined no-man's-land of forest and swamp. In the summer, small boats steamed along the larger rivers, but during the long winter the frozen streams or the narrow trails through the forests were the only routes for travel between the isolated villages and outposts. The nature of the terrain meant that the fighting during the winter would inevitably be a subal- terns' war. It was impossible for much staff control to be exercised. The isolated outposts, under the command of junior officers, would be very much on their own.

In Archangel, a civil government under an elderly and ideal- istic Social-Revolutionary attempted in vain to administer the area. Often indecisive and incoherent, the government had little success in attracting popular support. Constant "advice" from Poole had further limited its popularity and sharply reduced its freedom of action. A military government under a White Russian general with the unlikely name of Eugen de Miller replaced it. But de Miller was even less successful in fostering popular support. Eventually his administration recog- nized the authority of the all-Russian, anti-Bolshevik govern- ment under Admiral Alexander Kolchak in distant Omsk, but this did nothing to lessen the widespread apathy. Throughout, most of the people of northern Russia remained indifferent to Bolsheviks and anti-Bolsheviks alike. They did not even talk about the conflict. Ironside found on his trips to the various fronts that their conversation was "always the price of food and drink and the condition of the health of friends and relations. Nobody took any interest in what we were doing."[13]

Colonel Sharman was not surprised at the indifference he saw among the Russian peasants. He was never sanguine about their allegiance. Writing in August 1919, after his return to England, he recalled that one of the original purposes of the Allied expeditionary force had been

> ... the encouragement of the local Russians who were reported as eagerly awaiting the arrival of the allies, to organize and fight the Bolsheviks and restore stable government to Russia. In my opinion, these expectations were too optimistic. . . . The average Russian peasant was genuinely afraid of the Bolsheviks, if not a Bolshevik himself, but his chief desire was for both sides to go and fight somewhere else and leave him to his comparatively wretched but peaceful existence. As soon as he realized the small size of the Allied force, he was afraid to assist it in view of certain reprisals from the Bolsheviks in the event of his village coming into their possession and in many cases this led to active co-operation with the enemy intelligence agents. It was established that at all times more than 50 percent of all the inhabitants of Archangel were pro Bolshevik.[14]

The Allies and White Russians had little success in transforming the disinterested or suspicious young men of northern Russia into enthusiastic and efficient opponents of Bolshevism. Any early expectations of raising a mighty army were soon proved to be illusory. The few recruits or conscripts who were obtained were generally uncooperative, recalcitrant, or soon influenced by the omnipresent communist propaganda; so much so, in fact, that several major mutinies would occur in the White Russian forces during the spring of 1919.

Ironside never had much time to give to the long-term and basic problems posed by a largely indifferent or even hostile local populace. The pressing need to ensure the safety of his scattered forces on the five-finger front over the coming winter left him little time to think of anything else. To satisfy himself about the defensive arrangements and the welfare and morale of his troops, Ironside travelled constantly, visiting the columns. These military responsibilities, however onerous, were a relief from the political tasks, which he could never quite shake off. Ultimately, there was no escape from the fact that he had been assigned the impossible dual task of commanding an army in the field and at the same time of winning the support of a suspicious local populace by encouraging wise and benevolent civil government and inducing the local White Russian leaders to forsake autocratic methods. In his dual role, Ironside received little assistance from the ambassadors of the United States, France, and Italy, or from the former British minister, all of whom had remained in Petrograd as long as possible before seeking safety in Archangel. Now the time had arrived when they could not, given the ambiguous attitudes of their governments towards Russia, serve any further useful purpose. Their own safety was in question, with the landing of the Allies in northern Russia and in Vladivostok. The ailing United States ambassador sailed from Archangel shortly after Ironside arrived, and the other diplomats who had found shelter in the port gradually departed.

It was soon clear to both Ironside and Maynard that, whatever the theory, they had in fact been given independent commands in the fullest sense over the winter 1918-19. During the hectic, confused, and protracted peace negotiations in Paris, few Allied statesmen or generals had much time to think about the forces they had hurriedly sent to northern Russia and which were still there although the war was over. It was left entirely to Ironside and Maynard to decide on the disposition of their troops. They were, moreover, without any considered instructions about what attitudes they should take towards political developments in the area, and they never received any precise instructions from London about what they were to do after the Armistice.

At first, the Allied troops accepted their assignments in northern Russia without question. A young Canadian with the Royal Air Force recalled years later:

> . . . the average junior officer or the "other ranks" knew little or nothing of what was going on, or why, except in the units closely knit with his own local venture. As a member of "Elope", we accepted the explanation that the Germans must be kept from Murmansk, and the supplies at Archangel must be salvaged and not

allowed to fall into enemy hands. We also knew that Kolchak and Denikin were "on our side" somewhere in the northeast and the southeast, respectively. Except for that, I doubt that anyone below the rank of Brigadier knew much of the political significance, nor even cared.[15]

After the Armistice, however, this attitude of indifference among the troops changed gradually, becoming increasingly questioning about why the Allies were still in Russia.

Colonel Sharman described the Dvina front, where the Canadian gunners were sent after their arrival, as "in the air". It was isolated, exposed, and 250 miles inland. It was made up of two separate columns on the Vaga and Dvina rivers, between which it was difficult to communicate. Major Anoldi's 67th Battery was ordered to the Dvina and Major Hyde's 68th Battery to the Vaga, a tributary of the Dvina. Sharman selected the village of Piander, near the confluence of the two rivers, as his brigade headquarters.

For more than 200 miles southeastward from Archangel, the brigade travelled together. Twenty-eight filthy lumber barges towed by tugs carried them and their guns. The barges, generally 200 feet long and forty wide, were open to the weather, having only one small deck-house. There were no toilets other than the sides of the barges. The prospect of a week in such accommodation—travelling against the current was very slow—appealed to no one, least of all to soldiers who on the Western Front had developed scrounging into an art. Before their departure from Archangel, "the transformation which took place overnight in [one] barge will remain in my memory as a monument to the ingenuity, resourcefulness and acquisitiveness of our men," Hyde wrote later.[16] His abiding recollection of their departure from Archangel on October 8 was of the sudden appearance of the captain of the *Stephen*, which had brought them to northern Russia. Suitcase in hand, the captain wryly demanded either the return of everything that had been stolen from his ship or at least the command of the barge that now contained virtually all of the *Stephen*'s removable parts.

As Arnoldi's battery turned up the Vaga River, Hyde's battery continued to make its way up the Dvina. Two guns were detached so that an offensive, planned before Ironside's arrival, might have artillery support. Where the Yempsta River flows into the Dvina, the two guns and their crews were transferred to another barge that carried them thirty miles up the smaller river to the village of Seletskoe. From there, they made their way overland to the point from which the attack on Bolshevik forces farther down the railroad was to be made. Hyde wrote:

> Progress from Seletskoe had to be made overland, and I say overland advisedly, for roads in that part of the country were merely forest tracks, which wound in and around tree stumps, over rocks, and through streams or pools. Field artillery, according to the text books, is light artillery and is designed to be capable of negotiating rough country. But the man who wrote the text books on artillery training and the man who designed the eighteen-pounder gun had never met a North Russian horse when they stipulated that field artillery should be "horse-drawn". How we admired our staff that morning when the local Supply and Transport Officer finally convinced us that the menagerie he had assembled for our use were to be accepted as "Horses Draught". The Shetland pony is a sturdy animal and so is the highland sheep-dog, but a cross between the two seemed incongruous, and estimation of their value in terms of horse-power was futile. But the guns must go forward, so the task of acquainting the Russky horse with the British gun was started. Imagine harness, split new out of ordnance crates, harness designed for horses of twelve hands or more. Imagine, on the other hand, horses so small that the feet of an average driver dragged on the ground when mounted. To add further interest to the situation, each Russian horse had with it its owner, whose whole aim in life seemed to be to frustrate co-operative effort. Eventually, however, the harness and the hairies were reconciled and with ten and twelve animals to each gun hitch, amidst terrific shouting, shoving and kicking, the guns moved off toward the front.[17]

Every man in the brigade had been equipped with a rifle, and two machine guns had been assigned to each battery— unorthodox equipment for gunners, but there was never anything very orthodox about the fighting in northern Russia. Each man had to be ready to fight as an infantryman, whatever his training. Thus the Canadian guns went into action in northern Russia.

While Hyde and the remainder of the 68th Battery turned southward up the Vaga River, Arnoldi and the men of the 67th Battery headed for Seletskoe on the Dvina River. They reached that place on October 13, only to find that the local British commander had decided, against Sharman's urgent advice, to evacuate the village in order to take up what he considered to be a better line of defence running across the Dvina from the village of Kurgomen to Tulgas. All that day, the 67th Battery was in action, helping to keep the Bolsheviks at a distance as United States infantrymen, three companies of Royal Scots, and some raw White Russian recruits withdrew with great difficulty along the almost impassable road through swamp and forest. The 950 Allied troops, although facing an estimated total of 3,000 Bolsheviks with three batteries of field artillery, made their way safely to their new positions. The British colonel had, however, carried out the ill-considered withdrawal in such haste and had lost so many stores in doing so that General Ironside soon relieved him of his command.

Some of the Bolsheviks were badly trained, and generally they were incompetently led. But neither the British nor the Americans were first-class soldiers either. The Royal Scots were of "B" category—men considered fit only for service at a base. One observer later described them rather unkindly, in view of the courage and endurance they exhibited, as "an earnest body of Scots of the clerk type".[18]

None of the United States infantrymen had ever been in action. For Canadians who had served for several years on the Western Front, it was almost second nature to handle eighteen-pounders with enemy shells bursting around them. They quickly began to teach the Scots and the Americans some of the lessons they had learned in Flanders. An American officer was particularly impressed with what he observed after one battle:

> During this fight, or rather after it, the Canadians taught our boys their first lesson in looting the persons of the dead. Our men had been rather respectful and gentle with the Bolo dead who were

quite numerous. . . . But the Canadians, veterans of four years fighting, immediately went through the pockets of the dead for roubles or knives and even took the boots off the dead as they were pretty fair boots.[19]

Soon the Allied troops were established along the new defensive line from Kurgomen to Tulgas, which was not as good as the one evacuated. The month of October for these men of the Dvina column was marked by a series of minor attacks and counterattacks. They dug themselves in by constructing a chain of log blockhouses protected by that indispensable feature of warfare on the Western Front, barbed wire.

A careful watch was kept on enemy movements, partly by two Royal Air Force flights. After they had uncrated and assembled their aircraft early in October, "A" Flight, flying DH 4 biplanes, was assigned to Obozerskaya on the Vaga River, while "B" Flight, flying RE 8s, Nieuport 17s, and Sopwith Strutters (the latter discovered among the Allied supplies sent to Archangel the year before) went to Bereznik where the joint headquarters for the R.A.F. Elope Expedition was established aboard a river barge. Of the thirty pilots and observers in the two flights, almost half were Canadians.* Most were young officers who had recently completed their flying training in England and had less than twenty hours of flying experience. Their training and abilities were, however, soon tested. One of the Canadian airmen later wrote, "It was not a Billy Bishop war nor were there any specific episodes. It was plain, routine disciplinary procedure." But he added a few details revealing that the flying the novice airmen had to do was, in fact, anything but routine.

> Obsolete aircraft, poorly chosen; cruel weather for both machines and crew; distances great and landing fields far. Even so, except for

---

* Among the aircrew were Bernard A. "Pop" Heeney and Frederick A. Bradley, both from Alberta; Frank J. Shrive of Hamilton, Ontario; R.E. Gordon and P.V. Dobby, both of Montreal; Francis E. Tattam of Winnipeg; George W. Jones of Moncton; A.E. White of Vancouver; and James McDonnell of Alexandria, Ontario. Dugald MacDougall of Lockport, Manitoba, joined the unit after its arrival; he had come to Murmansk in July as one of the seaplane pilots aboard H.M.S. Nairana.

bad weather, daily flights were constantly carried out. Of course, keeping the machines serviceable was a heroic task for our mechanics. The hangars were tents, much like a marquee, and the oil had to be drained after each flight, then heated before being put back . . . just prior to taking off. Machine guns had to be stored in a warm shack and mounted just before departure. We had no bomb racks except for the 200-pounders and placed usually eight Cooper 20-pounders on the floor of the observer's cockpit. These were thrown over by the observer at appropriate times.[20]

With the approach of winter, everyone, Allied and Bolshevik, thought increasingly in terms of mere survival. The natural inclination to avoid the perils of a major offensive in sub-zero weather was reinforced by the uncertainties about what the troops in northern Russia were to do. The Armistice had undercut all previous rationalizations and explanations. The war was over. The Germans were withdrawing from Finland. In any case, it was becoming obvious that the White Russian forces in western Siberia would be unable to join with those which, it was hoped, would advance from Murmansk and Archangel. This grand strategy was revealed as the illusion it always had been by the reverses the White Russian forces suffered in western Siberia. Against this confused background, Ironside and Maynard were ordered by the War Office to remain on the defensive, holding on to their positions so as to retain forward starting-points in case an offensive were to become desirable in the spring. Maynard was also instructed to keep open an overland route to Archangel which, being ice-bound during the winter, would be more vulnerable than Murmansk.

Not all of the Canadians made the barge trip up the Dvina. Immediately after their arrival in Archangel, three officers, twenty gunners, and three signallers were detached temporarily to help man an armoured train on the railway front, through terrain that reminded them of the densely wooded country of northern Ontario. They relieved Royal Marines who had captured a Red armoured train intact a few weeks before. Two of the officers and six men (to act as telephonists) were appointed to the railway headquarters staff which had been established in passenger cars on a siding. The third officer and seventeen gunners joined the armoured train, under a commander of the Royal Navy. In front of the locomotive was a flat car with sandbags protecting a machine-gun emplacement. Then came a second car with an eighteen-pounder and another machine gun. The wood-burning locomotive was partly protected by steel plates. Immediately after it came a car with two small naval guns and more machine guns. In the rear were sleeping-cars and mess-cars for the officers and men. A second armoured train was operated by a mixed force of Polish officers, British sergeants, and Russian gunners. Later, a third train, manned by French gunners with their famous "French 75s", was added.

The principal problem facing the men on the armoured trains was not counterattack by Red Guards but rather the difficulties of operating their trains on a single track vulnerable to sabotage. Wooden bridges were demolished and tracks torn up. Even the Russian railwaymen on the Allied supply trains could not be trusted. One crew ran its engine up the track at full speed, deliberately smashing into the sleeping-cars of the White Russian gunners. Life on the armoured trains was, however, decidedly easier than on the other fronts. A bunk and organized messing in a heated passenger car or at least a converted box-car were always available. Daily trains brought supplies and carried away any sick. By mid December, a small cinema had even been established at the headquarters of the armoured trains. On Christmas Day the twenty gunners watched a fellow Canadian, Mary Pickford, in a Hollywood film. However, such amenities were soon to end for them. Early in January they returned to their battery on the Dvina.

The Armistice on the Western Front brought no change in the daily life of Syren or Elope. Neither General Maynard nor General Ironside received any new instructions from either London or the Supreme Allied Council in Paris after the fighting ended on November 11. Their orders remained the same, although circumstances were now fundamentally changed. There was no further need for a front in the east, the Central

Powers having been defeated. But the Allied force was nevertheless to hold on in northern Russia until the local government could organize itself and its army. The Chief of the Imperial General Staff explained the problem well when he wrote candidly on December 1:

> [The intervention] having been initiated as an anti-German measure, the signature of the German armistice robbed the campaign of its original purpose. It may then be asked why we did not immediately withdraw our troops from North Russia in November, 1918. There were two main obstacles in the way of doing this. In the first place, owing to climatic conditions, we could not be sure of being able to remove the whole force from Archangel before the Port was closed by ice. In the second place, the prosecution of our anti-German policy had involved us in obligations to those loyal Russians who had remained true to the Allied cause and had thereby compromised themselves with the Soviet Government. We could not precipitately abandon these without doing our utmost to ensure their subsequent safety.
>
> The Allied Governments consequently found themselves committed to the retention of their contingents at Archangel throughout the winter, although they had not decided on any definite policy with regard to the Bolsheviks.
>
> The difficulties of the Entente in formulating a Russian policy have, indeed, proved insurmountable, since in no Allied country has there been sufficient weight of public opinion to justify armed intervention against the Bolsheviks on a decisive scale, with the inevitable result that military operations have lacked cohesion and purpose.
>
> In these circumstances the action of our Commanders on the spot has been dictated largely by exigencies of the immediate situation on their front, which itself has been continally changing, thereby adding still further to their difficulties.[21]

Certain British leaders, principally Winston Churchill, Walter Long, and Lord Robert Cecil, looked beyond these immediate considerations and argued that the White Russian forces had to prevail over the Reds if any lasting peace was to be established and the new boundaries of eastern Europe secured. But all such rationalizations for the continued presence of Allied units in northern Russia during the winter of 1918-19 failed to impress many of the soldiers themselves. They were increasingly persistent in their inquiries about why they remained there when the original reason for their presence had disappeared with the German capitulation. When the Chief of the Imperial General Staff could give no more than the uncertain explanation noted above, Ironside and Maynard could only issue vaguely hopeful replies to the soldiers' questions.

Such attempts at explanation really posed more questions than they answered. Certainly, the generals did not know the answers. There were, in fact, no answers. The Supreme Allied Council, faced with a multitude of other pressing questions, continued either to neglect the problem of Russia or to fail to reach agreement about what should be done.

The Dvina began to freeze during the last days of October. But unexpectedly the weather became milder again. Bolshevik gunboats on the river had one more chance before the final freeze to use their long-range guns in support of an attack by Red Guards on the Allied line between Kurgomen and Tulgas.

Elsewhere in the world on November 11, 1918, men breathed a profound sigh of relief that a war that had begun in such a carefree way over four long years before was finally at an end. But, for one section of the 67th Battery, November 11 was the first day of fighting. Early that morning, five weeks after disembarking in Archangel, the section bore the brunt of a surprise attack on Tulgas. The thick morning mist on the Dvina River concealed the Red Guards who suddenly landed on both banks while their gunboats began to pound the blockhouses the Allied troops had been building as shelter from enemy attack and from the severity of the coming winter. While some Red Guards engaged a company of the 339th United States Infantry, about 500 others took advantage of the swirling mist to elude Allied patrols in the surrounding woods. They approached the two Canadian guns from behind. Near the guns were the huts of their crews and the stables of their horses. It was from these log buildings that twenty-three drivers and a batman, a cook, and the battery's veterinary sergeant rushed out with their rifles to help defend the guns from the surprise attack from the rear. One driver, W. Colville, fell dead, shot as he raced for the door of his hut, and the signals corporal, S.B. Wareham, was later killed in a gun-pit. The drivers were soon forced to fall back on the guns, but in the face of their repeated fire the impetus of the attack slackened, giving the steadfast gunners, under the direction of Lieutenant William J. Bradshaw, enough time to manhandle one of their two guns around 180 degrees to help meet the onslaught. Weeks before, Bradshaw had had the foresight to construct a gun-pit facing both ways. It now proved invaluable. Twenty-five Royal Scots advanced steadily under heavy fire to help the gunners and drivers. They joined in holding back the nearest enemy while shrapnel from the two Canadian guns took a mounting toll of those farther back.

The gun-line held. Several Bolshevik attempts to rush the guns were driven back in hand-to-hand fighting by the United States infantrymen and the Royal Scots. Colonel Sharman, who was visiting the four Canadian guns across the river at Kurgomen when the attack on Tulgas began, soon crossed over. He counted more than thirty enemy dead. During the next two days, the Bolsheviks continued their offensive by frequent bombardment from gunboats and a second frontal assault on November 14. The Dvina column was not, however, again in the kind of danger it had been in during the opening hour of the action on November 11, and with the freezing of the river the Red gunboats had to withdraw.

Bradshaw was proud of his men. They had played a crucial role in a fierce encounter that had cost the lives of twenty-eight British, Canadian, American, and White Russian soldiers. Writing to General Turner in London two months later, Sharman recorded with satisfaction: "General Ironside told me a few days ago the exploit of the 67th Battery at Tulgas on November 11, where the drivers saved the guns . . . is one which has only occurred twice before in the history of the British Artillery, once in the South African War and once in 1811."* Bradshaw

* PAC, RG 9, III; GAQ file 10-28. The reference to the South African War is to an action on April 13, 1901, near Brakpan, Transvaal, when "P" Battery of the Royal Horse Artillery was almost overrun by Boers. Ironside was evidently unaware of another occasion when guns had faced both ways–the guns of Major W.B. King's battery at the Battle of Ypres on April 22, 1915.

received the Military Cross and several of his men the Distinguished Conduct Medal or the Military Medal.

This notable action on Armistice Day was such as to warrant accounts—suitably censored—in British and Canadian newspapers. The reaction in most Canadian editorials was not, however, simply one of pride in the fortitude and skill of the gunners. The dispatches drew the attention of Canadians at home to the fact that Canadian soldiers were fighting in northern Russia on the same day that their comrades on the Western Front had finally been able to lay down their arms. Thereafter, the Canadian government was increasingly bothered by awkward questions posed in editorials and at public meetings. Post-war problems were difficult enough without the complex task of explaining why Canadians were still in combat in northern Russia. Concurrently, plans for a large Canadian expeditionary force for service in Siberia were rapidly going forward. Justification for both forces would now have to be offered by the government on new grounds. No longer was it sufficient to refer vaguely to Allied strategic needs. From Ottawa, Newton Rowell, the President of the Privy Council and Acting Prime Minister, anxiously wired Sir Robert Borden in London on November 28:

> People here have been much surprised to read reports of engagements of Canadian troops at Murman [sic] and Archangel, there having been no prior announcement to Canadian people that any of our troops had gone to Northern Russia. . . . What we need is a statement giving reasons why we sent troops to Archangel and the number sent. Already some of the influential papers are demanding withdrawal. . . . Personally I believe Canadian people will support all reasonable governmental action provided they are kept fully informed of the reasons therefor. Please have Overseas Minister cable statement without delay which can be published here.[22]

After clearance by Borden and by the War Office, the following announcement was finally released in Ottawa on December 27, a full six weeks after the Armistice Day battle at Tulgas and a month after Rowell's plea for a public explanation:

> The Canadian Force operating in Northern Russia, which was recently reported to have been in action against the Bolsheviks,

consists of two six-gun batteries of 18-pounders, with a personnel of 375 [sic] officers and men, and in addition, 88 [sic] officers and non-commissioned officers serving with a local force, raised in the vicinity of Archangel [i.e., Murmansk] under the authority of the Russian Government of Archangel; all the members of this force volunteered for this service. The Archangel Government is headed by M. Tchaikovsky, a well-known social revolutionary, who has taken a leading part in opposing the Bolsheviks.

. . . The Artillery was required for co-operation with British and American infantry sent to enable the Northern Russians to resist Bolshevik aggression and to prevent the Bolsheviks from seizing huge stores of war supplies at Archangel and elsewhere which had been provided by the British Government. As publicity would have defeated the purpose of the expedition no announcement could be made at the time the force was despatched to the Murman [sic] Coast, otherwise both the Germans and the Bolshevists would have been acquainted with the programme. As large reinforcements of artillery were available at the time, the application for assistance by the War Office was granted. . . . It was necessary that the force should comprise officers and men accustomed to the climatic conditions of the region.[23]

For the moment, this statement seemed to still misgivings in Canada about the forces in northern Russia. It suggested that the Canadian soldiers were not supporting Russian reactionaries but rather the liberal social revolutionaries; they were in northern Russia alongside British and United States soldiers; and they were preventing the purloining of valuable Allied supplies by Bolsheviks who were seen by some as simply collaborators of the Germans. For the moment, this explanation sufficed. In the immediate aftermath of the Armistice, men were thinking of what peace, that unfamiliar state, would mean for them, individually and collectively, but in the long run popular opposition to intervention could not be stilled by explanations such as this.

For the men of the 16th Brigade, the immediate dangers of the civil war pressed in on them, leaving them little time to question why they were still in northern Russia. The Bolsheviks, for example, had heavy guns of over 8,500 yards' range; the Allies did not. Consequently, the Allied line along the Dvina was subject to intermittent bombardment to which the Canadian eighteen-pounders, with their much shorter range, could not respond. On December 5, however, the Canadian gunners decided that they would risk a reply. They boldly mounted one of their guns on a heavy sleigh and drove it 1,500 yards in front of the most advanced Allied outposts. Inexplicably, the Bolsheviks did not attempt any direct counterattack. The strategem was repeated frequently thereafter. It was a daring expediency which, until the arrival of heavier guns, did much to redress the balance between the opposing artillery.

For the remainder of November and into December the brigade was "continuously in touch with the enemy . . . but outside of patrol encounters nothing of a serious nature developed." One such excursion was typical of several.

> . . . an officers patrol went out to investigate a Bolo patrol reported to be between our defences, on the island in the middle of the river. Not finding the enemy patrol, they decided to put on a little show of their own advancing . . . some 5,000 yards in front of our outposts and behind his. They opened up five rounds rapid into his billets, then sat back and watched the excitement, he went wild, opening up with his artillery and machine guns, apparently thinking we were trying a surprise attack. As soon as they quietened down they gave them another dose and came home without mishap.[24]

Vaga column and the Dvina column both readied themselves for the long winter now fast approaching. There could be no war of movement in sub-zero weather with the forests deep in snow. Preparations for the winter were based on the assumption that both the Allies and the Bolsheviks would remain on the defensive.

> Positions were selected to which the several units might retire, in case either a forced or a voluntary retreat became necessary. Ammunition was carefully distributed at such positions, so that in case of a hasty or prolonged retirement a minimum would be lost. Such comprehensive reconnaissance work demonstrated that the Russian military maps were hopelessly inaccurate and incomplete. To remedy this, maps were prepared in the field. In spite of a lack

of proper facilities for such work, these maps were drawn to scale and showed very many important details that were not indicated on the Russian maps.

The gun emplacements used during the winter were substantially constructed of logs. They were kept as nearly as possible at a temperature of 50 degrees F., in order to avoid the effects that wide variations of temperature would have on the ammunition.[25]

When General Ironside visited the Dvina and Vaga columns early in December, he found the troops well settled in their log huts. They were apparently comfortable enough, but there were disturbing and persistent questions about why they were required in Russia now that the Great War was over. Among the Russian peasants there was also no enthusiasm. Ironside found only apathy:

> They were all much confused about the fighting going on. They knew nothing about the Provisional Government in Archangel, and all of them thought that if they came out they were helping the Allies in a private quarrel with the Bolsheviks. . . . I searched everywhere for news of a local leader who might be able to lead a guerrilla movement against the Bolsheviks, but without any success. It was curious how no Russian I met had any desire to lead any movement against the enemy.[26]

The autumn and early winter proved to be quieter for Major Hyde's men than it had for Major Arnoldi's. For them there were no significant actions comparable to the Armistice Day battle of the 67th Battery. Yet two days later, on November 13, the 68th Battery also lost two men. Bombardier D. Fraser and Gunner F. H. Russell had volunteered for a small mounted reconnaissance patrol that was ambushed on a snow-covered trail in the woods. Their frozen, bullet-ridden bodies were eventually found, mutilated almost beyond recognition by blows of an axe.

For Hyde, the month of December was enlivened by an order he received to attempt a difficult and potentially explosive task. He was instructed to arrest Prince Aristoff, the Cossack leader who had participated in the September *coup d'état* in Archangel. Suspected of taking that opportunity to empty the local banks of four million rubles, Aristoff was wanted for trial by the

Social-Revolutionary authorities in Archangel. Most White Russian troops were afraid of his 500 Caucasian Cossacks, and the task of arresting him was eventually assigned to Hyde. Accompanied by a guard of honour and employing all his tact, Hyde calmly visited the Cossack prince, read out his orders, and got Aristoff to agree to go to Archangel. The old brigand was most obliging, having had enough, apparently, of northern Russia. Hyde was not surprised to learn two years later that Aristoff was living quietly and opulently on the shores of the Mediterranean, presumably on the assets of the Archangel banks.

One of the constant preoccupations of both General Ironside and Colonel Sharman was the morale of their men. No one, including Ironside, could answer satisfactorily their questions about why they were still in Russia now that the Germans had gone. And both Ironside and Sharman were fully aware of what the prolonged gloom of an arctic winter can do to a man's morale. (In the middle of the winter, there were only two hours of daylight.) Even more than the peripatetic Ironside, Sharman constantly travelled by dog sleigh or on snow-shoe, both of which he had learned to use during his two years of service in the Yukon. He found that the cold winter days were for most of his men simply long hours of boredom in their log block-houses. The Y.M.C.A. provided the only small diversions. By the end of December, Captain William J. Halliday of the Canadian Y.M.C.A. had joined with two American Y.M.C.A. representatives in establishing eight small recreation centres in the Archangel region. Soap and other small luxuries provided by the Y.M.C.A. had to be rationed, but there were frequent concerts, lectures, and church services. Despite the deep snow and the few hours of daylight, games of soccer and baseball were organized between different sections of the 68th Battery. Volleyball became a popular sport at brigade headquarters and a friendly rivalry in soccer sprang up with the Royal Scots.

Christmas was a welcome respite from the tedium of being on the defensive in a country locked in a hard winter. Hyde's men decorated a large Christmas tree for the children from the town of Shenkursk, a sight that pleased the peasants as much as it delighted their children. Arnoldi's battery dined on soup, wild fowl, beef, and plum pudding, with beer, candy, and cigars in special issue, "every one putting in the cheeriest day possible under the circumstances".[27] It was the fifth consecutive Christmas on active duty for many of the men. At brigade headquarters a yet more elaborate menu was prepared by Sergeant Cipriani of the Sussex Regiment, a former cook at Scott's Restaurant in Piccadilly, whom Sharman had obtained for his officers' mess.

> All officers had dinner with the men in a very well decorated mess room. The menu consisted of tomato soup, sardines on toast, roast mutton and potatoes, roast riabchik [a type of Russian woodcock], Christmas pudding and rum or tea. During dinner Russians manned our blockhouses so all Canadians were able to be present. In the evening the Canadians gave a dance to the villagers. In the two rooms of the largest cabin in the village, the guests were served with white bread, salmon sandwiches, and tea. The heat was terrific and the rooms very overcrowded, but everyone had a good time.[28]

The Russian Orthodox Christmas on January 7 was also celebrated by the Canadians, who held parties for Russian children and their parents, pleasing them in particular by their vigorous singing of "Alouette".

The year 1918 ended with Sharman writing in his personal diary:

> ... busy all day preparing Canadian recommendations for Honours List. It is quite a formidable one but a lot of good work has been done. We have only been in the country three months and two sections at different times have had hand-to-hand scraps with the enemy. We have many times sent guns out several miles in front of our outposts and shot at the Bolos and have sent a gun 65 miles through snow to shoot up a Bolo stronghold. Men who do stunts like that, especially in a country where morale and offensive spirit is everything, deserve to be rewarded.[29]

The new year found Sharman temporarily the senior Allied officer on the Dvina. Pending the arrival of a more senior British officer, Sharman was to be the man in over-all command during a difficult period when the Bolsheviks would make their one major drive towards Archangel.

Shenkursk, in pre-war years something of a summer resort as well as a garrison town and market-place, was the principal town in the Dvina region. Not surprisingly, it was against Shenkursk that the Bolsheviks directed an offensive in January 1919. Their reason for hazarding an attack in the worst months of the winter had little to do with events in northern Russia itself. During the first week of January, the White Russian forces based at Omsk had succeeded in driving westward to within 400 miles of Ironside's outposts. Trotsky was determined to prevent the juncture of White forces from the east and north. The chaos on the Siberian supply lines and weaknesses in White Russian morale would eventually spell defeat for the Omsk troops, but Trotsky could not be certain. He assigned most of the Sixth Red Army to the task of attempting to push in on Archangel and outlying Allied posts, while a major counterattack was launched against the Whites advancing from Omsk.

The first Allied outpost defending Shenkursk was near the village of Ust Padenga, eighteen miles to the south. From dawn on January 19 that outpost, garrisoned by 100 United States and White Russian infantrymen and two Canadian guns, was bombarded intermittently but heavily for two days. That the bombardment had been meant as something more than the usual harassment became clear on January 22 when large numbers of Red soldiers, some camouflaged against the snow in long white smocks, converged on Ust Padenga. To help defend themselves, the Allied garrison had two eighteen-pounders, alternately manned by Canadian and White Russian gunners. When the attack came on January 22, the United States commanding officer in Ust Padenga, doubtful about the relia-bility of the White Russians, immediately asked for Canadians to help stiffen their resolve. A detachment of eight gunners from the 68th Battery under Lieutenant J. Douglas Winslow of Woodstock, New Brunswick, was sent forward. In temperatures dropping to forty-five degrees below zero, Fahrenheit, the detachment was instrumental in slowing the attack, Winslow at times threatening the White Russians with his pistol to keep them at their guns. One United States account contained this passage. "The Canadian gunners were in full swing, and their shrapnel was horribly effective against the Soviet soldiers attempting to cross the open valley below. At fantastic cost in dead and wounded, the Communists succeeded in occupying the deserted houses of Ust Padenga, but they made no headway against Visorka Gora."[30] In Visorka Gora, a small village about 1,100 yards in the rear of Ust Padenga, were the two White Russian guns. Here the infantry from Ust Padenga regrouped in the log blockhouses around the gun emplacements, after seventeen United States infantrymen had been lost.

But Visorka Gora also had soon to be abandoned. Allied aircraft constantly bombed and strafed the gathering Red forces, but they could not prevent their advance. Intelligence reported that a large concentration was beginning to threaten Shenkursk itself. The troops in Visorka Gora were ordered to fall back on the next Allied line at Spasskoe, to help defend Shenkursk. On the evening of January 22 the evacuation began. The Russian drivers of the artillery horse teams gave up their efforts to control their horses, half-crazed by the shelling, and abandoned two guns. Winslow, by withdrawing his men who were manning machine guns in the rearguard, managed to bring away one gun and to remove the breech block and sights of the other.

Winslow and his exhausted gunners returned direct to Shenkursk, while Captain Oliver A. Mowat of Campbelltown, New Brunswick, with one eighteen-pounder, came up to help cover the withdrawal of the Americans and White Russians from Visorka Gora to Spasskoe. The "Bolos" were soon on their heels. Mowat and a small infantry detachment in Spasskoe joined with the survivors of the garrison from Ust Padenga in momentarily holding off the Red Guards who were now advancing on the village from the east and west, as well as from the south.

White Russian and R.A.F. reconnaissance flights, mounted patrols, and spies all reported large Bolshevik forces converging on Shenkursk from every side in the hope of surrounding it. The Allied garrison was now in a precarious position, rendered yet more so by the sudden defection to the Bolsheviks of a company of White Russian troops. Reinforcements in any number were out of the question since roads were either impassable or already in Bolshevik hands. The British colonel commanding the garrison wired that Shenkursk was now untenable.

On the evening of January 23, Sharman ordered the R.A.F. "B" Flight at Bereznik to have an aircraft ready at dawn to reconnoitre a trail from Shenkursk that passed through twelve miles of woods and frozen swamp before it joined a small road to Shegovary. Alexander Kazakov, a Russian ace of the war, and Frank Shriver of Hamilton, Ontario, deliberately flew the whole length of the trail at no more than 300 feet, but they drew no fire. The trail appeared to be still free of Red Guards, presumably because they were convinced it was unusable.

At 10:00 in the morning on January 24, 1919, an overwhelming Bolshevik force of about 700 men, supported by five guns, attacked the outpost of Spasskoe. From the tower of the village church, Mowat directed the fire of his single eighteen-pounder on the advancing troops. The Bolshevik troops immediately went to ground, for the Canadian gunners had won "a vicious reputation among the Bolsheviks for the calm skill with which they used shrapnel as a short-range weapon against foot soldiers".[31] Five Red guns then concentrated on attempting to knock out the single Canadian gun. Eventually they succeeded. During the afternoon, while Mowat was encouraging his men at the gun, an enemy shell finally found the emplacement. C. J. Worthington, the battery's farrier corporal, was killed and Mowat and another corporal were seriously wounded. With the Canadian gun damaged, there was no hope of holding off the advancing Red infantry. In the evening, Spasskoe too was abandoned, along with the remnants of the Canadian gun. Now it was the turn of Shenkursk.

With the town under bombardment from heavy guns whose range the Allies could not match, Sharman decided—"to my infinite sorrow"—to utilize the option given him by Ironside during a visit to Shenkursk five days before. He approved the recommendation of the British colonel at Shenkursk to destroy all Allied stores and to withdraw.

A night retreat is hazardous at any time. It was especially so at Shenkursk, where the column was encumbered by the wounded and by over 500 civilian refugees who could not be left to the mercies of the Red Guards. Plans were immediately drawn up, the rearguard assigned, and the order of march laid down. The preparation of ninety suitable horse-drawn sleighs to carry the 180 stretcher cases took longer than had been anticipated. Instead of beginning at 11:00 on the night of January 24, the withdrawal did not in fact begin until 2:30 the following morning. Less than five hours remained before daylight. The temperature was twenty-five degrees below zero, Fahrenheit. What then happened has been well recorded in the history of the 16th Brigade.

> To fully appreciate the situation in Shenkursk . . . and to fully realize the difficulties to be overcome in a successful evacuation of the town, it must be remembered that to our certain knowledge the Bolo Forces were in possession of every exit from the town but one: that the population of the town which at all times had been more prosperous than any other in the area of the Allied activity, had been increased in the summer and fall of 1918 by a great number of refugees from Petrograd and the districts between Shankhursk [sic] and Petrograd: that this largely increased population was, generally speaking, pro Ally, but that at the same time there existed the Pro Bolo element and of course a number of agents and spies. Had any indication or hint of our proposed evacuation been allowed to leak out it is clearly obvious that the last exit from the town would have been denied us and whereas the Force was sufficiently large to cope with any hostile force which might be met with on any one road, hampered as we must be by ninety sleigh loads of our own wounded it would have been sheer folly to have even attempted the withdrawal had any warning of it been allowed to leak out.
>
> For these reasons it was impossible for us to destroy by blowing up or by fire any guns or material which on account of shortage of horses it was impossible for us to bring with us. As it was the Canadian Field Artillery had to supply the Russian Battery with a hitch of twelve horses to enable [it] to withdraw one of their guns. The other guns before departure were rendered useless by one means and another.

And still when we started to withdraw from the town without having been able to warn any friends that might have been made in the town or to offer them an opportunity for flight we one and all felt that any undertaking was nothing more or less than the better of two evils—the staying in Shankhursk in an attempt to withstand a siege from which there could be no hope or possibility of relief, or attempting to slide out in the dead of night along a single road which by chance might not be in the hands of the enemy. No one entertained any doubts as to what the outcome would be had we met with enemy opposition and, therefore, it would be readily understood why the order issued to all troops to take nothing with them but three days' rations was so universally obeyed.[32]

Almost twenty years later a United States infantry officer could still recall the scene vividly.

... the column forming on the road, the bedlam of the streets merge into a single line ... Cossacks in the lead on panting horses, fidgeting to be away; Russian Infantry, undisciplined and sullen; a section of Canadian Field Artillery, grim and fine, veterans of Flanders and the Marne ... the sleighs of wounded stretch for half a verst; behind them in the snow the rear guard waits. The wounded moaning as the dope wears off, or sending up the heart-catching chatter of delirium, the Yanks of the rear guard mustering their strength for another march and fight.[33]

Among the 100 wounded were seven Canadians, including Captain Mowat, whose leg injury worsened. The body of Corporal Worthington was hastily buried in the local cemetery.

When finally under way, the column of almost 2,000 covered more than a mile of the icy trail. The Canadian guns were well up in the column, ready to help blast a way through if a Bolshevik force was encountered. In the cold, still night air, the Red guns could be heard shelling the now-deserted Shenkursk, but not a single Bolshevik was met on the trail.

The evacuation of Shenkursk and the withdrawal to Shegovary over the rough, snow-covered trail was, surprisingly, a complete success. Since they had met no opposition in their retreat, the exhausted Allied soldiers had wondered whether they were walking into a trap. Strung out between Shenkursk and Shegovary, in snow occasionally four feet deep, they were in a highly vulnerable position. As villages *en route* were evacuated, increasing numbers of refugees, uncertain about their future under the Bolsheviks, began to clog the road northward. Sharman had spent the night of the retreat concentrating as many troops as he could at Shegovary to form a rear-guard to cover the final stage of the withdrawal into the town, which was completed on the afternoon of January 25. He and his headquarters staff were also instrumental in making arrangements for the feeding, control, and transport of the refugees as they later made their way towards Archangel.[34]

The Bolsheviks had won a significant victory in the capture of Shenkursk, in both military and propaganda terms. But a further attempted advance was soon brought to a halt. New defensive positions were established near Bolshaya Vistafka, some twenty miles from where the Vaga and Dvina rivers join. There, the British and United States infantrymen, the Canadian gunners, and the White Russians, joined by British artillerymen, were subjected to frequent harassment from Bolshevik snipers and artillery, but they held the line.

Throughout February, despite the extreme cold, the 68th Battery was kept fully occupied in building a small log village. The Canadians were determined not to move again. Their morale did not flag, but they felt the loss of Mowat, who had died on January 27 of the wounds he had received five days earlier at Spasskoe. Amputation of his leg had not saved him. He never regained consciousness, dying in Sharman's arms. In war, casualties are soon accepted with a certain fatalism. But not even the hardened veterans of Mowat's unit were prepared to see his body left in Russia. With the tacit concurrence of Sharman, Mowat's body was frozen and then buried temporarily at Piander until the brigade's departure from Russia.

Along the new defensive line, February was a trying month.

> Heavy fighting followed at intervals, involving the eventual total destruction by shell fire of Vistafka . . . and the artillery moved back to Ignatofskaya where it could command both flanks of our position. The 68 Battery, which had been continuously in action for

six weeks with hardly any rest day or night, was by now very much exhausted. The column had been very severely handled and it had so happened that more and more of the work and responsibility had to be undertaken by the CFA [Canadian Field Artillery] due to the lack of knowledge or energy on the part of the others. Position after position had to be built, including accommodation for all ranks and horses, the enormous drain on men for machine gun guards gave them only one night in three, standto's at night were very frequent and the days occupied with hard manual labour.[35]

The Canadian gunners were at a marked disadvantage in their new positions. The Reds facing them had long-range guns. The morale of Allied troops was not helped by their inability to reply to the sporadic long-range bombardments to which they were subjected. Again the Canadians on occasion ran out their eighteen-pounders well in front of the Allied lines, but this was risky and, in any case, difficult in the deep snow. The only bright spot in the dreary and dangerous month of February was the arrival of a Y.M.C.A. officer with "almost forgotten luxuries such as tooth paste and soap".

The need for heavier artillery had been recognized from the beginning. Three sixty-pound guns had arrived from England in the autumn, but the ship carrying their ammunition had sunk *en route*. A month had been lost awaiting its arrival. By then the White Sea was frozen. Further delays resulted in a duplicate shipment not leaving England until March 1. Anticipating the arrival of the ammunition, Sharman sent Captain Andrew Alfred Gillis and Farrier Sergeant E. Dunford of the 67th Battery to Archangel to attempt to devise a way to haul the guns to the Dvina front. British ordnance officers had stated flatly that the heavy guns could not go forward until after the spring thaw, when the roads would be firm again. But Sharman and Gillis were determined not to wait. During January, Gillis and Dunford supervised the construction in Archangel of special sleighs, none of which when loaded could exceed two tons since the frail bridges on the way to the front would not take heavier loads. They dismantled and loaded the three guns and set out, with as many as ten horses pulling each sleigh. Sharman travelled to Archangel early in March to oversee the departure of the guns and to ensure that the ammunition coming from England was also dispatched immediately, before the roads began to thaw.

It remained doubtful to the last moment whether the ammunition would arrive in time. The *Wardown*, a new freighter carrying the shells, reached Murmansk from England at the end of the first week in March. It took the next three weeks and the efforts of five icebreakers to move her the relatively short distance from Murmansk to Archangel. On March 31, the *Wardown* staggered into port, almost sinking from ice damage.*
At the dock special trains were ready to take her long-awaited cargo to the point on the rail-line where the shells had to be shifted to sleighs for the final stage of their journey to the front. Lieutenant J. Roberts noted in his diary for April 3:

> The long promised 60 pounder gun actually arrived at Malaya Beresnik and it was astonishing the sense of extra security that the possession of one such gun gave to the Column even though most of us had been in France where the presence or absence of one or more guns was not of sufficient importance to mention. But this was a distinct event in our life in Russia as it meant that at least we had range supremacy and could "talk back" however weakly, a thing we had not as yet been able to do.[36]

The fall of Shenkursk and the consequential greater vulnerability of Ironside's force had led the War Office to order Maynard in Murmansk to transfer 2,500 of his men to Archangel. While the Allies were thus regrouping to hold off the Red Guards, they pressed the Whites to reorganize their forces and to recruit new ones. Ironside had been informed that the Allies were most unlikely to stay in northern Russia beyond the late summer of 1919. In his desire to help revitalize the anti-Bolshevik forces, he constantly urged the White officers to adopt

---

* R. Barry O'Brien gives a graphic account of the long struggle to get the Wardown to Archangel in "Icebreaking Operations in the White Sea 1918-19" (Journal of the Royal United Service Institution, Vol. LXXVI, No. 503, August 1931, and No. 504, November 1931). Two of the icebreakers involved had been raised from the mouth of the Dvina where the Bolsheviks had hurriedly sunk them in their effort to stop the landing of the Elope force.

less autocratic attitudes towards their unsettled troops.

Ironside went to the length of almost emptying the overflowing Archangel gaol in the hope that the prisoners would be willing to fight with determination in return for their freedom. Immediately after his arrival in Archangel, he decided that many of the prisoners in the gaol might be put to work unloading the vast quantities of supplies that were arriving. As he noted later, "Many of them were of the worst imaginable type, the very riff-raff of a revolution. Archangel had become the last refuge of criminal or political fugitives from the horrors behind them."[37]

It was a gamble. But, in fact, Ironside had little choice, since it had proved difficult to provide sufficient guards, and the prisoners were of little use where they were. He put the released prisoners in the charge of a young Canadian, Captain Royce Dyer, a former NCO of the 8th Battalion, "the Little Black Devils". Dyer and his adjutant, Patrick Burke, an Australian serving in the New Zealand army, managed to form them into an efficient and hard-working gang of stevedores for work on the docks.

When Ironside decided to add the convicts to the ranks of the Slavo-British Legion, a force composed of Russians in British uniforms under the joint command of British and Russian officers, he looked again to Dyer and before long began to believe that his much-criticized gamble was going to pay dividends. When Dyer's unit of the Slavo-British Legion was first put into the line, it performed well. Dyer himself died of pneumonia and was spared the humiliation of seeing his men involved in a mutiny: on July 7, 1919, the ex-convicts of the Third Company joined with other men of the 1st Battalion of the Slavo-British Legion and the Machine Gun Company of the 4th Northern Rifle Regiment in a mutiny that took the lives of two British officers, Burke the New Zealander, and four Russians.

III *Murmansk· Operation Syren*

On the Archangel front, the Canadian gunners were involved from the beginning in fighting between sizeable numbers of troops. Four hundred miles to the northwest, the Canadians who had been sent to Murmansk were eventually involved in smaller skirmishes, but no less vicious, bloody, and bitter. But at first they had less contact with the enemy than their compatriots around Archangel.

Immediately after their arrival in Murmansk during the early summer of 1918, the Canadian volunteers for Syren were sent through the region to help defend it against anticipated Bolshevik attacks. General Maynard, upon his arrival late in June 1918, had ordered the occupation of Pechenga, a small port on the Barrents Sea about 100 miles west of Murmansk, near the Norwegian border. The War Office feared that the Germans might attempt to seize Pechenga as a U-boat base. At first Maynard had been able to send as a garrison only a few Royal Marines and Serbs, backed up by the guns of H.M.S. *Cochrane* off shore. Reinforcements were needed, if vague rumours of an early Fenno-German advance on Pechenga were well founded.

Major Angus McArthur of New Glasgow, Nova Scotia, Captains J. K. Nesbit, J. W. Hunter, and E. D. Allen, and eighteen NCOs were assigned to the Pechenga garrison on September 27, the day they arrived in Murmansk on board the *Leicestershire*. They re-embarked almost immediately with two British infantry companies, a machine-gun company, and a few engineers, in a filthy little collier that had just discharged a load of coal. Although they were happy to leave such a ship, the troops were hardly overjoyed at what awaited them as barracks in Pechenga: a bleak, bare monastery dating from the sixteenth century.

> The actual place of pilgrimage in honour of one Zosimus, a saint previously unknown to us, was five or six miles inland. The "lower monastery" represented a kind of reception centre for pilgrims at the highest point of navigation. It had the considerable advantage from an invader's point of view of including, clustered round the onion-topped church and its detached belfry, two or three quite large and weatherproof timber resthouses.

Here, as they arrived, platoons made themselves at home, undeterred by a certain odour of sanctity, or it may have been a combination of primaeval dirt and non-existent sanitation. There was hardly a whisper of German-Finn raiders, and few, except "Intelligence", believed it evenly remotely possible that any sizeable force could make its way over 200 miles of dirt road in tundra country at that season. In fact, everyone felt thoroughly comfortable, with the solitary exception of one young officer, something of a Don Juan, who, having been apprised of the nature of the establishment, entered it with obvious misgiving.

. . . the authorities played safe, and on the hypothesis [Pechenga] *might* be attacked in strength during the months when it *might* be blocked by ice, decided to render it self-sufficient for the winter. The garrison pressed on with fortifying the beach-head at the lower monastery, with an outer perimeter of block-houses running from height to height right across the valleys converging on the fjord. As further troops arrived, including a field battery and French *skieurs*, room was made for them by infantry platoons moving out to man the block-houses.[38]

The Pechenga garrison, once its defensive works were completed, set about ensuring that it could, in an emergency, retreat across country to Murmansk. This would have to be done through deep snow and the British officers in the small garrison understandably looked to McArthur and the other Canadians for instructions in skiing. But not all of the Canadians were skiers. One squad of British troops soon found that they, and especially one of their officers who had skied in Switzerland before the war, spent much of their time restoring their Canadian instructor to his feet. "In the end almost everyone, including the instructor, became reasonably proficient."[39] Skiing, snow-shoeing, and football on beaten snow became popular pastimes once the garrison was being properly fed. During the first weeks, food was strictly rationed, for no one knew whether it would be possible to supply the garrison regularly over the winter. Then it became evident that trawlers, sometimes with the help of an icebreaker, could safely unload on the firm ice near the shore. Normal rations were resumed and, thereafter, the 250 Canadians, British, Serbs, and French stationed at Pechenga passed a reasonably comfortable if very boring winter.

At Murmansk, as on the Archangel front, it was necessary to take precautions against an enemy within, "against insurrection and riot within the limits of occupation". General Maynard later recalled that there "existed still a strong undercurrent of Bolshevism, evidenced by agitations and strikes, and by persistent efforts to create trouble between the Allies and the local population. This culminated at times in demonstrations of active hostility, such as the destruction of railway-bridges and attempts to derail trains."[40] There was no easy way for the Allies to deal with problems of civilian unrest and hostility. The only real solution lay with the White Russians. But their cause seemed to many Russian peasants to be similar to, if not identical with, that of the hated tsarist régime. The generally reactionary attitude of the White officers gave them little cause for hope of a new life.

It must have been with some relief that Maynard turned from the complex and often puzzling problems of civil administration to the more familiar questions of defence and offence. A man who favoured the offensive, he soon after arrival launched a three-pronged attack against all known Bolshevik emplacements within striking distance of Murmansk. The offensive was intended to render the Allied force as secure from attack as possible, to mislead the Germans in Finland about its real size, and to open new areas for White Russian recruiting. One of Maynard's three columns, consisting of 150 British and Serbs from Soroka, pushed the Bolsheviks southward along the rail-line. The other two columns set out westward towards the Finnish border. One of these, composed of a unit of Red Finn volunteers (known as the Finnish Legion), led by twenty-eight-year-old Major Robert Bruce Stalker Burton of Winnipeg, made its way from Kandalaksha to the Finnish frontier, driving White Finn patrols before it. On October 3, after a final clash, Burton pushed the last of the White Finns across the frontier. The three columns returned safely to their bases at Soroka, Kandalaksha, and Kem. Burton was so well pleased with the performance of his Red Finns that he asked Leckie to order from England 1,200 sets of Canadian Army maple leaf badges for them to wear. Burton clearly felt that there was no higher honour he could bestow on them. British headquarters in Murmansk did not authorize the order.

Murmansk was now as secure from the approaching winter as Maynard could make it. Any worry about the Germans attempting to use White Finn units to invade northern Russia disappeared when the Germans in Finland were withdrawn to reinforce their hard-pressed armies in Flanders. Maynard's small autumn offensive southward, combined with the approaching armistice on the Western Front, ended any real Bolshevik threat to Murmansk.

Most of the Canadians in the Murmansk region were initially stationed at Kola, a small fishing village which the Royal Navy had briefly bombarded seventy years before during the Crimean War. There, General Maynard made his headquarters, secure from the uncertainties of restless Murmansk. The surrounding barren countryside reminded Colonel Leckie of the sparsely populated northern shore of Lake Superior, but the village itself was crowded. In addition to Canadians, there were a battalion of Italians, the 11th Battalion of the Royal Sussex Regiment, detachments of Royal Engineers and Royal Artillery, a few Poles and Letts, and one Australian NCO (Poles and Letts were not strangers to the area; some had worked with the Chinese and Korean labourers and German prisoners-of-war who had built the railway.) Accommodation in the dirty, malodorous village was meagre. Under the guidance of Major Peter Anderson,* a former building contractor from Edmonton, the Canadians immediately strengthened the dilapidated log huts assigned to them. Impatient with the slowness of the local workmen, they built themselves new log barracks and a large officers' mess (soon known locally as "Canatski Inn").

As October passed into November, the Canadians settled in at Kola. They helped to strengthen its defences, improve its

---

* *Anderson (1868-1945) was born in Newborg, Denmark, and arrived in Edmonton as a young man. He served in France with the First Division, was captured, and became the first Canadian to escape from a German prisoner-of-war camp.*

buildings, and construct kennels for the sleigh dogs expected from Canada. Anderson, with several sergeants to help, cut large quantities of birch in the surrounding forests. With sawmill equipment at Soroka, they soon produced thirty-two Yukon-style dog sleighs, based on a design prepared by a Sergeant Janes working under the supervision of Captain R. D. "Wolf" Adams, a former Klondike gold prospector and a pioneer of Nome, Alaska.

The Canadians were much in demand, for they knew something of construction work in northern climes. Their largest undertaking was to build several miles of narrow-gauge railway from the main rail-line to supply the garrison huts.

> Three weeks from the time the main party reached Kola, the Canadians were found to be lumbering up the river; in charge of sections of other troops on details of unloading and storing of supplies; undertaking duties as railway transport officers; arranging for regulation of railway traffic; and on the general administration of the camp. The detachment was commended on more than one occasion on its efficiency, adaptability and the capacity of the officers and sergeants to carry out any work to which they were assigned.[41]

Following the first heavy snowfall, six of the sergeants began the task they were to continue throughout the winter, the supervision of Lapp reindeer drivers who were the only communication with several outposts.

During their leisure time, the Canadians made friends among the local people, thanks in part to the fluent Russian of Captain Victor Ernest Klanitzki Weldie of the Canadian Field Artillery—an architect in civilian life, who was born in Russia—and to the hospitality of the local Russian railway superintendent who organized a dance to welcome them. The detachment returned the hospitality with film shows and concerts. Soon there were few evenings without some entertainment. Indulgence in the modest pleasures of Kola was, however, short-lived. On November 11, the day of the Armistice on the Western Front, thirty-three of the Canadians were moved from Kola to Soroka, about 400 miles south on the White Sea coast. On November 18, seven weeks after his arrival in northern Russia,

Leckie, now promoted full colonel, assumed command of all Allied troops—including the United States railwaymen—in Soroka and the surrounding district, the advance outpost of Syren force.

By the end of November, all the Canadians but a few who remained at Kola and three who were stationed at Kem (and, of course, those in the Pechenga garrison) were at Soroka. As Syren's southernmost garrison, they organized a small depot for the use of a "super mobile force" that patrolled on skis through the silent forests, watching for any sign of enemy movement. For those Canadians who were not included in such reconnaissance patrols, December was a tiresome month.

Almost on the Arctic Circle, Soroka had little daylight during the winter months and was intensely cold (sixty-four degrees below zero, Fahrenheit, was recorded by the garrison). The sun appeared only briefly on the horizon. The wilderness of the bare coast offered no diversions. Captain Norman Rawson, a twenty-six-year-old Y.M.C.A. welfare officer who had served in France with the Royal Canadian Engineers, set about doing what he could to provide recreation and pastimes. With the help of a unit of Italians, the Canadians built a large log hut which the imaginative and energetic Rawson stocked with writing paper and such English books and magazines as he could obtain. He organized language lessons (Russian was studied by several Canadians), concerts, and church services on Sundays. (After the war, Rawson became a Presbyterian clergyman and had churches in Ottawa and Hamilton.) A well-educated half-Ukrainian, half-Italian refugee girl, whose father had been shot by the Bolsheviks, was found to speak some French. She gratefully left the box-car in which she had taken shelter with other refugees to become an interpreter and an assistant to Rawson.

The local people were generally friendly, if a little reserved. The adjutant of the Canadians noted with some understatement:

> The problem of the future of Russia appears to be one of some little complexity in this part of the country. It would appear that a very large majority of the inhabitants are very favourably disposed toward the Allies and eager to restore a degree of order requisite to the successful future of the country . . . [but] until a definite Allied

policy is decided on it is probable that many will be inclined to
watch the general trend of events rather than [give] an undissenting
committal to the Allied Powers.[42]

The Russian women, for their part, generally did not prove very
attractive even to the Canadians, well known for their catholic
taste in all shapes and forms feminine. The younger women did
the heavy labour, not the men, and they generally showed the
effect. Older women were occasionally the village bath-house
or *sauna* attendants. Armed with birch twigs, they flayed the
astonished troops. Romantic escape from the monotony of
northern Russia was not to be found with such Amazons.

All the villages were crude, the log houses dirty and ugly. The
food was little better. As on the Western Front, the staples of
the military diet were bully beef, hard biscuit, jam, and the
infamous "M&V", which was something like a concentrated
Irish stew. Lime juice and rum were issued in small quantities.
Occasionally eggs and potatoes, purchased from peasants at
exorbitant prices, added some variety to the otherwise dull diet.
Christmas provided some relief. At Soroka, Captain Calvin Fee
presided as Santa Claus at a party given by the officers for the
local people. "The end of the year closed with a mess dinner
. . . and the New Year was ushered in by 'Auld Lang Syne' being
sung in the customary manner with crossed hands of Canadian,
Imperial, French, Serbian, Polish, and Russian Officers,
followed by selections on the bagpipes by the Canadian
piper."[43]

Inactivity is often the soldier's worst enemy. The Canadians at
Soroka welcomed an opportunity in January, after a largely
uneventful autumn, to perform a service that called on all their
skills and recollections of northland travel. On the Archangel
front, the Soviet capture of Shenkursk had led the War Office
to fear a possible threat to Archangel itself. General Maynard
was accordingly ordered to transfer from his more secure
Murmansk theatre to Archangel 2,500 of his men (the 6th and
13th Yorkshire battalions, one battalion of the Liverpool Regiment, and the 280th Machine Gun Company). Five hundred

could be transported on the most powerful of the available icebreakers, but no other ship could force its way through the ice. Colonel Leckie and several of his officers were charged with the daunting task of moving the other 2,000 men overland more than 300 miles from Soroka to Archangel, in sub-zero weather.

Six hundred reindeer sleighs and drivers were assembled at Soroka, the rail-point where the troops detrained for their overland march to Archangel. Only then was it fully realized that their route along the White Sea was so desolate that it was devoid even of the moss on which reindeer live. It was decided that small, indigenous ponies would be more adaptable and, in any case, more manageable than reindeer, which had to be harnessed as many as six abreast. Enough ponies were quickly gathered along with sleighs on which they were able to pull up to 800 pounds.

A third means of transport was provided by sleigh dogs but they, like the reindeer, were not an unqualified success. A correspondent of a London newspaper was more enthusiastic about the dogs than those who had to use them.

> The animals employed were of the Siwash tribe of Canadian Transport Dog [a cross-breed of huskies and malamutes], and were brought from the Dominion for this Expedition. They were useful for those parts where reindeer could not be employed because of the lack of moss beds. The sleighs were of the light Shackleton type, long and narrow, but capable of taking 600 lb. when properly stacked. Special Canadian drivers had to be engaged, for the dogs need very careful understanding and handling.[44]

Before leaving Canada, Captain T. P. O'Kelly of Vancouver had selected twenty-five soldiers with experience as sleigh drivers and purchased 232 dogs in areas around lakes Nipigon and Athabaska and the Mackenzie River. This special unit had arrived in Murmansk late in January (bringing the total number of Canadian personnel in the theatre to 135). Approximately 150 dogs were sent to Kola and the remainder to Soroka. They proved of little use. The first time the dogs met reindeer on the trail, "the *mêlée* that followed [made] Headquarters decide quickly and absolutely that the dogs must go".[45]

The 2,000 troops, by marching in groups of 300 with their supplies on accompanying pony-drawn sleighs, were safely transferred to Archangel in the sub-zero temperatures.

Following the transfer of so many of his troops to Archangel, Maynard moved part of the Pechenga detachment back to Murmansk to bolster its depleted garrison. There was no longer any threat of a German advance on Pechenga for the simple reason that there were no longer any German troops in Finland. Captain E. M. Squairey of Newfoundland led 170 of the 11th Battalion of the Royal Sussex Regiment from Pechenga to Murmansk. With 200 sleighs and 600 reindeer, they covered the 115 miles on skis in three and one-half days. The skiing lessons in Pechenga had proved their worth.

When Winston Churchill became Secretary of State for War on January 14, 1919, he was faced with the practical implications of the Imperial War Cabinet's resolutions of the previous months to send troops to northern and southern Russia and to Siberia, decisions in which he had played no part. Churchill was also faced with the particular implications of the Cabinet's conclusion of a fortnight earlier that no further British troops would be sent to northern Russia until Allied policy with regard to Lenin's government was decided upon by the Paris Conference.

Following the transfer of 2,500 men from Murmansk, there was little else that could be done by the Allies to bolster the Archangel front. With further reinforcement impossible, either overland from Murmansk or across the frozen White Sea, the Archangel force would be in an especially precarious position if the Bolsheviks were able to mount a major and determined offensive. Murmansk itself, even with its depleted Allied garrison, was secure enough, since it could be protected by British warships in its ice-free harbour. But Allied forces in both theatres remained highly vulnerable, especially the isolated units that were spread over difficult terrain south of the two ports.

Local White Russian units might have provided some relief, but recruiting efforts had been notably unsuccessful. A general mobilization decree by the regional government produced only a handful of additional—and untrained—soldiers. A larger

THE WHITE SEA SECTOR / 95

recruiting area might produce better results. An Allied advance to the south would not only enlarge the potential recruiting area but would, it was believed, keep the Bolsheviks off balance and forestall any enemy plans to close in on Murmansk. On the Archangel front, an advance southward was out of the question in the wake of the Allied defeat at Shenkursk.

For the first months of 1919, the scene of the principal fighting in northern Russia shifted from the Archangel front to the Murmansk front. Maynard and the White Russian authorities planned a southward offensive for February. Maynard's hand was, however, forced by the Red Guards, who were also seeking recruits and spreading propaganda in the area south of Murmansk. Intelligence agents reported the threat of a Bolshevik attack against an Allied outpost about eighty miles west of Soroka. To check this movement, Maynard on January 13 authorized a "mobile force" of five Canadian sergeants and seven Finns, under Captain "Wolf" Adams, to reconnoitre the area around the village of Rugozero, whence the Bolshevik attack was to be launched. Adams was allowed the option of attempting to seize the village if it did not appear to be held in strength. This he did on January 16, killing two Bolsheviks and capturing two others. The attack also yielded a large number of documents on which accurate plans for further Allied advances could be based. Adams was awarded the Military Cross for his daring, the first decoration to be won by a Canadian in the Murmansk theatre. Such sorties as these, dangerous though they often were, provided a welcome escape from increasing boredom and from the continuing perplexity about why Allied troops were being kept in the desolation of northern Russia after the end of the Great War.

Maynard, with his western flank now reasonably secure, turned his attention directly southward. Ever eager to be on the offensive, he organized in February an advance along the railline, "to keep the initiative" and to open new areas for White Russian recruiting. Maynard let it be thought that the troops he ordered to Soroka in preparation for the push southward were additional reinforcements for the Archangel front. Leckie was assigned the over-all command of the 600 men of the four-column attacking force. His second-in-command, Major

Mackenzie, headed the eastern column while Major Alfred Eastham commanded one of the two centre columns. Nineteen Canadians served under Mackenzie, twenty-one under Eastham, and a few in the other two columns, along with British machine-gunners, French skiers, and White Russian and Serbian infantry. Captain J. Walter Hunter was responsible for the transportation arrangements for Mackenzie's column and Captain Adams for those of Eastham's column.

The common objective of all four columns was the town of Segezha, about seventy-five miles south of Soroka. Surprise would be impossible if the total force simply advanced along the rail-line. Bolshevik outposts stood in the way and, in any case, Red Guards would very likely destroy the wooden railway bridges near Segezha unless the town could be taken from the flank. In a wide encircling movement, Mackenzie's column set out on February 15 in weather "pitilessly cold, the temperature dropping to over forty degrees below zero, with a biting wind and heavy snow squalls".[46] Ahead lay 115 miles of frozen tundra and snow-covered woods.

Mounting an offensive in such weather and over such terrain was a dangerous, complex, and trying operation. During the next three days only Mackenzie's and one other column were able to reach Segezha in time for the scheduled attack. When the two columns converged on the town, they caught the Bolsheviks unaware and captured the nearby rail bridges intact. The fighting was brief but bitter. House-to-house fighting in Segezha was the climax of a three-day offensive that cost the Allies three dead and eleven wounded. The Bolsheviks lost an estimated fifty dead (including the district commissar) and large amounts of arms and supplies.* A recently trained White Russian unit

---

* Included among captured rail wagons were six manufactured by the Eastern Car Company of Trenton, Nova Scotia, originally sent to Archangel as part of the Allied supplies for the tsarist forces. From the first months of the war, the Imperial Russian government had placed orders for arms, munitions, and other equipment in Canada. Snow-shoes, shells, rifles, bayonets, saddles, and railway equipment (including locomotives), and even icebreakers had been purchased. (The Canadian government icebreakers Earl Grey, which was renamed Canada, and Minto were delivered in 1915 to work in the White Sea.)

participating in the advance had performed well, much to the satisfaction of its British and Canadian instructors. Gratification with the offensive was general and awards were promptly made; both Mackenzie and Eastham received the Distinguished Service Order for their leadership.

March was a generally quiet month. The country was still locked in winter and neither side was inclined to hazard the offensive again. For most of the Canadians, March was a month of patrolling and of escorting supplies. But spring was approaching and with its arrival fighting would probably begin in earnest.

Brigadier-General G. D. Price, the British officer commanding the 237th Brigade (to which Leckie's men were attached), was not happy at the prospect. He wrote to Leckie on March 4: "I heard awful accounts of the Archangel front, place and troops seething with discontent and troops refusing to do their job. Ironside has a hard furrow to plough. . . . Lots of things here too at Kem have gone arseways and I feel one wants about four heads."[47]

Price's fears about unrest on the Murmansk front as well as on the Archangel front were well founded. On April 9 Leckie reported to him that, four days earlier, Red railway workers and Bolshevik sympathizers among the White soldiers had planned to hold a banquet to which the Allied officers at Soroka would be invited and then either seized or murdered. The plot was discovered the day before, only just in time to be frustrated.

By the end of March, arrangements had been made for the Canadians of the Pechenga garrison on the Barents Sea to leave their monastery and rejoin the main group. By the first week of April, all of the Canadians, except small detachments at Kola and Segezha, were again stationed at Soroka. Some acted as instructors for newly raised White Russian units, including one composed of 100 boys who had volunteered for a work party command by Captain Hunter. Despite the language barrier, friendships sprang up between the Canadian instructors and the young Russians. Sergeant R. J. Forbes later took an orphan to Canada where he eventually became a railway stationmaster in Ontario.

On April 10, Major Anderson, who had replaced Eastham in command of the 300 troops at Segezha, received information that a major Bolshevik attack was imminent. Anderson had already distinguished himself for his daring during a long-distance patrol at the time of the capture of the town whose Allied garrison he now commanded. Characteristically, he again decided to seize the initiative and, without awaiting approval from headquarters, to attack the much larger Red garrison at Urosozero, twenty miles south of Segezha on the rail-line. On April 11, Anderson moved southward on a French armoured train carrying forty-one French, thirty-six Russian, nineteen Canadian, seven British, and one American soldiers. Despite the heavy odds in favour of the Bolsheviks—they were estimated to number as many as 500—the surprise raid was a complete success. The Bolsheviks' own offensive was not yet ready when Anderson put an end to their planning by steaming boldly into the Urosozero station and detraining his troops. More than thirty Red Guards were killed and forty taken prisoner. One Canadian, Sergeant C. I. Erickson of the Engineers, was killed, the first Canadian casualty on the Murmansk front. Two field guns and 7,000 shells were captured, along with a machine gun, 100 rifles, and 100 pairs of skis. Most of the shells were found to be of Canadian manufacture, sent to Russia as part of the wartime supplies. Anderson eventually received the D.S.O. and was promoted to lieutenant-colonel for his successful daring, although Maynard's first reaction had been displeasure on learning that the wilful and energetic Anderson had launched the attack without first seeking the concurrence of headquarters. Anderson's extension of the Allied line in turn led to a further small offensive to secure the flank of Urosozero. In the capture of Vojmosalmi in April, Major Eastham, five other Canadian officers, and twelve sergeants participated.

IV   *Withdrawal*

Spring was coming to northern Russia. The silence of the woods, heavy with snow, gave way to the first sounds and movements of spring. The season was approaching when a major offensive could be launched, leading into the hinterland of Russia. There was, however, no such aggressive intention at Allied headquarters and there were insufficient White Russian troops to launch a major offensive. During the late autumn of 1918, it had seemed for a brief moment that the White Russian forces in the Urals, if supported by the much more efficient Czech Legion, might be able to effect a juncture with the Whites of northern Russia. But that brief hope had soon flickered out. By the spring of 1919, it was evident that, after a winter of confusion, corruption, defeat, and withdrawal, the anti-Bolshevik forces were everywhere in retreat and everywhere in disorder. There could no longer be any hope of a grand convergence of White Russians from the east and north.

In any event, the pressures for the return to Britain of the "duration only" men serving in northern Russia had been increasing rapidly since the Armistice. The soldiers themselves were restless, resentful about being detained in the army when their comrades from the Western Front had, months before, been returned home for discharge. Further, some in the War Office itself questioned whether the regular army soldiers would not better serve Imperial interests elsewhere in the world. In war-weary Britain, there was a widespread urge to return as quickly as possible to "normalcy" and to avoid interference in the affairs of others. In the ranks of the opposition Labour Party, suspicions were strong about why the troops had been left in northern Russia over the winter.

The intervention was cited as evidence of a capitalist conspiracy to stifle the first socialist state (however imperfect it might be), to restore an autocratic régime, and to regain Russian recognition of the enormous debts the tsarist government had incurred with British and French bond-holders. The fact that the right wing of the London press was so vociferous in its condemnation of Lenin's government was regarded as evidence of a concerted plot on the part of the British upper classes, industrialists, bankers, press barons, and the Conservative Party to overthrow the new government of Russia.

Many more than Labour supporters and radical Liberals saw

in the Allied military intervention a violation of one of the basic principles over which the Great War had been fought. No nation or group of nations should attempt to impose its will on another.

Winston Churchill, Secretary of State for War, had the various opponents of intervention in mind when he rose in the House of Commons on March 3 to introduce the army estimates.

> It is no use people raising prejudice against these expeditions. . . . They were sent as part of our operations against Germany. It was vitally necessary to take every measure in regard to Russia during the war which would keep as many German troops as possible on the Russian front, and reduce that formidable movement of the German armies which carried more than a million men to the Western Front. . . .
>
> That reason has passed away, but the troops sent in obedience to it are still on these wild northern coasts, locked in the depth of winter and we must neglect nothing required for their safety and well-being.
>
> Further, we have incurred heavy commitments towards the people of these districts who have espoused our cause, and to the Russian armies, which were encouraged and called into being largely by the Allies and largely for our own purposes during the period of the German war. It has been the custom in this country to pay particular attention to matters of this kind and always to endeavour, to the very best of our ability, to do our duty by those who have put their trust in us, and who have run into danger in consequence of action which we have advised them to take.[48]

Planning for the relief of the Murmansk and Archangel contingents was going on, even as Churchill spoke (as early as February 16, a War Office memorandum had urged the need for a "forward defensive movement"). On March 4, the day following Churchill's statement in the House, the War Cabinet decided that all British (including Canadian) troops should be out of northern Russia by June. On April 3, Churchill received Lloyd George's approval for a large "Rescue Force" which the War Office intended to undertake, a general offensive designed in part to ensure that the White Russians would have the largest possible area under their control before the Allies withdrew. The North Russia Expeditionary Force, refugees, and, finally, the relief force itself could then be evacuated in an orderly fashion, well away from the front lines. There were to be no hairbreadth escapes of the Dunsterforce type.

In these circumstances, the War Office hastened to implement the second of the two suggestions made by the Director of Military Operations and sent the following somewhat flowery message to Ironside and Maynard on April 4 for promulgation to their troops:

Although you are cut off from your country by ice, you are not forgotten. Your safety and well-being, on the contrary, is one of the main anxieties of the War Office, and we are determined to do everything in our power to help you and bring you safely home. You were sent to North Russia to help draw off the Germans from attacking our armies in France, and undoubtedly you helped last year to keep large numbers of German troops away from the battlefield and so enabled a decisive victory to be won.

Whatever may be the plan of action towards Russia decided on by The League of Nations, *we intend to relieve you at the earliest possible moment*, and either bring the whole force away or replace you by fresh men. These reliefs are being prepared now, and will come through the ice to your aid at the earliest possible moment when the ships can break through. Meanwhile, your lives and your chance of again seeing your home and friends and your fellow-countrymen, who are looking forward to give you a hearty welcome, depend absolutely on your discipline and dogged British fighting qualities. All eyes are upon you now, and you represent the British Army which has fought and won and which is watching you confidently and earnestly. *You will be back home in time to see this year's harvest gathered in*, if you continue to display that undaunted British spirit which has so often got us through in spite of heavy odds and great hardships. Only a few more months of resolute and faithful service against this ferocious enemy and your task will have been discharged. Carry on like Britons fighting for dear life and dearer honour, and set an example in these difficult circumstances to the troops of every other country. Reinforcement and relief on the way. We send you this personal message with the most heartful [*sic*] wishes for your speedy, safe and honourable return.[49]

The troops were perhaps more heartened by the tangible

evidence around them that the long winter was finally ending and that the port of Archangel would soon be reopened.

During the first months of 1919, low morale, disaffection, and the severe cold, rather than the strength of the enemy, had been the fundamental problems confronting the Allied units in northern Russia. Normally the troops remained in their warm blockhouses. Neither side was very eager to attack during the sub-arctic winter. Men's thoughts were concentrated on how to stay alive in the cold. To survive was enough; there would be ample time in the spring to fight, if fight they must. What worried General Ironside much more than the possibility of a Bolshevik offensive was the incipient unrest among his own troops.

As early as October 17, only a fortnight after his arrival, Ironside had cabled the War Office that the French 21st Colonial Battalion had shown great restiveness when rumours had reached it of an approaching armistice on the Western Front. But, in 1919, it was British troops rather than French who were the first to refuse to obey orders. Ironside telegraphed the War Office on February 23 that some of the men of the 13th Battalion of the Yorkshires had "refused to go in support and relief of Russian and British troops". He suggested that announcement in the United States that the American troops were to be withdrawn "at an early date" had probably contributed to the low morale. By February 26, men of the Army Service Corps and the Royal Army Medical Corps had also disobeyed orders. Three NCOs and thirty soldiers were court-martialled and two sergeants who were the ringleaders were sentenced to be shot. However, standing orders of King George V issued after the Armistice required the commutation of the sentences to life imprisonment. Ironside knew that even such harsh sentences would not by themselves counteract the growing unrest in his mixed force. Within a fortnight of the British mutiny, men of the French 21st Colonial Battalion, on leave in Archangel, exhibited serious disaffection by refusing to return to the line. The soldiers informed the French consul that they would assist in the defence of the port of Archangel if this proved necessary in order to secure an escape route for the Allied force, but that they would not participate in any further offensive action against men with whom they had no quarrel. Two hundred French *skieurs* on the Murmansk front followed their example. United States troops also showed increasing signs of restiveness, including resentment at serving under British officers of some-times doubtful quality.* An Australian sergeant later recalled that "on signing of the Armistice . . . things began to take a more serious aspect. There appeared to be only one line of thought among all ranks and nationalities. On every side was heard nothing but, 'What are we here for?' 'Can't these Ruskies do a bit for themselves?' 'If they have such a good cause, why don't they do their own fighting?', and so on."[50]

With this rapidly increasing unrest in mind, the Director of Military Operations at the War Office wrote to the Deputy Chief of the Imperial General Staff on March 27 that the troops are a

> . . . heterogenous assortment of all nationalities and were never of
> a high quality. They are now tired, dispirited, homesick and
> inclined to be mutinous; their moral [sic] is undoubtedly so low as
> to render them a prey to the very active and insidious Bolshevik
> propaganda which the enemy are carrying out with increasing
> energy and skill.[51]

In order to help counter this gradual deterioration in morale, the Director of Military Operations proposed the appointment to northern Russia of relief officers of proven ability and the granting of authority to Maynard and Ironside to announce that all soldiers entitled to demobilization would be replaced at the earliest possible date. But, before the War Office took any decisions on these sensible recommendations, further signs of deteriorating morale manifested themselves.

On March 29, Company I of the 339th U.S. Infantry Regiment refused briefly to return to the front. The Canadians were not

---

* A contemporary complaint by a Y.M.C.A. officer, reflecting the general dissatisfaction among the United States troops about the British officers placed over them, is Ralph Albertson's Fighting Without a War (New York: Harcourt, Brace and Howe, 1920).

entirely immune from this growing contagion. In a letter to the Chief of the Canadian General Staff on April 13, 1919, Colonel Sharman reported that one section had briefly refused to obey orders.* The explanation was contained in a cable Ironside had sent to the War Office four days before:

> Will you put strongly in front of Canadian Government the fact that neither Arctic pay nor weekly bonus are being drawn by Canadian Officers and Men here. The Canadians out here, especially the artillery brigade, have been the backbone of the expedition; but owing to the above grievance one section definitely refused to obey orders for 24 hours. The matter was settled, but the fine service of the Canadians would be completed without further incident by the grant of allowances similar to British.[52]

Two months before, on February 6, Ottawa had declined to pay the equivalent of the additional daily British arctic allowance of one shilling for NCOs and sixpence for privates. But a letter of April 13 from Ironside and a long, detailed report by Sharman in favour of the allowance (which he sent to London the following day) eventually convinced Ottawa. The Director of Military Operations at the War Office wrote to Sir Edward Kemp on April 14, strongly supporting Ironside's plea:

> I cannot speak too highly of the work of these troops and think that everything possible should be done to allay any grievances. . . . I realize that the Canadian troops are paid better than the British and therefore have no very clear grounds for their request but it is sometimes difficult to convince men who are at the front of the justice of cold logic.[53]

After further unexplained delays on the part of the army headquarters in Ottawa, the proposal was finally submitted to the cabinet on May 27 and was promptly approved. The authority to pay the Canadians the arctic allowance arrived in Archangel only shortly before they departed from northern Russia. Until then, their ineligibility was resented not only in itself; it

---

* This incident received no publicity, but a passing reference to it occurs unexpectedly in John Harris's novel about the fighting in southern Russia, Light Cavalry Action (London: Hutchinson, 1967).

also became a focus for the frustrations and perplexities of men still on combat duty when their comrades-in-arms from the Western Front were returning home and taking, so it seemed, all the best civilian jobs.

The Great War was over. Most other Allied soldiers had by the spring of 1919 been demobilized. To those in northern Russia, there appeared to be no justification for their continued presence in the homeland of an "enemy" against whom many felt no animosity. The reasons for the unrest naturally varied from man to man and from unit to unit. The Americans were dissatisfied with the British, the Allies were dissatisfied with the White Russians, no one was sanguine about the future, and most were deeply puzzled to know why they were fighting men who had overthrown a hated autocratic régime. Further, food was sometimes meagre and generally of low quality. Accommodation was bad and the weather severe. It is not surprising that Bolshevik propaganda, crude though it generally was, made some headway, while agitation at home for the return of the Allied troops became more and more insistent.

The morale of the White Russian forces was even worse. Many of their private soldiers agreed with much or all of what Lenin and Trotsky were proclaiming in Moscow. White Russian officers were often so reactionary that even the more conservative or unthinking among the private soldiers were alienated. Where there was no commitment to communism, there was often indifference among Russian soldiers as well as civilians. In these circumstances, the position of the Allied forces was rendered difficult by the disinterested, if not hostile, attitude of many of the local Russians with whom they were supposed to be co-operating. It was rendered positively dangerous by the unreliable attitude of some of the White Russian units forming part of the common front against the Red Army.

One of the worst cases of mutiny occurred in the Dvina column on the morning of April 25. Earlier in the month, the defence of the left bank of the river had been assigned to approximately 1,000 White Russian troops who had been trained by the Allies. Their officers had pressed for an independent command. Now they had it.

The artillery fire that awakened the Canadian gunners at 5:00 in the morning on April 25 was clearly coming from the White battery of four guns on the other side of the river. But at whom the White Russians were firing was not at all clear. "The guns seemed to be firing almost at point blank range to their front, rear and right flank." There was no response to repeated wireless calls or signal lamps. The river was almost impassable, with great fissures and open spaces in the ice. Some of it was already shifting and breaking into huge blocks. By 6:30, the Allied troops felt they could no longer remain inactive; the Canadian gunners laid down a light box barrage around the Russian camp on the opposite side of the river so as to deter anyone from either entering or leaving the area. By 8:00, a Russian artillery officer and three of his gunners, under heavy machine-gun and rifle fire, managed to cross the ice-choked river, alternately dragging and rowing a boat over the moving ice.

They brought the disturbing news that the White Russian infantrymen had mutinied, murdered their officers, and declared themselves for the Reds. However, the White Russian gunners, who had been trained by the Canadians, remained loyal. It was they who were shelling both their mutinous compatriots and the Red units advancing in support of the mutineers.

As the mutineers had foreseen, the Allied troops could not cross the ice-choked river in any numbers. The Canadian gunners did, however, open fire across the mile-and-one-half of river on every point where the disaffected troops were known to be. Although acting in unison through lamp signals, the combined fire of the Canadian and loyal White gunners could not by itself prevent the mutineers and the Red Guards from pressing in on the White Russian artillery. By 9:30, their position was becoming untenable. Their signal lamps flashed to the Canadians: "Cannot hold out any longer; support withdrawal of guns." A brief hiatus in the Bolshevik advance gave the White Russian gunners time to limber their guns and to escape, through encircling mutineers and Red Guards, to new positions seven miles down the river.

This withdrawal immediately rendered the position of the Allied force on the opposite bank of the Dvina very difficult. With the riverside directly opposite and for several miles downstream now in Bolshevik hands, the Allied troops were vulnerable to bombardment. The Bolsheviks had gained a number of advantages as a result of the disaffection of the White units. From Tulgas, which was on higher ground, they now overlooked all of the Allied positions around the village of Kurgomen. The total of Red forces in the area had suddenly increased to an estimated 2,500, while the Allies had been reduced to only 550 (including about 160 Royal Scots, 140 Canadian gunners, and seventy-five White Russians). Even more important, the Reds could also outgun the Canadians. Not only did they have artillery of greater range, but the Dvina thawed inland before it thawed at its mouth, with the result that the Bolsheviks were able to bring the six-inch guns of their gunboats into use before the British could get their gunboats up the ice-filled river from Archangel.

After the mutiny on April 25, the Bolsheviks were able to shell the Allied positions in and around Kurgomen constantly, taking advantage of the fact that there was now about twenty hours of daylight. Red infantry was discouraged from attempting any direct attack by a judicious use of artillery, but there was nothing the Canadians could do with their eighteen-pounders to silence the longer-range guns on the other side of the river.

The Allied position improved greatly on May 6 when a Royal Navy monitor managed to force its way through the ice to Kurgomen. The Allies now had an effective answer to the Red gunboats. Two more British monitors (which two years before had been shelling Turks on the River Tigris) and four gunboats arrived the next day and were placed under Sharman's command. Under cover of their five-inch and six-inch guns, and of the Canadian artillery in Kurgomen, the Royal Scots crossed safely to the point downriver where the loyal White Russian artillery had established itself after its withdrawal from Tulgas. On May 18, after careful planning and preliminary bombing by

R.A.F. aircraft, an Allied counterattack was launched to drive the Bolsheviks from Tulgas. If the Allied position at Kurgomen was to be secure, the counterattack had to succeed. By the late afternoon of May 18, the Allies had retaken Tulgas and captured thirty prisoners, and their position was restored to what it had been three weeks before. Incredible though it seemed, not an Allied soldier had been lost during those three precarious weeks.

The Allied position was, however, far from secure. The same day as the recapture of Tulgas, Ironside had telegraphed the War Office that two companies of White Russians at Pinega had mutinied, killing two of their officers. "I regret to report that I had to shoot fifteen."

The spring weather of April and May also brought new dangers for the men of the 68th Battery attached to the Vaga Column. They knew that the ice up the river would break up before the ice at Archangel. Hence the Bolshevik gunboats on the Vaga were in the same advantageous position as those on the Dvina: they could begin operations before the British gunboats that had wintered in Archangel. With the support of their gunboats, the Red forces, to mark May Day, began a general attack that lasted from morning to night. Despite their advantage, the Red units failed in their attack. Their artillery and the Canadian gunners shelled each other throughout the day, but with little effect. The men of the Liverpool Regiment were not to be dislodged and their casualties were few. The Bolsheviks, on the other hand, suffered an estimated sixty-six dead, and thirty-eight were taken prisoner.

The arrival of the Royal Navy gunboats "was the beginning of the end as far as our work in the Vaga Column was concerned. For almost immediately, that is on May 12th and 14th, Russian personnel reported to the Column to take over from us."[54] The 68th Battery was, however, in action once more before departing for Archangel. It was decided that the White Russians should be given one more opportunity to advance with the support of Allied units before they withdrew. On May 20, the White Russian forces, backed by Allied troops, captured seventy-one more Bolsheviks and killed twenty-two in a final advance intended to render their positions as secure as possible and to protect the withdrawal of the Allied troops.

As in the case of Archangel, so also in the Murmansk sector a general advance was made southward to open new recruiting territory, to give the White Russian forces as much opportunity as possible to fight alongside the steadier Allied troops, and to win defensive positions capable of being held by the relief force while the original units were withdrawn. Maynard telegraphed the War Office on April 25, "Russian leaders are urging me very strongly to press forward, stating that unless they are permitted to follow up recent successes the morale of the troops will suffer. They affirm too that the advance will open up the most hopeful of all recruiting areas, and do more than anything else to stop Bolshevik agitation throughout the occupied [sic] areas. . . . I feel justified, under the circumstances, in further aggressive action, providing good results are promised."

The offensive south of Murmansk began after the thaw, on May 1, with three columns advancing over a sixty-mile front towards Lake Onega. In the centre column, Colonel Leckie commanded a detachment of thirty Canadians (in which Major Anderson played a prominent part), 100 Royal Marines, 100 Russians, thirty Americans, and sections of British and French artillery. Even Captain Norman Rawson, the Y.M.C.A. officer, joined in by serving with the British gunners. After forty-eight hours of continuous fighting, the column stormed and captured Morskaya Maselga on May 3. Pushing on southward, and fighting from rail-siding to rail-siding wherever they were opposed, the three columns converged on Medvyejya Gora, repairing sabotaged track as they advanced. The town fell on May 21 to the column led by Leckie.

During June, Maynard jumped his troops forward from village to village down the western side of Lake Onega, aiming at Kiappeselga, a point on the railway where defensive lines for the summer could best be established. Of Leckie's column, one of his officers wrote:

> When Colonel Leckie developed his attack, the garrison of Dianova Gora retired, and as they came down the road in twos and threes

some of them dragging machine guns on wheel mountings . . . [we] captured them all and had a pretty gang of Bolsheviks and equipment to hand over. . . . In the afternoon with motorcycle-mounted machine guns and a few men, we captured Unitza, another village to the southwest.[55]

In hot, humid weather, with mosquitoes now a constant torment, the three columns converged on Kiappeselga. The town surrendered late in the night on July 5. With the seizure of the northern and much of the western shore of Lake Onega, Maynard had completed the advance sanctioned by the War Office. However, local opposition to Bolshevik rule in nearby areas seemed to him to require an Allied response and this help was given. The Allied line was thereby further extended. By mid July, large sections of the west and east sides of Lake Onega had been occupied.

When Maynard ended the offensive and Allied positions on Lake Onega were secure, Leckie moved his headquarters from Soroka to Povenetz on the lake's northern shore. Installations to service the armed motor boats and seaplanes that had arrived from England at the end of May were quickly constructed along the shallow lake-side. The Bolsheviks had an armed flotilla on the lake, but it was outclassed in every way by the Royal Navy and American motor boats, backed up by the Fairey 3C and Shorts seaplanes of the R.A.F. operating from a hastily built base near Medvyejya Gora.

The White Russians were now in control from Murmansk to Kiappeselga, and within this vast area they sought actively, if not very successfully, to recruit or conscript young men. Canadians at Maselga and Medvyejya Gora found themselves once again acting as instructors. Lawrence Mackenzie, who had been promoted to lieutenant-colonel on May 28, commanded the Canadians in the region, while Captain Calvin Fee acted as their quartermaster. The Russian-speaking Captain Victor Weldie served as an intelligence officer, helping to evaluate information obtained about the dispositions and intentions of the Red Army.

Despite appearances, the position of the White Russian forces was basically insecure. White reaction and brutality and Red propaganda had combined to stimulate pro-Bolshevik sentiment among a growing number of White soldiers. Around Lake Onega, communist agitators and propagandists either had remained behind when the area had passed to White control or had infiltrated the Allied lines. Their efforts to subvert whole units of the restless White troops almost succeeded at Maselga. On July 5, Canadian officers serving there had learned from several Russian privates that some of the other soldiers were plotting to murder their own officers, and also the Canadians if they got in their way, and then go over to the Reds. The ringleaders were promptly arrested, summarily court-martialled, and executed by the same White Russian officers who were to have been their victims.

The rot of disaffection was equally evident on the Archangel front. A major mutiny occurred there two days after the Maselga incident. A fortnight later, on the White Sea coast, the garrison at Onega handed the town over to the Bolsheviks. For three weeks it remained in their hands, rendering the rail-line near Soroka vulnerable to sabotage. But, before any real destruction occurred, the town was retaken on August 10 by the Serbs. These and other mutinies underlined the precarious nature of the White Russian hold on the whole northern area. The Allied military presence had given the Whites the opportunity over the winter to demonstrate their ability to win popular support. They had failed utterly.

By late May, ice conditions in the White Sea had finally improved enough to allow the entry of the British relief force, totalling 8,000 all ranks. The relief ships reached Murmansk on May 26 and Archangel on June 6. The orders the relief force brought were simple in content, if not of execution. Having helped to assure the safe withdrawal of the Allied troops from Murmansk and Archangel by driving back the Red Army, they were themselves to withdraw by October, before ice again became a navigational hazard. They would, some still hoped, leave the Archangel region in the hands of trained White Russian troops able to withstand Bolshevik attacks until White forces elsewhere in Russia could overcome the communists.

They were well-trained and well-equipped veterans who soon

took over the lines, permitting the withdrawal of most of the troops that had served in northern Russia throughout the winter.* Nine Canadians with especially long service in France and with pressing family responsibilities at home left Murmansk for England at the end of May, along with the French gunners and *skieurs*. (The Royal Marines embarked on June 7, the Italian infantry early in July, and the United States railway troops on July 15.) The main group of Canadians in the Murmansk sector—Colonel Leckie and his 100-odd men—was at this time in the Lake Onega area with more than ten weeks of action still ahead.

The War Office had planned for the 16th Brigade to be replaced in the Archangel sector by White Russian and British gunners from the relief force. It was, accordingly, part of a well-considered plan that, on May 28, after firing two final rounds at the Bolsheviks, the 67th Battery was withdrawn from the line and loaded with its guns onto scows. Pulled by tugboats, the battery sailed down the river to Archangel. Major Arnoldi was justifiably proud of his men. He later wrote of them:

> Many times in France, I had talked with other chaps and discussed what a corker of an outfit one could make if one had the choice of men from the whole Corps. Well, I had them. Men from every unit, at least every brigade, including new men from Canada. Picked from a reserve of some 8,500, including the cream of the School of Gunnery. The men were even beyond my expectation and never during our eight months' existence on the front were there any signs of discontent among them. Always game for a fight or a laugh and it was generally both.[56]

A fortnight later, at 3:00 in the morning on June 7, 1919, the 68th Battery boarded barges and began its trip down the Vaga and Dvina. In the warm weather, clouds of black flies and mosquitoes, as virulent as those of the Canadian north, accompanied the barges. The body of Captain Mowat was exhumed and

---

* *The volunteers of the relief force were generally men whose wartime experiences had become more familiar to them than the peacetime life of Britain and who welcomed the chance of further military service. The same phenomenon was to be seen in the volunteers for the Canadian force sent to Siberia.*

placed on the last barge in a specially constructed square box (to escape detection, it having been decided that the Allied dead would be left in northern Russia). Thus it made the initial stage of its long voyage to New Brunswick.

Colonel Sharman paraded his men twice during the hot day of June 10, before their embarkation. In the morning they were inspected by General de Miller, the military governor of northern Russia, who praised the brigade warmly. Four Canadian officers had already received Russian decorations for gallantry during the course of the winter. Now Sharman was given the Order of Stanislas. (He and Major Hyde had already received the Order of St. Vladimir.) All of the other Canadian officers were presented with the Order of Ste. Anne. General de Miller also presented ten St. George Medals to the brigade, which was the only Allied unit in the north to be so honoured. In accordance with the Russian military custom, Sharman left it to his men to choose the ten bravest among them to receive the medals. In the afternoon, the brigade also paraded for Ironside, with whom Sharman had developed a pronounced mutual admiration, and heard him state that "over and over again the CFA [Canadian Field Artillery] had saved the Force from destruction and that the highest traditions of the Canadian Corps had been fully maintained".[57]

Sir Edward Kemp was no less pleased with the performance of the 16th Brigade. In referring to the Canadians in Russia during a speech in the House of Commons on May 27, 1919, he somewhat immodestly stated: "Our men have been the backbone of that expedition, because they are physically fit and understood their work, and I have no hesitation in saying that they were the best of the troops sent there."

Sharman was more reticent. From his veteran gunners he had asked and received much, but even those who did not have the good fortune to be gunners had exceeded his expectations. He noted in his final report:

> The attached officers, Medical, Veterinary, Dental, Pay and
> Y.M.C.A. had been specially selected by their respective
> departments, at my request, the requisite qualifications, in addition
> to their departmental fitness, being that they should be strong, in

good health and optimists. The latter is a particularly valuable asset, as I found in previous service in Klondike, and it was a great pleasure to see how these officers cheerfully undertook duties far in excess of their normal and travelled . . . over hundreds of miles to properly perform their work. Before we had been a month in the country an occasion arose when every available man on Brigade H.Q. was on outpost duty . . . with the Medical, Veterinary and Dental officers each in charge of patrols.[58]

At 5:00 in the afternoon on June 11, twenty-two officers and 455 other ranks of the brigade sailed for England in the converted Cunard liner Czarista. Also aboard were most of the Canadian pilots and observers who had flown with the two R.A.F. detachments.* Mowat's body, too, was aboard, but those of six other Canadian dead had to be left behind.† "On arrival at Leith, Scotland, on June 18, everyone was given ten days' leave and . . . a few hectic days (and nights) [were spent] preparing unnumerable forms in quintuplicate, which was cheerfully undergone as a preliminary to getting home and into civilian life again."[59] At York on Dominion Day, the brigade paraded for the last time, to be inspected by General Turner. It sailed for Canada on July 4, 1919, by which time some of the men had been away from home for almost five years.‡

During the spring of 1919, Canadian newspapers, clubs, trade unions, and private individuals had increasingly pressed Ottawa to explain what Canadian interest the troops in northern Russia were serving. Ottawa had no real answer and urged on London

* Lieutenant Francis F. Tattam of Winnipeg did not embark with the other aircrew. On March 31 he and two British wireless operators had been ambushed. The two British were killed and he was captured. Tattam was repatriated during the autumn of 1919, along with most other Allied soldiers captured in northern Russia.

† Five Canadians had been killed in action and a sixth, Gunner J. J. McDonald, had died of an illness contracted during the winter.

‡ In accordance with the established practice for Canadian units supplied by the British Army, the War Office sent Ottawa a bill of £49,407/18/10 (approximately one-quarter of a million dollars at the then rate of exchange) for supplies used by the brigade in northern Russia.

their early return. As early as April 3, Sir Henry Wilson wrote Churchill from Paris that the "Canadians propose to withdraw certain men from their two batteries at Archangel at once and without relief." The War Office, however, appeared to procrastinate. At the London headquarters of the Canadian forces, the patience of the Chief of Staff, General Turner, ran out when the War Office continued to return evasive replies to his inquiries about the plans being made for the repatriation of the Canadians in Murmansk and Archangel. On May 15, Turner wrote to Colonel Gordon Harrington, the Deputy Minister of Overseas Military Forces of Canada (and a future premier of Nova Scotia):

> I think that the Ministry should put up a very strong protest at the continued retention of our people in this area. The Archangel front is now open and Imperial [i.e., British] Forces appear to consider they will suit themselves as to whether they will or will not return our people. I do not think this attitude should be tolerated any longer, and, if necessary, now the premier is here, I think some action should be taken.[60]

Turner's letter had the desired effect. At luncheon on May 17, Harrington emphasized to Borden the points Turner had made to him. Borden undertook to raise the question himself with the War Office, having already been pressed by Winston Churchill, the Secretary of State for War, to leave Canadian troops in Siberia. The following day Borden sent a stiff letter to Churchill.

> Beyond question it is imperative that the Canadian Forces now at Archangel should be withdrawn without delay. The demobilization of the Canadian Corps and the withdrawal of Canadian Troops from Siberia render any further continuance of our forces at Archangel absolutely impracticable. On the 10th of March the War Office suggested that Canadian Troops could not be withdrawn until the port of Archangel should be opened for navigation. The period thus indicated has now arrived. However, on 30th April a letter from the War Office indicates that it is not proposed to withdraw them until late summer or autumn. Many of these troops were sent in the first instance for instructional purposes. Doubtless they have not objected to the active service which has been substituted for the original purpose. Recently, there has been unfortunate evidence of keen resentment on their part at the continued delay. A few weeks

ago a very capable Canadian officer who had just arrived from
Archangel emphasized the very trying effects of long continued
service in that region [and] told me that not only the Canadians but
all the forces at Archangel and Murmansk who have been there
more than six or eight months should be relieved as soon as
conditions of navigation permit.

However, I have no right to speak for the others; but I do insist
that the Canadians shall be withdrawn immediately.[61]

Borden sent Lloyd George a copy of his letter to Churchill. In
a covering note he added the terse comment: "It will be most
unfortunate if the War Office persists in its apparent determination to extend the period of service for the Canadians . . . I
must insist that they shall be withdrawn without the slightest
unnecessary delay."

Borden received no reply to either letter. In fact, without
bothering to inform him, the War Office was arranging for the
replacement of the Canadian artillery brigade in the Archangel
theatre by White Russian and British gunners. And there was
no intimation of when Leckie's men might be withdrawn from
Murmansk. Harrington accordingly wrote to the Secretary of the
War Office on June 13. For all its verbosity and circumlocution,
the letter reflects the complete loss of patience by Canadians
with the way British were dealing with the men loaned to them.

I am to state that it is apprehended no discourtesy has been
intended in this regard [Harrington wrote acidly], yet it would
appear that approximately a month is ample time in which to
dispatch a reply to the foregoing communication [Borden's letter of
May 18]. I am to inform you that the continuation of Canadian
troops in North Russia is no longer sanctioned, and I am to express
the hope that your convenience will permit a reply being dispatched
to this office in the immediate future, with the information that the
withdrawal of these Canadian troops has actually commenced.[62]

The War Office took six days to reply to this broadside. In
a reply of June 19, it was confirmed that the artillery brigade was
already on its way from Archangel to England. The Canadian
"instructors" were, however, still needed in the Murmansk
theatre. Maynard found them of the greatest assistance. Could
Maynard accordingly call for volunteers among the Canadians

to remain with the relief force? From Ottawa on June 28, Mewburn agreed as long as any such volunteers transferred formally from the Canadian to the British army. However, when Harrington replied to the War Office query he simply said that no volunteers were approved, omitting even Mewburn's concession.

The War Office then did nothing until July 10, when it finally informed Maynard that the Canadian government had ordered the immediate evacuation of all Canadians. The War Office added, however, that "their move . . . must not jeopardize the safety of the British and Allied troops in this area".[63] Maynard, taking his cue from the War Office message, responded promptly, calling for the continuation of the Canadians' assignment. On July 21 a telegram was on its way from Churchill to Borden urgently requesting the retention of the Canadians in the Murmansk theatre: "I cannot take the responsibility of transmitting an order . . . which would lead to an immediate disaster and to the destruction of British troops."[64] This was an exaggerated compliment to the prowess of the Canadians, but there could be only one response to such an appeal. From Ottawa, the Minister of Trade and Commerce and Acting Prime Minister, Sir George Foster, agreed the following day to Maynard's request. The Chief of the Canadian General Staff also wired the War Office sanctioning the continued service of the men in the Murmansk region until September—but not beyond. On August 13, a full three months after receiving the first request for the return of the Canadian troops, the Secretary of the War Office had the satisfaction of writing to Harrington, noting that "the Canadian Government has agreed to the temporary retention of the Officers and other ranks whose withdrawal would prejudice the position of the remaining British troops."[65]

Colonel Leckie and the other Canadian volunteers in the Murmansk sector did not finally embark for Glasgow until August 21, following their replacement on the shores of Lake Onega by the British relief force.

On September 18, a month after Colonel Leckie and his men embarked on the first stage of their long journey home, the final

Allied advance ended thirty miles north of the major town of Petrozavodsk. Along with large amounts of equipment, the line was turned over to the White Russian forces a few days later. The Allied troops were then withdrawn to Murmansk, and the last of them sailed from there on October 12, 1919, nineteen months after the Royal Marines had first landed. An Australian infantry officer later wrote of their departure:

> Thus ended another of the many pathetic side-shows of the Great War. It achieved nothing, cost the British taxpayer many hundreds of thousands of pounds, but the most tragic thing of all was the number of splendid men who lost their lives in the venture—men who, having passed through the dangers of France, Gallipoli and other theatres of war, deserved a better fate.[66]

The final stage in the sorry history of the White Russian forces in the Murmansk theatre is one of almost unrelieved defeat, mutiny, and growing disorder. The peasants were increasingly indifferent or hostile. The "Bolos", on the other hand, displayed growing confidence and efficiency. All along the route northward, as the Whites were driven back, reprisals were frequent. During the winter months, the Bolsheviks rapidly made their way up the rail-line to Murmansk, which they seized without much opposition on February 21, 1920, two days after another Bolshevik force had marched into Vladivostok.

For most Canadians, the year of service in northern Russia had been demanding and dangerous in a conflict marked by brutality and cruelty on both sides. But, for one Canadian, the experience ended not in fighting but in furthering an act of concord and reconciliation. Major Burton had throughout the winter commanded the Finnish Legion, a force of over 1,000 Red Finns. They were bitterly opposed to General Mannerheim's White Finns, who, supported by German troops, had driven the communists from power in Helsinki early in the summer of 1918. The Germans in Finland were also the enemies of the Allies. Thus the interests of the Allies and Red Finns had coincided as long as the Germans remained in Finland. But, when the last Germans withdrew in December 1918, Allied enthusiasm in opposing Mannerheim declined sharply and the confidence of the Red Finns in the Allies rapidly dwindled. Soon the Legion was entrusted only with guard duties along the railway near Kandalaksha, well away from the front line where temptation to switch their allegiance to fellow communists might be stronger.

By late February, the unrest in the Finnish Legion had become so pronounced that General Maynard ordered it to be concentrated in Kandalaksha while the outcome of general elections in Finland in March was awaited. If Mannerheim's conservative government was returned, the Legion might attempt to cross the frontier into Finland as part of an armed revolt against Mannerheim.

When Mannerheim was re-elected, Maynard wanted to forestall trouble by arresting the most active communists in the Legion. He dispatched Royal Marines from H.M.S. *Glory* and two platoons of the Sussex Regiment to apprehend the suspected ringleaders. Burton, who knew what a powder-keg he had handled all winter, was not now going to have Maynard precipitate an explosion. He gave his word to Lehtimaki, the leader of the Red Finns, that he and his closest collaborators would be allowed to cross over to the Bolsheviks if the remaining Finns would undertake to do nothing detrimental to the Allied cause while negotiations for their repatriation were under way.

To this end, the British legation in Helsinki discussed the question of repatriation with Mannerheim's government, but in such a leisurely way—or so it seemed to Maynard—that he obtained permission from London to send his G.S.O.1, Lieutenant-Colonel E. O. Lewin, and Burton to Helsinki to hasten the agreement of the Finnish government. On May 20, 1919, Lewin, Burton, and two Red Finns sailed for Bergen, Norway, in the French cruiser *Montcalm*. From there they made their way overland via Stockholm to Finland. Maynard's instructions to them were brief:

> The task alloted to you is the making of an agreement with the
> Finnish Government by which members of the Finnish Legion now
> serving under my command in the Murmansk region as are
> desirous of repatriation to their own country, and are not debarred

from returning by virtue of sentences passed for criminal offences by a properly established Finnish Court of Law may return to their homes without fear of arrest by order of the Finnish Government for political offences committed prior to the date of their repatriation or of molestation at the hand of their compatriots.[67]

These instructions proved much easier for Maynard to issue than for Lewin and Burton to carry out.

The negotiations with representatives of the Finnish government began in Revel on June 2. A new amnesty law would, it was anticipated, permit the repatriation of most of the Red Finns. Burton and the two Red Finns arrived back in Murmansk via Copenhagen on June 20 to report the good news to the Legion. Lewin, however, soon learned that the amnesty law would not include the Legion and, with the support of the British Legation in Helsinki, engaged for the next month in negotiations with the Finnish prime minister, foreign minister, war minister, and attorney-general. Their memory of the brutal "Red terror" in Helsinki early in February was too fresh for them to welcome the idea of a Red legion entering their fragile state. Lewin, however, persisted. By mid July he was able to report to Maynard that he had successfully carried out his orders.

According to the agreement, men of the Legion who wanted to return home (a few chose instead to join the Russian Bolsheviks) were to be given a suit of civilian clothes and taken to Finland on a British ship. The overland route would have been much shorter, but the Finnish government was taking no chances on the Legion crossing a remote part of the frontier as an armed unit. Dressed in civilian clothing sent for them from England, nine officers and 1,025 other ranks of the Legion sailed from Murmansk on September 1. Aboard the *Kursk* with them were Burton, four British officers, and thirty-five other ranks to act as an escort. Upon their arrival in Helsinki, some of the Red Finns underwent a form of court martial, as had been previously agreed between Lewin and Mannerheim's government. Burton acted as an advocate for the defence. Several of the more prominent Red Finns were sentenced to short terms in prison, but the majority were allowed to go quietly to their homes. In many cases, Burton accompanied the men to their native villages where he personally supervised the final arrangements with the local authorities for their return to civilian life.

In northern Russia throughout the summer of 1919, the increasing frequency of desertions and other signs of insubordination—the mutinies of "Dyer's Battalion" and of the Onega garrison occurred during July—underlined the precarious position of the White Army in northern Russia. By September, despite large-scale provision of advice, money, equipment, and combat support by the Allies, the White Russian authorities in the region had still not been able to organize a dependable army, though they had scored a few initial successes against the Bolsheviks. On August 17, more than one thousand White Russians "voted with their feet", sailing into exile on a British ship, the first of many thousands of White Russians who would seek safety abroad. When General Ironside sailed from Archangel on September 27, and General Maynard from Murmansk on October 12, leaving behind 327 British dead, it was clear that the incompetence and reaction of the White leaders, the apathy of the Russian recruits, and the appeal of communist social and land reform to the peasants would very likely frustrate any hope of a successful stand against the advancing Red Army.

Nevertheless, a small British liaison staff remained with General de Miller, and a Canadian company sergeant-major and a sergeant volunteered to serve with it. Before the war, Jack Colton of Edmonton had been a travelling salesman in Winnipeg. C. H. Turnbull, also of Edmonton, was formerly a Royal North West Mounted Policeman. After service in France, they had volunteered for Murmansk where they were attached to a Karelian unit. When the other Canadians left Murmansk, they elected to remain with the British mission, for which they carried dispatches between Helsinki and Archangel. Their last journey from Helsinki was early in February 1920. Along with a British major named Turner, the two Canadians made their way without opposition over the frozen, snow-covered countryside from Helsinki to Medvyejya Gora, then to Soroka and Onega on the White Sea coast. There, however, they were stopped by Bolsheviks. At a rate unknown to the three travellers, the whole of northern Russia was passing into the hands of the communists, whose morale and military skills had risen as those of the White Russians had fallen.

The horror which Colton, Turnbull, and Turner witnessed during the next few days they were never able to describe dispassionately. The White Russians had not been gentle with the Bolsheviks. Now a vengeful Red terror spread over northern Russia, with wholesale executions of those who had collaborated with the Whites. Fortunately for the two Canadians and for Turner, the new Bolshevik commissar in Onega was a friend from the days when the Canadians had served in Kem. Amidst summary executions that continued throughout the day, Turner, Colton, and Turnbull left Onega for Soroka, travelling under the commissar's safe conduct. From Soroka they hoped to be able to reach the safety of Finland. But in Soroka, and for several days as they made their way overland to Medvyejya Gora, they passed many scenes of slaughter as the Bolsheviks summarily executed and stripped the bodies of all those they suspected of being White supporters or sympathizers.

When the three Allied soldiers finally regained Medvyejya Gora, the Red Guards there were drunk on bourbon whisky that the American contingent had left behind in Murmansk. Suddenly the remnants of a White unit, 800 strong, swept through the town, slaughtering the inebriated Reds. Turner and the two Canadians joined the Whites as they fought their way to the safety of the Finnish frontier, where they were disarmed by the Finnish border guards. Their Red pursuers had anticipated such an outcome. Knowing that the Finnish border guards were few in number, they called on the White officers to return or they would cross the border and kill them and their now disarmed troops. The opposite happened. When the Reds approached the border, the Whites took back their arms from the Finnish border guards. In a sudden counterattack, they killed a large number of Reds and drove the remainder off. Then they turned themselves over for internment in Finland. On crossing the border with them, Colton and Turnbull became the last Canadians who had served in northern Russia to leave the region. They had come close to being the final Canadian casualties.

The month before, in January 1920, as the disintegrating White forces were being rapidly pushed back on Archangel and Murmansk, the news had arrived that in Siberia the White forces had suffered major reverses and that the Allies had decided to reduce their blockade of Soviet Russia as a move towards restoring trade relations.

It was obvious to General de Miller that he could not hope to hold out much longer. He sailed from Archangel on the morning of February 19 aboard the icebreaker *Kosman Minim*. He embarked at the last minute, when Bolshevik troops were already entering the city, taking with him almost 1,000 government officials and their families, as well as his remaining staff and the British liaison staff.* The overcrowded icebreaker ran the gauntlet of shore batteries, pursued by the armed icebreaker *Canada* (the former *Earl Grey*) which had been seized by the Bolsheviks. Having eluded the *Canada*, the *Kosman Minim* reached safety in the Norwegian port of Tromsö. After provisioning, the ship sailed on to Trondheim where de Miller dispersed his party and, with many of them, headed for exile in western Europe. (De Miller himself disappeared in Paris in 1935, supposedly abducted by Soviet agents.)

Allied intervention in northern Russia thus ended in an Allied withdrawal and a White débâcle—a muddled conflict relieved only by occasional flashes of personal courage and fortitude. After studying the intervention, General Sir Henry Wilson, the Chief of the Imperial General Staff and a long-time opponent of British military involvement anywhere in Europe, concluded:

> ... there is one great lesson to be learned from the history of the campaign.
>
> It began with the landing of 150 marines at Murmansk in April, 1918. These were followed by 370 more at the end of May, which were in turn reinforced by 600 infantry and machine gunners on 23rd June. From that time onwards demands for reinforcement followed each other without intermission, and our commitments

---

* *A young British lieutenant of Danish birth, John Hundevad, who escaped on the* Kosman Minim, *emigrated to Canada where he later became editor of the Royal Canadian Legion's* The Legionary.

steadily grew without our being able to resist them, until the British contingent numbered 18,400.

The Mesopotamian campaign started with the despatch of 2 brigades and ultimately absorbed nearly 900,000 men before it was terminated.

The 6 divisions with which we entered upon the Great War in France and Belgium swelled to 63 before victory was achieved.

I think the moral of this is easy to point. It is that, once a military force is involved in operations on land it is almost impossible to limit the magnitude of its commitments.

In the present state of world chaos it will surely be wise to bear this principle in mind, for we may expect to receive continual appeals for troops, "even a company or two" from every part of three continents and the temptation to comply will often be difficult to resist. Therefore, I venture to urge that no such requests outside the British Empire may be acceded to by His Majesty's Government without the fullest and most careful consideration of the larger obligations which such compliance may ultimately involve.[68]

These were wise words. But they were the wisdom of hindsight. A year or more before, in the hectic days of the spring of 1918, no one in London or Paris had either the time or the inclination to give careful consideration to those "larger obligations" involved in Allied military intervention in Russia of which General Wilson wrote. In the urgent need to relieve the pressure on the Western Front by reopening the Eastern Front, few statesmen or soldiers considered whether moves intended to that end would subsequently create among the Allies a sense of obligation to go on assisting the White Russians, who had pledged themselves to uphold the Allied war aims. Long after the original reasons for the military intervention had vanished with the Armistice, there were many in the governments of France or Britain who were uneasy about simply cutting losses in Russia and abandoning their erstwhile allies to whatever fate awaited them. It was to be no less difficult to withdraw from Siberia than from northern Russia.

PART THREE

Siberia

I   The Rationale of Intervention

"Anyone who sets out to give in brief compass an adequate picture of the origins of the Siberian intervention imposes on himself an almost impossible task."[1] If the challenge of presenting an adequate picture was daunting to George Kennan, to whom subsequent students of Allied intervention in Russia are indebted, how much more daunting it is to attempt to present briefly that protracted and sorry tale as background to an account of the Canadian contingent.

The operations of Dunsterforce were almost entirely a reaction to the real or supposed intentions of the Central Powers in Transcaucasia and on the approaches to India. The intervention in northern Russia was based on the urgent Allied desire to reopen the Eastern Front and the fears of a resurgent Germany able to exploit new opportunities in Russia after the revolution. Even the Allied military intervention in Siberia, which occurred for the most part after the Armistice, was decided upon when the Great War was still being fought and there was a frantic desire in London and Paris to reopen the Eastern Front. None of the Allies believed that intervention across Siberia could bring any dramatic results during 1918. But it was widely assumed that the war would continue into 1919 or even 1920. A War Office study argued that intervention in Siberia would begin to pay major dividends in 1919 (and not in 1918). In the Committee of Prime Ministers, which the Imperial War Cabinet had established, in June 1918, Borden concurred in the conclusion that "rather than run the risk of failure to reach a decision on the Western Front in 1919, with its disastrous results on the moral [sic] of the British and French, and perhaps even of the American Armies, the Committee would prefer to postpone an attempt until 1920".[2] In the meantime, it was fondly hoped by the British and French that White Russian armies from Siberia, supported by Allied forces, could force the Central Powers to withdraw troops from the Western Front to meet a new threat from the east.

After their seizure of power in October 1917, the Bolsheviks had quickly attempted to establish their writ throughout Siberia. During the following months, local strife between them and the various Russian factions opposing them was constant. But in Siberia, as elsewhere, the response of White Russians to the challenge of the Bolsheviks was ineffectual, largely because of their disunity. Various rival groups, ranging from left-wing Social-Revolutionaries to tsarist reactionaries, competed for the allegiance of those in Siberia who did not welcome the prospect of communism. Unable to agree among themselves on common social or economic programs, they failed to win any widespread support. The collection of taxes and the conscription of soldiers by White forces became increasingly difficult in the face of the growing apathy of the great majority of peasants. In any case, some anti-Bolshevik forces were dependent on the assistance of the Japanese, who opposed the establishment of any strong government in Siberia capable of countering their efforts to gain at least economic hegemony there.

From early 1918, Japanese, British, and United States warships had been at anchor in Vladivostok harbour.* At first they did

---

* The Japanese cruiser Iwami arrived on January 12, the British cruiser H.M.S. Suffolk on January 14, the Japanese cruiser Asahi on January 18, and the United States cruiser U.S.S. Brooklyn during the latter half of February.

nothing to intervene in local affairs. However, the situation

... as of early March was one of growing tension: the Communists becoming increasingly resentful of the inhibitions placed upon them by the spectacle of the foreign warships in the harbor, the Allied consular representatives increasingly irritated by the harassment of their nationals and the suppression of normal business activity in the port. Suspicion and antagonism were mounting on both sides.

... the European war—the factor that affected so strongly the attitudes of the western Allied chancelleries—was remote and unreal. The fear of "driving the Russians into the arms of the Germans" that more than any other consideration moved the western governments to observe forbearance in their attitude toward the Bolsheviki, was scarcely present in the cities of the Far East. The general tone of discussion in Allied circles there was uninhibitedly anti-Bolshevik. ... The repercussions of all this anti-communist activity and intrigue in the Far Eastern capitals did much to confirm the suspicions with which the Soviet leaders were congenitally inclined to view the Allied governments and their offers of military aid.[3]

In the port of Vladivostok, as at Archangel, there had accumulated vast quantities of Allied munitions and stores, sent to aid the tsarist forces against the Central Powers. By the end of 1917, an estimated 648,000 tons of *matériel* were choking the port. The tsarist government had ordered the supplies without much thought about how the Trans-Siberian railway was to carry them inland. As the flow to Vladivostok increased, the railway had become more and more overburdened and less and less able to move the shipments westward. Goods were piled on the docks or on barges until, eventually, recently arrived supplies had to be placed in temporary shelters in the hills near the city or even left in the open, frequently without any covering. It became impossible to be certain exactly how much there was or what was either rotten or stolen. When the main Allied contingents arrived late in the autumn of 1918, a special correspondent of the *New York Times* noted:

During the war scores of great warehouses were constructed to house the perishable goods, and when these were stacked to the rafters and it became impossible to erect buildings as fast as the supplies came, everything, from cotton to unassembled motor-lorries, were piled in open fields and lots and covered with tarpaulins. Outside the city . . . are hills and fields of munitions and materials, rotting, rusting, decaying and wasting. There is a hill of cotton shipped from the United States tucked under mounds of tarpaulin. There are 37,000 railway truck-wheels and heavy steel rails in such quantities as to make it possible to build a third track from the Pacific to Petrograd. There is enough barbed wire to fence Siberia. There are field guns, millions of rounds of ammunition, and a submarine; automobiles, shoes, copper and lead ingots.[4]

The same indignation and the same misgivings that affected Allied thinking about the Bolshevik seizure of the stores at Archangel influenced Allied thinking about Siberia. The Bolsheviks, it was feared, would attempt to ship the *matériel* westward where, intentionally or unintentionally, it might find its way into German hands.

Yet another element in Allied thinking about Siberia was what the released German and Austrian prisoners-of-war in Russia might do. Upon the signature of the Treaty of Brest-Litovsk, they ceased being prisoners-of-war and became "displaced persons". Their numbers were estimated as high as 1,600,000. But, whatever their exact number, given the evidence that most of them wanted to do no more than leave Russia as quickly as possible, the Allies need not have feared that they would form any sort of fifth column working to hand over Russia with all its natural resources to the Central Powers. But it was precisely this fear that the Germans might be able to organize a fifth column that deeply troubled some Allied statesmen and military leaders. After four years of most exhausting and destructive conflict, the belligerents were apt to believe almost anything in that final uncertain winter of the war.

In reality, some of the prisoners-of-war were pro-Ally rather than pro-German. The majority were from the Austro-Hungarian army, but among them there were many who were neither Austrian nor Hungarian. Some were Czechs or Slovaks, for the most part moderate socialists and staunchly pro-Ally.

They, and Czechs and Slovaks who had joined the Russian Army at the beginning of the war, had formed the Czech Legion, one of the very few coherent military elements in Russia.

With Russia officially at peace with the Central Powers, Lenin and his colleagues decided upon the expulsion from Russia of these strongly pro-Ally Czechoslovaks. Some Czechoslovak units had volunteered to fight alongside the Red Army against the Germans during various skirmishes that had preceded the Treaty of Brest-Litovsk. But, thereafter, they had proved immune to communist propaganda and their continued presence in Russia had become a liability rather than an asset to Lenin and Trotsky. The Legion's eagerness to see the defeat of the Central Powers and the dissolution of the Austro-Hungarian Empire could provoke further friction with the Germans. This in turn might upset the precarious peace on which the Bolsheviks had gambled everything to gain breathing space in order to consolidate their position and make Russia the centre of a world revolution.

The fate of the Legion became another major factor in Allied thinking about intervention in Siberia. Eventually, there were approximately 70,000 members, scattered all the way from the Urals to Vladivostok. With Russian uniforms (bearing the insignia of the rampant lion of Bohemia on a red and white ribbon) and ample rifles and machine guns, they were well equipped, but they lacked both artillery and senior officers. They had, however, one distinct advantage over both the Red and the White Russian forces: a strong sense of comradeship and national purpose knit them into an efficient military unit. The Allies, especially the French, desperate for men on the Western Front, welcomed the prospect of the arrival of 70,000 experienced and determined soldiers. Thomas Masaryk and the other Czechoslovak nationalist leaders were, for their part, eager to transfer their men to the Western Front where the fate of the Hapsburg Empire and the future of Bohemia and Slovakia would finally be decided.

The only safe route to the west was via the east. The Legion would have to congregate in Vladivostok where Allied ships would pick it up and take it to the west coast of Canada and the

United States. From there, it would travel by rail to Atlantic ports where it would embark for France, to join in the long war of attrition against the Central Powers. Masaryk went to Moscow to arrange with the Bolsheviks for the Legion, which he himself had done so much to create, to be transported to Vladivostok. Having reached agreement by early March on the evacuation of the Legion, Masaryk travelled from Moscow to Vladivostok and Japan and, after passing through Vancouver on April 29, 1918, visited Washington before returning to Paris where he resumed the leadership of the Czechoslovak nationalist movement.

However, at the same time that these plans were being made to dispatch the Czech Legion to the Western Front, it began to appear to some British and even to certain local Czech leaders that the Legion might after all prove more useful where it was. Some Czechoslovaks and a large number of Allied observers were convinced that the Bolsheviks had sold themselves to the Germans.

> They felt, accordingly, that by fighting to keep Siberia out of Bolshevik hands they were actually keeping it out of the hands of the Central Powers and rendering an important service to the cause of the Allies. Beyond this, they felt . . . a responsibility to the White Russian faction which had aided them in their uprising. . . . They were reluctant to abandon these White Russian comrades, who had not yet had time to organize any serious armed force, to the reprisals of the vengeful Bolsheviki. Finally, the Czechs were well aware that the Allied governments had made no practical preparations for removing them from Vladivostok, even if they could get there. No ships had yet been sent. The Czechs who had reached Vladivostok at the beginning of May were still there and had no idea when, if ever, they would be evacuated.[5]

While the Bolsheviks were attempting to hasten the departure of the Czech Legion from Siberia, Lenin and his followers began to have second thoughts about allowing the Legion to congregate in eastern Siberia. Grigori Semenov, a Cossack brigand in eastern Siberia, was known to be the recipient of some Allied (mainly Japanese) help. Following the landing of the Japanese marines in Vladivostok on April 5, Lenin became even more doubtful about the wisdom of introducing the Czech Legion into Siberia where it might co-operate with Semenov's units. Semenov, the twenty-seven-year-old leader of a small, tough band of anti-Bolshevik Cossacks operating along the Siberian-Manchurian border, had seemed to both the French and the British during the early spring of 1918 to be an ally deserving financial support. It soon became evident, however, that Semenov was no better than a criminal interested only in personal gain and that he was completely uninterested in the grand strategy of reopening an eastern front. British financial support was withdrawn, but by mid March Japanese "advisers" had stepped in and made Semenov their creature. The Japanese, eager to extend their own influence in eastern Siberia and therefore opposed to the establishment of any viable Russian authority, had no scruples about employing even such a criminal as Semenov.*

Throughout the spring of 1918, the Allies, confronted with a German offensive so successful that the French government began to evacuate Paris, exaggerated the new resources that a blockaded Germany would be able to draw on in Russia, and equally exaggerated the need to reopen the Eastern Front. In an almost desperate state of mind, they looked everywhere for soldiers, finally turning to Japan, the one ally with no land forces in Europe and from which real help might come at only a marginal cost to the other Allied states. Britain, in particular, was anxious to obtain the re-establishment of the Eastern Front, principally by the Japanese. The War Office gradually deluded itself into believing (a) that Tokyo would be willing to send troops as far west as Omsk (where they would still be 1,500 miles from the nearest German forces); (b) that large numbers of fully equipped Japanese troops could be transported quickly across Siberia and supported west of the Urals by a ramshackle

---

* When the Bolsheviks finally occupied eastern Siberia in 1922, Semenov fled to the United States, and later to France, via Vancouver. A note about his brief visit to Vancouver and the support given to him while he was there by three Canadian army officers appears in Appendix "B".

railroad;* and (c) that Russians would remain passive or even be co-operative in the face of what they would regard as a Japanese invasion of their country. It illustrates how unclear the Allies were about what they wanted and what was possible in Russia, that they should have considered for a moment, let alone attempted to further, such an impossible project.

The Japanese were intensely interested in everything pertaining to Siberia and eager to increase their influence there. They were fully aware of United States opposition to their supremacy and, equally aware of the hopes of the United States, and to a lesser extent of the Allies, to find major new markets in Siberia. They had viewed with suspicion the dispatch by President Woodrow Wilson of a "Russian Railway Service Corps" to advise on and assist in the operation of the Trans-Siberian railway. Tokyo also resented what it regarded as British and French determination to retain a major voice in Siberia so as to ensure recognition of the huge pre-war investments of British and French capitalists in railways and mines. Nevertheless, the wary Japanese had no intention of intervening in Siberia until such a move was fully supported by other Allies (unless, of course, Japanese vital interests or nationals were directly threatened).

Japanese-British-American relations during the first months of 1918 resemble an elaborate chess game. A piece is moved and eventually a response is made, but not before elaborate skirmishing and manoeuvring betray mutual suspicions. Japan is eager to enter Siberia yet reluctant to do so without the agreement of its Allies; Britain pursues policies that are often inconsistent, due, in part, to the contradictions between the short-term military factors advanced by the War Office and the longer-term political and economic considerations urged by the Foreign Office; and the United States is torn by conflicting suspicions of Japanese motives, a desire to meet the wishes of its Allies for some form or other of intervention, reluctance to become

---

* *The Japanese general staff was more realistic; it estimated that three years might be required to transport the men and equipment of the minimum number of divisions required, given the condition of the Trans-Siberian railway.*

involved in the internal affairs of Russia, and the expectation of major new markets in Siberia.

The arrival of Allied cruisers in Vladivostok in January and February of 1918 has been considered by some as the first step in intervention. But the landing of 500 Japanese marines on April 5 to protect Japanese nationals in the restless port was a more significant step in an involvement that was to last for over three years and would eventually include more than 100,000 Allied soldiers. Not surprisingly, the Bolsheviks did not believe that the Japanese marines had landed simply to protect Japanese citizens in the city. They feared that the Japanese marines (to which fifty British were soon added for the protection of the British consulate-general) were the vanguard of a much larger force that would join with the Czechoslovaks in an anti-Bolshevik drive westward, while White Russian and Allied forces closed in on Moscow and Petrograd from the north and south.

At this same time, the Germans were protesting to Moscow about Soviet acquiescence in the transfer of such a large and well-trained force as the Czech Legion to the Western Front. The eastward movement of the Legion, strung out along the Trans-Siberian railway, was in fact stopped early in April on orders from Lenin, after the Japanese landing in Vladivostok. Intermittent discussions between Bolshevik and Czechoslovak leaders led nowhere. Finally, on May 25, 1918, at the instance of Trotsky, the Bolsheviks ordered the immediate disarming of the Czechoslovaks.

> Every armed Czechoslovak found on the railway is to be shot on the spot; every train in which even one armed man is found shall be unloaded, and its soldiers shall be interned in a war prisoners' camp. Local war commissars must proceed at once to carry out this order; every delay will be considered treason and will bring the offender severe punishment . . . [6]

On almost the same day, in London, Anglo-French discussions led to an agreement, endorsed by the Supreme War Council in Versailles on June 3, that the detachments of Czechoslovaks who were erroneously believed to be making their way to Archangel and Murmansk should remain in northern Russia to co-operate with White Russians and with Allied contingents to be dispatched there. The remainder of the Legion could proceed to Vladivostok, and, once there, arrangements would be made for some of them to be embarked on Japanese ships. These ideas were symptomatic of the confusion in Allied thinking about Russia. The Czechoslovaks had been stopped on their way to Vladivostok, and in any case no firm decision had been made by the Allies about what the Czechoslovaks in Siberia were to do.

The Czechoslovaks' reaction to Bolshevik attempts to prevent their further progress towards Vladivostok was as abrupt as Moscow's order had been. The Legion seized control of the Trans-Siberian railway from the Urals to Lake Baikal. Well-armed and well-disciplined, it soon overcame any local opposition. In late May, with the support of various anti-Bolshevik factions along the line, the Czechoslovaks themselves began to operate the railway so as to ensure their own safe passage to Vladivostok. The first contingents of any size arrived in the port early in May, only to find the situation there uncertain and worrisome. The quiet withdrawal by April 25 of all the Japanese and British marines (three weeks after their landing) had not ended the quarrels and disorders between the local socialists and conservatives. A Soviet was nominally in control of Vladivostok, yet even within this Soviet there was dissension. The Czechoslovaks had not seized almost 4,000 miles of railway only to leave its terminal in the hands of men they could not rely on. On June 29, at the same time that the British and French were landing in distant Murmansk, the 15,000 Czechoslovaks in Vladivostok took control of the city. On July 6, the British, French, American, Japanese, and Czechoslovak representatives in the city proclaimed that the Allies had placed the whole area under their "temporary protection".

One month before, on June 8, 1918, when Sir Robert Borden and his Minister of Militia and Defence, Major-General C. S. Mewburn, arrived in London to attend the second series of meetings of the Imperial War Cabinet, Borden was aware that the Allies and the United States had been unable to agree about the desirability of intervention in Siberia. American acquiescence was still a month away. This had not, however, deterred the War Office from inquiring whether Canada would provide units for a British infantry brigade to be sent to Siberia. The War Office was eager to have as large a British Empire contingent as possible in the Allied force—it always seemed eager to participate in all such forces everywhere—but, when it came to finding troops, its enthusiasm encountered practical obstacles. Not a man could be spared from the Western Front during that crucial early summer of 1918. A purely Japanese force would be unacceptable to the Russians, whether Red or White, and might only encourage the Bolsheviks to seek help from the Germans. It occurred to the War Office that there could be troops in Canada either completing their training or unfit for further service on the Western Front who might be able to meet the somewhat less rigorous requirements somehow foreseen for service in Siberia.

Clearly the first step was to convince Borden of the general necessity for Allied military intervention. Then the more specific question of Canadian troops could be raised. Leopold Amery, an Assistant Secretary of both the British Cabinet and the Imperial War Cabinet (with special responsibilities for Russian affairs) and a personal friend of Borden, sent him on June 11 a copy of a long memorandum written by General Knox, a man who was regarded—and who regarded himself—as one of Britain's leading experts on Russia. Knox was in no doubt about the imperative need for an Allied force in Siberia.

> Intervention from the Far East is our only chance of closing to the Central Powers in 1919 the material resources of Asia, and of bringing to bear against them a part of the enormous Allied manpower of that continent. It is our only chance of winning this war and of preventing another disastrous war in the near future.[7]

For the most part, Knox's memorandum was closely reasoned and detailed, even if the reasoning was sometimes based on false premises or was unduly optimistic. A paper that the War Office had prepared took a somewhat more poetic approach. One of its recommendations read: "Good results may be expected also if the Russian Vanguard that precedes the Allied Armies is accompanied by prominent churchmen to give the movement the character of a crusade with the object of restoring Russia's lost Church and nationality." This crusading touch was never entirely absent from official Allied—particularly British— thinking about Siberia, but neither were more mundane commercial aspects. Amery mentioned the trade opportunities to Borden, emphasizing the possibilities for Canada in Siberia. Borden was already conversant with the commercial arguments, thanks to optimistic forecasts by the Canadian Department of Trade and Commerce.*

The same day Borden received Knox's outspoken and detailed, if speculative, memorandum, he attended a meeting of the Imperial War Cabinet. At the meeting, and subsequently in the Committee of Prime Ministers, Lloyd George described the situation on the Western Front in bleak terms. The defeat and occupation of France could not be ruled out. In the light of such a possibility, a new eastern front, an urgent necessity at any time, became imperative, since only there and in Italy would Britain and the United States then be able to strike directly at the Central Powers. But the United States, Lloyd George noted, remained opposed to Allied intervention in Siberia.

By the end of June, despite persistent efforts by the British, there was still no word from Washington of willingness to join in an Allied expeditionary force for Siberia. On July 2, one final appeal was addressed to President Wilson by the Supreme War Council. This plea, combined with the seizure of Vladivostok by the Czech Legion on June 29, convinced Wilson that he should send a contingent to Siberia as part of a wider Allied effort to encourage all those Russians still willing to fight the Germans—this meant, in effect, the anti-Bolsheviks—and to ensure the safety of the Czechoslovaks. As Wilson saw it, the Czech Legion would, if necessary, be "rescued" by the dispatch of United States and Japanese troops inland to cover the joining up of Czechoslovaks still west of Irkutsk with those already in

* See pp. 225-6.

Vladivostok. Wilson had earlier agreed to the use of United States troops in Murmansk and Archangel, and the United States Railway Mission was providing some badly needed help in keeping the Trans-Siberian railway running. But Wilson had long been suspicious of the ambitions of the Japanese in eastern Siberia as well as in China and Manchuria and had been reluctant to take a step that would open the way for them to enter. The United States could hardly oppose Japanese intervention once it had intervened itself.

A predecessor of Wilson's, Theodore Roosevelt, had helped bring peace to the Far East twelve years before, limiting Japanese demands and conquest. But now Wilson acceded to the insistent pleas from Britain, France, and Italy to provide United States troops for an international force that would inescapably include a large Japanese contingent. The other Allies sought the establishment of a stable Russian government willing to rejoin the struggle against the Central Powers and, in time, to honour the massive debts of the tsarist régime. The Japanese, it could be assumed, would regard the landing of a joint Allied force in Siberia as an opportunity to extend their own influence there. Against these considerations, however, Wilson saw pressing reasons why the United States should assist the Czechoslovaks, representative as they were of those European national entities that, he was convinced, must be freed. When, on July 6, 1918, Wilson finally decided to supply 7,000 troops for Siberia, he did so on the understanding that the British would also provide 7,000 and that the Japanese force would not exceed 40,000 (in fact, it eventually grew to 70,000). Now assured of United States participation, the other Allies quickly began to dispatch small contingents to join the 15,000 Czechoslovaks already in Vladivostok.

The way was at last clear for joint Allied intervention. Yet, even as the force was being formed, there were signs of discord. Dissension was inevitable in a force that included both Japanese and United States troops, the Japanese bent on extending their influence and the Americans determined to hinder them. As already noted, the Japanese worked against the establishment of a strong Russian government able to forestall their plans, while the Americans and the other Allies wished to see the growth of a popular and viable government capable of standing on its own feet, resuming the fight against the Central Powers, honouring Russia's debts, and playing a major role in international trade. To complicate matters further, the British and French did not entirely share the scruples of the Americans about intervening in what the Americans, at least, considered to be the internal affairs of Russia.

The likelihood of disagreements involving Japan, Britain, France, and the United States was yet further increased by the fact that Major-General William Graves, the United States commander, was sent to Vladivostok with little more enlightenment about what American interests in Russia actually were than the high-minded but vague and contradictory *aide-mémoire* that Wilson himself had typed to justify, first to himself and then to the American people, the dispatch of United States troops to Siberia.

But dissension among the Allies was still only incipient. The first Allied soldiers began to embark for Vladivostok. The vanguard came not from nearby Japan but rather from the British garrison in Hong Kong. The 25th Battalion of the Middlesex Regiment was composed of 1,000 "C-class" men, all unfit for combat service. They sailed for Vladivostok late in July—still in tropical uniform—as part of a British brigade in which, it was envisaged in the War Office, Canadian troops would form the major element.

On July 10, 1918, only four days after Wilson finally sanctioned the dispatch of American troops, the War Office formally asked Borden whether Canadian units could be made available for service in Siberia "to restore order and a stable government", to assist the Czechoslovaks, and, most of all, to help reopen an eastern front. Little more than these few simple justifications were given for Canadian participation.

Earlier, as the Great War dragged on, Borden had argued that the co-operation of the Dominions could hardly be expected if they were not involved in the making of basic decisions through

Imperial consultation. Since Borden had been consulted, to
some extent, about the situation in Siberia, his strong sense of
responsibility, when joined with his exaggerated optimism
about trade prospects, led him to approve the War Office's
request. However, he pointed out that a final decision could only
be taken by the Canadian cabinet as a whole. There then
ensued long telegraphic exchanges between Borden (and those
few members of his cabinet who were with him in London) and
their colleagues in the Union government in Ottawa. A decision
was rendered more difficult by the fact that, only two days after
Borden received the War Office proposal for troops for Siberia,
Canadian headquarters in London received a request for an
infantry battalion for service in northern Russia. As we have
seen, the request could not possibly be met, when every able-
bodied Canadian soldier was required to reinforce the hard-
pressed units on the Western Front. To be "able-bodied" was
not, however, considered an essential requirement for service in
Siberia.

Major-General Sir Thomas Bridges, the head of the British
military mission in Washington, was sent to Ottawa during the
first days of July to further the War Office's request. He was told
by the Chief of the Canadian General Staff that it might be
feasible to raise two battalions of discharged soldiers, but that
no first-class units would be available. This suggestion was in
turn picked up by Major-General Percy Pollexfen de Blaquière
Radcliffe, the Director of Military Operations at the War
Office.* He pressed it on Newton Wesley Rowell, the President
of the Privy Council, who was in London on his way to visit the
Western Front and who, like Borden, was greatly interested in
Canada's evolving international role and status. Rowell assured
Radcliffe two days later that he had discussed the idea with both
Borden and Mewburn and that they had agreed that "the matter
can be satisfactorily arranged".[8] Mewburn and Rowell would
accordingly call on Radcliffe "to go into the matter further". On

---

* Two months before, Radcliffe (1874-1934) had been serving on the Western Front
as Brigadier-General, General Staff, Canadian Corps. "P.de B." became Director of
Military Operations at the War Office on April 22, 1918.

July 12, Mewburn discussed the request with Radcliffe, who outlined the size of the contingent the War Office hoped Canada would provide. He added that Lord Balfour, the Foreign Secretary, had asked that its destination not be made public, "in view of the present delicate situation as regards negotiation for intervention in Siberia".[9] However, Radcliffe could not answer the two specific questions uppermost in Mewburn's mind: what the duties of the force would be and under whose control it would come.

The first intimation of the British request seems to have reached the cabinet in Ottawa through the office of the Governor General, more than a fortnight after Borden had received it. To the request, the Minister of Justice replied direct to Borden on July 28: "Council approves principle of sending expedition, leaving you to arrange cost and other detail."[10] Borden, however, did not regard this informal decision as sufficient authority for the organization and dispatch of the force. He wired Ottawa on August 7, urging that the necessary order-in-council be passed immediately.

A reply from Ottawa two days later made it clear that some cabinet members had in the interim begun to have serious doubts about the wisdom of Canadian participation. Specifically, they wanted to know what would be the relationship of the Canadian force to the Japanese and American contingents and whether the British objectives were as limited as the American objectives (i.e., to help safeguard the Allied stores at Vladivostok and assist the departure of the Czech Legion). These were two highly important considerations, but Borden simply replied on August 12 that Mewburn was discussing "all questions" with the War Office.

Ministers in Ottawa remained doubtful, especially when it became increasingly evident that Canada, through its participation in the Allied force, might be faced with the dilemma of having to choose between United States and British positions. Canadian statesmen were generally happiest when they could work in co-operation with their two great English-speaking allies. To be confronted with a choice of siding with one against the other, especially in a confused and distant civil war, was a dilemma to be avoided. It appeared to some ministers that Canada was now quite gratuitously placing itself in a position where, for no tangible national advantage, it might have to elect between antagonizing either the United States or Britain. Indeed, some members of the government in Ottawa could not see what Canada stood to gain by participating in the Siberian intervention under any circumstances. It appeared to them especially foolish when the British were talking in sweeping terms of the necessity of re-establishing an eastern front and of defending India, while at the same time the United States was declaring emphatically that Allied military intervention in the Russian civil war (as opposed to garrison duty in Vladivostok) would only add to the existing "sad confusion" and would be of no help in the war against Germany. Here indeed were ample ingredients for later misunderstandings and confusion. Rowell, now back in Ottawa, put his finger on them when he wired Borden on August 9 inquiring what exactly the relations would be between the Canadian, American, and Japanese forces.[11] In addition to differences in British and American thinking, there was already some evidence of contradictions between Japanese and United States intentions. If any conflict between the Japanese and Americans developed in Siberia, Canadian public opinion would doubtless want the Canadian troops to side with the Americans. Yet the British, more friendly towards Japan than either Canada or the United States, would expect Canadian neutrality.*

These various misgivings in Ottawa notwithstanding, a Privy Council Order of August 12 authorized the force requested by the War Office (two subsequent Orders of August 23 and September 5 authorized additions). Three days later, in Port Hope, Ontario, Rowell publicly announced the government's decision, justifying the dispatch of "a small but thoroughly

---

* Britain had a Treaty of Friendship with Japan, first negotiated in 1902, which bound the signatories to assist each other if attacked by a third party (although, under an article added in 1911, Britain excluded the United States from the terms of the treaty).

effective force" in terms of helping the Czechoslovaks "and the Russian people of Siberia, who are courageously battling against Germany's effort to dominate and control Siberia, as she already dominates and controls western Russia". Rowell also contended that Canada's position "as a Pacific power" required it to take an active interest in the northern Pacific, a theme he later developed during a speaking tour of the Western provinces where opposition to the Allied intervention was especially pronounced.[12]

Rowell's justifications may have convinced some, but to several of his colleagues in the cabinet it was never very clear why Canada was sending soldiers to Siberia. Borden, on the other hand, was vulnerable to the continuing pressures and persuasions of London and privy to the thinking in the Imperial War Cabinet where the problem of Russia was discussed frequently, if with little solid information, understanding, or objectivity.

Mewburn, however, was also in London and he remained skeptical. He met with Borden at the Savoy Hotel on the morning of August 13. After their meeting they exchanged letters, Mewburn seeking written clarification of Canadian policy and Borden responding by setting forth guidelines for his Minister of Militia. Mewburn asked for a "final decision" on what the effect on Canadian opinion would be of sending troops to Siberia when there was already unrest and bitterness among some in Canada over the decision to use conscripts to reinforce the Canadian Corps in France. Mewburn further asked Borden how far he envisaged Canadian soldiers being committed when the United States was reluctant to become involved and Japan was not following "an offensive policy".[13]

Borden, in his brief reply to Mewburn, noted that he had explained at their morning meeting the reasons why he believed the Canadian Government was justified in sending "a small force" to Siberia.

> Intimate relations with the rapidly developing country will be of great advantage to Canada in the future. Other nations will make very vigorous and determined efforts to obtain a foothold and our

interposition with a small military force would tend to bring Canada into favourable notice by the strongest elements in that great community.[14]

What Borden had in mind was the trade opportunities which he, no less than the British, Americans, and Japanese, was convinced existed in Siberia. The constraints of tsarist despotism had been removed. Now, if a viable, popular government could be established in Siberia, the huge commercial potential of that vast area might gradually be realized.

The Americans must not be allowed to corner the market. The potential trade opportunities were, throughout, a fundamental consideration in deciding Borden in favour of sending both Canadian soldiers and an economic mission to Vladivostok.* Borden, however, did not respond to Mewburn's query about public opinion in Canada.

The Prime Minister was, by contrast, entirely clear in his own mind about who was to be responsible for decisions affecting the Canadian units. During the course of the war, Borden had actively sought to ensure Canadian control over Canadian troops (other than in over-all operations) and a distinct Canadian voice in the conduct of the war. He was determined that the predominantly Canadian brigade for Siberia would be controlled by Canadians and that Ottawa alone would decide on its disposition. No less an arrangement would be acceptable.

I am thoroughly of the opinion that the disposition of the force at so great a distance from Canada, and under conditions which are uncertain and practically unknown, should be left to the judgment of . . . the Canadian Officer who is to command our forces. This should be thoroughly understood with the War Office before the organization of the expedition is proceeded with. We would not be justified in despatching our force into the interior of the country without knowing with certainty what arrangements had been made for the conduct of the campaign, what forces are to co-operate with ours, and under whose direction and command, and what dispositions have been made to carry out the operations successfully and with due regard to the safety of the force.[15]

* See Part Four, III, for a description of the Canadian Economic Commission to Siberia.

At the same time, ministers in Ottawa appealed for a clear statement of the basic reasons for Allied intervention so that explanations might be given to the Canadian people. When no such statements were forthcoming and only muddled restatements of earlier British proclamations were issued, someone in the senior levels of the Department of Militia and Defence (the handwriting appears to be that of the private secretary to the minister) observed about British policy:

> It is damned, cold-hearted, facing-both-ways effusion, inspired by cowardice. It says nothing. It does not withdraw; it does not go forward. It is a normal stage in the English mismanagement of such affairs. A commitment is made; some fools get cold feet; the Government neither fishes nor cuts bait, but holds up progress without clearing out; a lot of people die unnecessarily.[16]

II *Canadian Expeditionary Force (Siberia)*

Whatever the doubts among the cabinet ministers about the prospects of Canadian participation, there was no question in the military mind about what should be done. Early in July, the British and Canadian military staffs in London had begun discussing the nature of the force envisaged, how it would be composed and equipped, and who would pay for it. Concurrently in Ottawa, the Chief of the Canadian General Staff, following receipt on July 12 of a telegram from Mewburn, had begun to organize in skeletal form a brigade headquarters, two battalions of infantry, a battery of field artillery, a machine-gun company, and various support services. The brigade would be equipped to serve in a distant theatre with a hostile climate and among an uncertain populace. It would have to be self-contained. There would be few local resources for it to draw on.

But, before planning could go very far, the commanding officer of the brigade had to be designated. Mewburn selected Brigadier-General James Harold Elmsley, a professional soldier who had been wounded in the Boer War and had commanded

The Canadian Prime Minister, Sir Robert Borden, reviewing Canadian infantry in France, July 1918.

DUNSTERFORCE,
MESOPOTAMIA.
1918.

Photograph courtesy G. S. Hopkins

(*Above*) British, Canadian, other Dominion, and White Russian reinforcements for Dunsterforce near Baghdad, April 1918. (*Opposite*) Dunsterforce's Ford vans at Birkandi in northern Persia, on the road to Enzeli on the Caspian Sea.

(Above) The reinforcement column for Dunsterforce making its way through the valleys of northern Persia, May 1918. The officer in the sola topi in the left foreground is Lieutenant-Colonel John Warden of Vancouver, the senior Canadian. *(Below)* Troops of the 7th North Staffordshire Regiment moving into position against the Turkish advance on Baku.

(Top) Pilots and observers of "C" Flight, No. 47 Squadron, Royal Air Force, in southern Russia. The squadron was commanded by Major Raymond Collishaw of Nanaimo, British Columbia (centre of middle row). *(Bottom)* DH 9s of "C" Flight, No. 47 Squadron, Royal Air Force, in front of tent hangars, probably at Ekaterinodar.

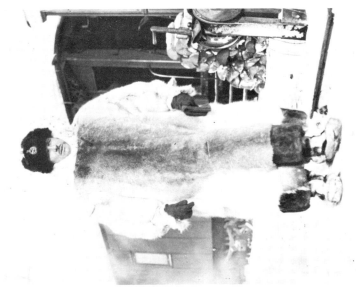

(*Above left*) Major-General Sir Edmund Ironside, commander of the North Russia Expeditionary Force. (*Above right*) Colonel John E. Leckie of Vancouver, senior Canadian officer on the Murmansk front.

(*Right*) Lieutenant-Colonel Charles H. L. Sharman, officer commanding the Sixteenth Brigade, Canadian Field Artillery, on the Archangel front. (*Far right*) Major-General James H. Elmsley, officer commanding the Canadian Expeditionary Force (Siberia).

Library of Congress, Washington

(*Above*) Horse-drawn Canadian eighteen-pounder on skis on the Archangel front. The gun and limber are in camouflage paint. (*Below*) Canadian dog team on the Murmansk front.

Imperial War Museum, London

(Above) Lieutenant J. Roberts and a gunner of the 68th Battery, Royal Canadian Artillery, with a refugee boy in northern Russia, February 1919. *(Below)* A street in Murmansk, in summer.

(Top) Shipping in Murmansk harbour. *(Above)* March past of Allied units in Murmansk, with Canadian guns passing the reviewing stand. *(Right)* Canadian gunners making tea on their supply barge on the Dvina River, on the Archangel front.

Canadian gunner supervising prisoners loading a barge at Yemetskoe in northern Russia, May 1919.

(*Middle*) An overnight camp of the 170 men of the 11th Battalion of the Royal Sussex Regiment who made their way on skis from Pechenga to Murmansk under the command of Captain E. M. Squairey of Newfoundland in February 1919, following the fall of Shenkursk.

(*Bottom*) Officers' mess, "B" Flight, Elope Squadron, Royal Air Force, at Bereznik in northern Russia, February 1919. From left to right: Major Mueller (British), Second Lieutenant Frank J. Shrive (Hamilton, Ontario), Lieutenant Green (British), Second Lieutenant George W. Jones (Moncton, New Brunswick), Second Lieutenant A. E. White (Vancouver), Lieutenant Dugald MacDougall, D.F.C. (Lockport, Manitoba, killed in northern Russia, August 1919), Lieutenant (?) Mills (British), Second Lieutenant P. V. Dobby (Montreal), Lieutenant (?) Derebezov (Russian), Lieutenant Biakok (Russian), and Lieutenant DeJanis (British).

Imperial War Museum, London

(Above) Two DH 9a aircraft and a Sopwith Snipe at Bereznik on the Murmansk front. Canadian pilots and observers flew sorties on both types of aircraft. Bombs ready for loading are near the aircraft's wheels. *(Below)* Springtime in northern Russia: gunners of the 68th Battery, Canadian Field Artillery, at Bereznik, May 1919.

Public Archives of Canada

The Canadian War Museum, The National Museum of Man, National Museums of Canada

(Above) Vladivostok harbour in 1919, showing war supplies piled outdoors. *(Below)* Canadian troops aboard the *Protesliaus* immediately before sailing for Vladivostok, December 1918.

Photograph courtesy of William Thompson

CANADIAN SPORTS DAY 19 & 19 VLADIVOSTOCK.

(Above) The Canada sports day at Vladivostok, April 19, 1919. *(Below)* Local labour unloading Canadian ordnance stores at Vladivostok — a sketch by Louis Keene. *(Opposite)* Canadian infantry outside their barracks near Vladivostok, early morning in winter — a painting by Louis Keene.

The Canadian War Museum, The National Museum of Man,
National Museums of Canada

(Right) A trooper of "B" Squadron of the Royal North West Mounted Police in full kit, near Vladivostok. *(Below)* Six officers of the Royal North West Mounted Police outside "B" Squadron's stables near Vladivostok, spring 1919. *(Bottom)* The "Advance Party" of the Canadian Expeditionary Force (Siberia) in the Allied victory parade at Vladivostok on November 15, 1919. Major-General Elmsley joined other senior Allied officers on the reviewing stand.

the 8th Canadian Infantry Brigade on the Western Front.* After Elmsley's transfer to London from the infantry reserve camp at Bramshott which he was commanding, the pace of planning quickened. Several weeks before formal approval for the formation of the brigade was issued in Ottawa, Mewburn and Elmsley met with London-based officers to begin making plans for the brigade and its various support services. As a result of this planning in London and Ottawa, the Canadian army was able in less than a fortnight after the Order-in-Council of August 12 to promulgate the "establishment" of the brigade.

The new infantry brigade was numbered the 16th. The 25th Battalion of the Middlesex Regiment, already in Vladivostok, would be included, but all other units would be Canadian. The brigade was planned as follows:

259th Canadian Infantry Battalion
260th Canadian Infantry Battalion
25th Battalion, Middlesex Regiment †
"B" Squadron, Royal North West Mounted Police
85th Battery, Canadian Field Artillery
16th Field Company, Canadian Engineers
6th Signal Company
20th Canadian Machine Gun Company
No. 1 Canadian Divisional Train
No. 16 Field Ambulance

---

* *Elmsley (1878-1954) was born in Toronto, but was educated primarily in England. He was commissioned in the Royal Canadian Dragoons in 1898. After recovering from his Boer War wounds, he served with the cavalry in India in 1906, attended staff college in 1912, and was on the Canadian staff in France from May 1915 to June 1916, when he was promoted brigadier-general and commanding the 8th Canadian Infantry Brigade. He was invalided in May 1918 to the command of the Canadian camp at Bramshott. After his service in Siberia, Elmsley returned to Ottawa and became Adjutant-General. From 1922 until his retirement in 1929, he commanded, successively, the military districts centred on Kingston, Toronto, and Winnipeg.*

† *A second British infantry battalion, the 1/9th of the Hampshire Regiment, was added in November. Some thought was given to sending several aircraft, to be purchased in the United States and piloted by Canadians. In the end, no aircraft were included in the British brigade, but the French Air Force provided nine pilots and 158 other ranks for service in Omsk and Vladivostok (in addition to an infantry battalion and an artillery brigade).*

No. 11 Stationary Hospital
No. 9 Ordnance Detachment

In Canada, volunteers were at once sought. Recruiting posters, with a picture of a sturdy Canadian soldier ready to do his duty, soon appeared in military camps and public buildings. The Middlesex battalion already in Siberia was to be transferred to Elmsley's command when the other units of the 16th Canadian Infantry Brigade arrived in Vladivostok. It was further agreed that, unlike the arrangement for Canadian troops in northern Russia, all the costs incurred by the brigade would be borne by Britain, except pay and the value of whatever equipment the contingent carried with it.

Before leaving England, Elmsley, now an acting major-general, settled these and other details with the War Office, operating from "The Headquarters, Canadian Expeditionary Force (Siberia), Oxford Circus House, London, W.1". He transferred his headquarters to Ottawa on September 19 when he sailed from England with a small group of officers he had selected to serve as the nucleus of his staff. Once in Ottawa, he consulted Mewburn on the appointment of all his senior officers, a subject in which the Minister took a personal interest. Brigadier-General Harold Childe Bickford of Toronto became Elmsley's deputy. Under him, Colonel Albert Edward "Dolly" Swift of Quebec City headed the 259th Battalion and Lieutenant-Colonel Frederick Charles Jamieson of Edmonton headed the 260th. Like Elmsley, both battalion commanders were Boer War veterans, Swift having served as a subaltern in the First Canadian Contingent and Jamieson in the ranks of the Second Canadian Contingent (in which Elmsley was a lieutenant). Swift and Jamieson were also veterans of the Western Front, both having gone overseas with the First Division. When Jamieson was appointed to command the 260th Battalion, he was on the staff of the Canadian recruiting centre in New York City.

The soldiers of the two battalions came from every province of Canada. Two companies of the 259th were mainly French-speaking from Quebec; the other two were English-speaking from Ontario. One hundred and thirty-five Russians who had served with the Canadian Corps on the Western Front were brought together in Bexhill, England, and attached to the brigade.* One company of the 260th was from the Atlantic provinces, another from Manitoba, the third from Saskatchewan and Alberta, and the fourth from British Columbia. The officers were mostly veterans of service in France, some of whom had been invalided home. Many of the NCOs were also veterans of the Western Front, but the men were mainly recent volunteers or conscripts.† Some had employed whatever influence they could to win appointment to the brigade.

Canadian Army headquarters in both Ottawa and London were flooded with applications from officers who sought either further military adventure or a continuation of wartime life, which was more attractive to them than the peacetime life to which they were due to return. There were, in fact, many more officer volunteers than could be employed—a Canadian manifestation of the same attitude that was seen in the British relief force sent to northern Russia in May 1919 and in the "Black and Tans", which were so readily raised for service in Ireland in 1920. For those for whom war had become a way of life, the issue was of less consequence than the opportunity to go on soldiering. The Canadian people might have had enough of war. Some of the soldiers had not.

---

* When the brigade was concentrated at Victoria, there was some evidence that among the Russo-Canadians were a number who were willing to fight Germans but could not see the point of fighting other Russians, however Red they might be. Some effort was made to weed out such men in the fear that they might contaminate the thinking of the other troops. The two platoons of Russian-speaking troops were broken up; thirty-five were discharged, and the remaining men assigned to other units.

† Several in the contingent were later to achieve eminence in public life. Among them were Thomas G. Murphy, a graduate of the Manitoba School of Pharmacy, who in 1924 became Mayor of Neepawa and in 1925 a Member of Parliament; he was defeated in the general election of 1926 but was re-elected in 1930 and, in the same year, R.B. Bennett appointed him Minister of the Interior. William Pate Mulock, a Toronto lawyer, was Member of Parliament for North York from 1939 to 1945 and Postmaster General under Mackenzie King from 1940 to 1945. Stuart Ramsay Thompson became a university professor and author of several books on Russian history. Raymond Massey, the brother of a future Governor General, won international fame as an actor.

Originally it had been intended that the force would be composed entirely of volunteers, but, when an insufficient number came forward, conscripts were included to the number of 1,653, or about one-third of the total contingent. The Canadian government was never happy about its decision to send men who, following the bitter conscription crisis of 1917, had been drafted only "to defend the realm". Siberia posed no threat to Canada. The government was uneasily aware that it might be charged with having abused its own contentious conscription legislation. Only the men of the Royal North West Mounted Police were true volunteers (all were experienced horsemen, including many ex-cowboys).*

With the recruitment of the force under way, Canadian Army headquarters turned its attention to the drafting of Elmsley's instructions. This proved to be unexpectedly difficult. Not surprisingly, the instructions suggested by the War Office envisaged Elmsley as acting exclusively under its direction. Furthermore, "as regards all local political or military political [sic] questions he will be in close touch and be guided by General Knox, who has been selected because of his unrivalled knowledge of Russia." Borden was having none of this. Neither the War Office nor Knox, the former military attaché in St. Petersburg who in mid July had been appointed head of the British Military Mission in Siberia, were to have exclusive control over Elmsley or his troops. Discussions between Ottawa and the London headquarters of the Overseas Military Forces of Canada eventually led to the acceptance by the War Office of two important additional phrases: "no appeal is to be decided against the General Officer Commanding . . . without consultation with the Canadian Government", and "without reference to the War Office or any outside body, direct correspondence may pass between General Officer Commanding . . . and the Cana-

* The Commissioner of the R.N.W.M.P. had been authorized by Rowell on August 17 to recruit six officers and 184 other ranks. Five volunteers died of influenza before the unit was officially transferred on October 1, 1918, to the Canadian Expeditionary Force (Siberia).

dian Government". The insertion of these two qualifications helped. But for Borden it was still not enough. He was increasingly concerned about what the British might attempt to do with the force and, more broadly, about the preservation of the status Canada had won by its contribution to victory on the Western Front. Borden, conscious of the way the British had frequently attempted to assume complete control of Dominion troops, personally prepared the following paragraph, to ensure that there could be no misunderstanding about where ultimate control resided:

> There will be direct communication regarding matters of policy and operations between the War Office and the Canadian Commander of the Force, and all orders sent to, or reports made by the Commander will be repeated to the Militia Department, Ottawa. The Canadian Government is to deal direct with all questions concerning the administration of the Force and on such matters there will be direct communication between the Commander of the Force and the Militia Department, Ottawa. All such communications being repeated to the War Office.
> Notwithstanding the foregoing, the Canadian Government has agreed that no disposition of the Force in the field shall be made, nor shall such Force be committed to any military operations without carrying the judgment of the Canadian General Officer Commanding and therefore the latter at all times shall have the right of direct communications with the Canadian Government.[17]

Borden's personal preoccupation with the exact terms under which the force was to operate in Siberia was a direct result of the persistent efforts he had made during the Great War to ensure that the Canadian government alone decided on the conditions of service of Canadian soldiers. Borden was determined that the status of the brigade should be no less than that of the Canadian formations on the Western Front.

In addition, Elmsley's relations with the Japanese had to be clarified. In theory Elmsley was under the over-all direction of the senior Allied officer in eastern Siberia, General Kikuzo Otani, a veteran of the Russo-Japanese War of 1905. In practice, however, Elmsley was given the right—and the Japanese were informed of this—to appeal to the War Office if an order from

Otani might, in Elmsley's judgment, place his force in unwarranted danger.

To make quite certain that Ottawa would never be left in ignorance about what was being planned or about what was happening in Siberia, Mewburn appointed Lieutenant-Colonel John Francis Lash, who was serving in London, to be his personal representative at the White headquarters in Omsk. Mewburn understood that both Sir Charles Eliot,* the British High Commissioner in Siberia, and Knox, the head of the Military Mission, would be stationed there. Mewburn accordingly gave Lash a letter of introduction to Eliot.

> Colonel Lash will be Major General Elmsley's representative at Allied Headquarters [i.e., at Omsk] and will, also, personally represent me in Siberia on matters arising in connection with the CEF [Canadian Expeditionary Force]. I will appreciate it if you will take Col. Lash into your confidence and consult with him in all matters wherein Canada is affected both from a military standpoint as well as from an economic and political.[18]

While these awkward questions of command and responsibility were being settled, an advance party was dispatched to Vladivostok to prepare for the arrival of the main contingent. As early as August 28, the War Office had urged on Ottawa the necessity of bolstering the Czech Legion by the early arrival of at least a token unit of Canadians, including the cavalry squadron from the R.N.W.M.P. Efforts were accordingly made to get some of the men on their way as soon as possible, but it was not until October 11, 1918, three months after the original request for troops had been received from the War Office and only a month before the Armistice, that Elmsley and the advance party of

---

* Charles N. E. Eliot "had been secretary . . . at the Petersburg Embassy [1887-92]; he knew something like twenty languages, and was recognized as one of the highest experts in questions of the Near East; but . . . his special hobby was the study of sea-slugs, of which he was believed to know more than anyone living. In Siberia he was extremely cautious, as indeed he might well be, and he was a very shrewd observer; but he was also very generous to the more optimistic view." (Pares, My Russian Memoirs, p. 499). Eliot had been High Commissioner in East Africa and, more recently, vice-chancellor of the University of Hong Kong. He was British Ambassador to Japan from 1919 to 1926.

680 (including one officer and twenty other ranks from the R.N.W.M.P.) sailed on the Canadian Pacific liner *Empress of Japan*, after a final inspection in Victoria by Mewburn. Fifteen days later, to the music of a Czechoslovak brass band, they disembarked in Vladivostok. Upon arrival, Elmsley was greeted aboard the ship by Leolyn Dana Wilgress, the young Canadian trade commissioner in Vladivostok. Wilgress came away from his first meeting with Elmsley with a favourable impression of a "modest, retiring man, sincere and upright".

The Base Headquarters was immediately established in the Pushkinskaya Theatre, "a large modern building" in the centre of Vladivostok that Wilgress had obtained with the help of the British Military Mission. There the Canadian headquarters were to remain throughout the brigade's service in Siberia. Arrangements for billeting the men of the headquarters staff were facilitated by Ross Owen, the local representative of the Canadian Pacific Railway Company, as well as by the staff of the British Military Mission. The first Allied activity in which the Canadians participated was a parade on November 15 to mark the Armistice on the Western Front. Sixty-two officers and men marched in the long lines of troops that passed before a reviewing stand where Elmsley stood with other Allied generals and senior naval officers.

The main task of the advance party was to find adequate accommodation for the Canadian contingent. Both the Japanese—in surprisingly large numbers—and the Americans had already arrived. They had naturally taken the best barracks. After the establishment of the headquarters offices, the advance party turned to the renovation of tsarist barracks at Second River, at Gournastai, and at East Barracks (at the east end of the "Golden Horn"), made available by the White authorities for use by the brigade. Some of the barracks were filthy, having been used by refugees, but all were of sound construction. In the refurbishing, the 31st United States Infantry Regiment was so helpful, lending everything from water carts to a bugle, that Elmsley asked Ottawa to convey his thanks formally to Washington.

During October, the main body of the Canadian force—for

whom the barracks at Vladivostok were being readied—gathered at the Willows Camp in Victoria to undergo three months of intensive training, which included frequent use of the rifle range at nearby Clover Point. The soldiers were housed first in tents and, when the December rains came, in the buildings of the Willows racetrack and exhibition grounds. During the autumn of 1918, an epidemic of Spanish influenza swept through the armies in Europe and across North America. The soldiers travelling to Victoria and those already there were not immune from the contagion: 100 died, mainly veterans weakened by combat in France. As a result of this high fatality rate and of the heavy rain, the men were placed in quarantine for a fortnight, their training program was reduced for several weeks, and only basic instruction was completed before embarkation.

The force proved more immune to the efforts of Bolshevik sympathizers in Victoria to induce them to desert. Anti-imperialist meetings in a local cinema were organized by communists every Saturday, until one evening six junior officers led the troops in the hall towards the stage in a menacing fashion. Then, "the speakers seemed willing enough to kiss the flag and sing 'God Save the King'. There were no more meetings!"[19]

While the two battalions and their various support services were concentrated at Victoria and the advance party was sailing for Siberia, there passed through Vladivostok on his way to Omsk a short, lonely man of forty-five who was to become, in little more than a month, the ruler of all Russia not under Bolshevik control. Rear-Admiral Alexander Vassilevich Kolchak, a patriot of the deep devotion that Russia seems especially prone to produce, had served with distinction in the Russo-Japanese War of 1905. In 1916 he was appointed commander-in-chief of the Black Sea fleet. After resigning his command during the Revolution, he volunteered to serve in the British Army on the Western Front. Known for his high sense of duty and personal integrity, Kolchak appeared to the British—and to Knox especially—to be the type of man who might be able to untangle the web of conspiracy and corruption encumbering the efforts of the anti-Bolshevik All-Russian Provisional Government in Omsk.

Somewhat reluctantly, Kolchak accepted the portfolios of war and navy in that unstable government. The task of reorganizing the White forces to crush the Red would have daunted a man less devoted to duty than Kolchak. With this same high sense of patriotism, he also assumed the new post of "Supreme Ruler of All Russia", when it was offered to him on November 18 by a conservative military clique in Omsk. Supported by Cossacks, the clique had overthrown the liberal directory the day before. Those involved in this *coup d'état* congratulated themselves on overcoming a government that they, from their ultra-conservative point of view, considered too radical. But they paid a heavy price for doing so. The Czech Legion, favourable to the moderate Social-Revolutionaries, was alienated. Thereafter, the Legion played an increasingly passive role in the civil war, generally restricting itself to holding open the Trans-Siberian railway. As early as November 28, Elmsley wrote to Ottawa and London about the likely effects of the Legion's growing disaffection.

> The Czechs' future attitude is the deciding factor. . . . If the Czechs withdraw their support, the Russian military, and possibly political, situation may collapse. . . . As the Czechs' future attitude is very doubtful, it might have a beneficial influence if the Canadian Government could now guarantee them active support, provided they continue their former policy of assistance to Russia.[20]

Before long, it became evident that Kolchak could not halt the rampant corruption or rectify the widespread incompetence that trammelled his government.* Kolchak was an inflexible and uninspiring man who stimulated little devotion among his troops. He was, moreover, too tolerant of the monumental selfishness of his own excessively numerous staff. However, he at least provided a centre for the allegiance of White Russians during the winter of 1918. Even Semenov eventually stated his willingness to recognize Kolchak's authority (although the Cossack brigand, supported by the Japanese, proved more of a hindrance than a help). In order to provide some tangible

* Trailing the Bolsheviki, *a book by a special correspondent of the* New York Times, *Carl Ackerman, gives on pp. 51-8 a graphic picture of the hazardous life in the overcrowded and unhappy city of Omsk during the winter of 1918.*

evidence of support for Kolchak's efforts to organize an offensive against Moscow, the British supplied large amounts of arms and clothing.* The 25th Battalion of the Middlesex Regiment, commanded by a redoubtable Labour Member of Parliament, John Ward, was dispatched from Vladivostok to Omsk as a further token of British support. † Early in September the Middlesex Battalion had joined with the Japanese in driving a small force of Bolsheviks from eastern Siberia, but in Omsk it did no fighting. However, it was, in the very centre of Russia, a tangible pledge of British support for Kolchak. Arriving in Omsk on October 18, the battalion remained "at the front" for seven months, helping in a very limited way to train White Russian forces.

Once Elmsley and the advance party were installed in Vladivostok, the Canadian government had its own sources of information about what was happening in Siberia. As early as November 2, Elmsley wrote to Mewburn:

> The general situation here is an extraordinary one—at first glance one assumes that everyone distrusts everyone else—the Japs being distrusted *more* than anyone else. Americans and Japs don't hit it off. The French keep a very close eye on the British, and the Russians as a whole appear to be indifferent of [sic] their country's needs so long as they can keep their women, have their vodka, and play cards all night until daylight. The Czecks [sic] appear to be the only honest and conscientious party amongst the Allies.
>   The whole situation here is so intricate and apparently full of intrigue that I have not yet been able to get a clear grasp of the situation. . . . It is, without doubt, a curious country and situation.[21]

* *By late November 1918, Britain had sent to Siberia 200 field guns and complete equipment for 100,000 men. Equipment for a further 100,000 was ordered to be sent in December (included in the arms shipments were three million rounds of .303 ammunition ordered in Canada on August 10, 1918).*

† *In a civil war where unlikely figures abounded, John Ward (1866-1934) was one of the most unlikely. The son of an artisan, a labourer on the Manchester Ship Canal, a veteran of the Sudan campaign of 1884-5, and a prominent Labour leader, Ward himself raised the 25th Battalion of the Middlesex Regiment. An obituary by Sir Bernard Pares, giving details of Ward's eventful life, is in* The Slavonic and East European Review, *vol. XIII, No. 39, April 1935.*

Such information only confirmed the worst fears of those in Ottawa who had been either sceptical or hostile about Canadian participation from the day it was first proposed. As it became increasingly evident that the fighting on the Western Front would soon end, the cabinet began to have still greater misgivings about what it had authorized at Borden's prompting. The advance party had sailed as originally planned, the Armistice then being one month away, but opposition in Canada to the dispatch of the main body grew apace, as October passed into November.

Anticipating the Armistice, the Chief of the Canadian General Staff in Ottawa, with the approval of Mewburn, wrote to the War Office on November 2, inquiring whether the force should not be disbanded since it was now obvious that there would be no further need for an eastern front. The reply from the War Office eight days later was both equivocal and complacent. It did not, in fact, answer the question at all.

> French and British activities are being co-ordinated and should succeed in denying Siberia to the anarchy which has overcome the rest of Russia and rendering its resources available for world reconstruction. Although the lack of direction in the American and Japanese assistance in this task renders it more difficult for the French and ourselves, the advantages to British trade will be correspondingly greater.[22]

The reply reflected the fact that the chimera of trade was always at least as great for the British as it was for Borden, but Ottawa was told nothing about what role was envisaged for the Allied forces in Siberia.

The Armistice was followed by a rapid and occasionally confusing exchange of telegrams between Borden in London and the acting prime minister in Ottawa and by frequent contacts between Borden and the War Office. (Borden was in Ottawa from August 24 until November 8, when he returned to London to participate in the preparations for the Paris Peace Conference.) The result was that decisions, often based on incomplete information, were regarded as final, only to be overturned on the arrival of further conflicting facts or opinion. Telegrams were quick. But they were never quick enough to prevent misunderstandings, doubts and confusion among the three principal actors—Borden, the War Office in London, and the cabinet in Ottawa—as each attempted to make sense of the fundamentally new situation in which they found themselves as a result of the Armistice.

There is no evidence that any cabinet minister, other than Borden himself, could identify after the Armistice any major benefit justifying Canadian participation. Scepticism among ministers in Ottawa deepened into grave doubt as public opposition and social unrest, especially in western Canada, became more acute. During November, for example, Sir Thomas White, the finance minister and, in the absence of Newton Rowell, the acting prime minister, wired Borden four times in three weeks, urging the early withdrawal of the Canadians from northern Russia and the termination of the plan to send troops to Siberia. On November 14, for example, White wired Kemp in London: "Please discuss Siberian Expedition with Prime Minister as soon as he arrives. All our colleagues are of opinion that public opinion here will not sustain us in continuing to send troops. . . . " The following day, and again on November 20, White urged on Borden the desirability of recalling even the advance party, and the Chief of the Canadian General Staff sent a similar message to the War Office.

Borden replied to White on November 20. He had personally ascertained that the War Office did not envisage using the brigade "offensively". General Radcliffe had urged that the presence of the Canadians would help to stabilize the situation in Siberia and would prove useful in the training of a new Russian army. (What, exactly, this new Russian army was to do was not explained.)

These reasons were not, however, paramount in Borden's own mind. He hoped, as all the Allies did to a greater or lesser extent, that Siberia would offer promising new markets. Borden not only favoured the retention of the advance party in Siberia, but he also urged that "the additional forces originally arranged for should proceed to Siberia for the purpose indicated as well as for economic considerations which are manifest."[23] If there was a strong current of opinion against sending troops under the controversial Military Service Act, volunteers might be found to form at least one battalion.

There was no doubt where Borden stood. At the same time, logistic considerations were also pressing in on the cabinet. The War Office, despite growing public opposition in Britain, had agreed to a request from Knox for a strong and experienced battalion to act as an example to Russians under training. In late October the 1/9th Battalion of the Hampshire Regiment had embarked in Bombay to join the Middlesex Battalion in Siberia.* The War Office informed Ottawa that the Hampshires, like the Middlesex, would become part of the 16th Canadian Infantry Brigade and urged that Elmsley leave immediately for Omsk, taking with him a headquarters staff for the two British battalions that would serve there. The War Office also hoped that "B" Squadron of the R.N.W.M.P. would go on to Omsk as soon as it arrived in Vladivostok, thereby providing cavalry support for the two infantry battalions. Presumably the War Office anticipated that if Elmsley, two of his four infantry battalions, the cavalry element, and a headquarters staff were all in Omsk, it would be difficult for Ottawa to resist the suggestion that the whole brigade should be based there. The first step was, however, to move a Canadian headquarters staff to Omsk. In this proposal, the War Office had—for the moment—a supporter in Elmsley, who had wired Ottawa as early as November 2 that he agreed with Sir Charles Eliot and General Knox—and also with the French and the Czechoslovaks—that the Canadian advance party "should be immediately despatched to Omsk and further West, if the situation demands."

When the cabinet met in Ottawa on November 21, it was under pressure to continue the original plans for the Canadian Expeditionary Force (Siberia) and to take further steps that would probably in time result in the brigade going to Omsk. At

---

* The original idea was that the Hampshires would replace the Middlesex but it was soon decided to keep both battalions in Siberia. The 977 officers and men of the Hampshires disembarked in Vladivostok on November 25, one month after the arrival of Elmsley and the Canadian advance party.

the meeting on November 21, there was, however, a bare quorum. Rowell, who presided, decided that the sparse attendance did not justify raising Borden's telegram of the previous day urging dispatch of the main body of troops. Rowell himself was unable to be present the next day, so he wrote to Sir Thomas White, who would preside, that in his view Canada "should go on with the expedition to the extent the Prime Minister has mentioned."

But this did not prove to be the consensus of the cabinet meeting. In its view, there was no real alternative to withdrawal. The dispatch of an entirely voluntary force was no longer feasible since this would require breaking up units already organized and partly trained. Yet a mixed force of volunteers and conscripts would be very unsatisfactory (eventually 36 per cent of the troops were conscripts). Questions were already being asked about the legal right of the government to send conscripts. Parents had protested about the inclusion of their sons who had joined the army only for "the defence of Canada". The bitter memories of the conscription issue that had rocked Canada to its foundations in 1917 were all too fresh. No one wanted to reopen those painful divisions within the Dominion.

Canadian public opinion, after the Armistice, was opposed to intervening in the Russian civil war. This was abundantly clear to the cabinet and to senior officials in Ottawa. Canadians had long regarded the Tsar's government as the most despotic régime in an otherwise increasingly democratic Europe. In the spring of 1917, most Canadians, as well as many Americans and British, had welcomed the overthrow of that régime. It was incomprehensible to many why, a year later, Canada appeared to be aligning itself with Russian reactionaries. Why should Canadian soldiers risk their lives to restore an illiberal régime in a distant land?

This was reason enough for ministers in Ottawa to have misgivings about Borden's conviction that Canadian units should participate in the Allied intervention. But an even more compelling reason for their uneasiness was the way in which Canadian participation in the Allied intervention in Russia had become an issue in the social turmoil attending the end of the war. All left-wing groups in Canada regarded intervention as one more indication of capitalist perfidy. Such groups were successful enough in identifying domestic causes for popular protest without adding an issue remote from immediate Canadian interests.

Public opposition to the Siberian policy continued to increase as the winter wore on and the effects of a sharp post-war economic recession began to impinge upon the Canadian economy. Rising unemployment, aggravated by the rapid discharge of servicemen, caused the government increasing concern. That concern was in turn heightened by the activities of radicals, many of whom enunciated ideas regarded by the authorities as Bolshevik in origin or content. The government's sensitivity had already been demonstrated when it passed an order-in-council in September barring certain socialist organizations deemed to be dangerous to the state. In the wake of that action, and as reports reached Ottawa of attempts by radicals and left-wing organizations to influence the troops destined for Vladivostok, both civil and military leaders became progressively more alarmed.

Most Canadians were not socialists, but like T. A. Crerar, the Minister of Agriculture, they were sick of strife and opposed to interfering in the affairs of another people. A colossal war had, in their view, been fought on just such a principle as non-interference. Some might not like the forces at work inside Russia, but to intervene would probably only unite a majority of the Russian people behind the Bolsheviks. On November 22 Crerar wrote to White that he "abolutely opposed" sending the force to Siberia. The Armistice had removed the original strategic justification. He asked White to put his views to the cabinet. Given this dissent, the cabinet decided to ask Mewburn to postpone the sailing of the *Monteagle*, which was to take additional men for the headquarters staff and 153 men of "B" Squadron, of the R.N.W.M.P. from Vancouver to Vladivostok.*

* *The* Monteagle *eventually carried 429 Canadian soldiers (including the R.N.W.M.P.), one nursing sister, and 292 horses of the R.N.W.M.P.*

While White, a cautious man preoccupied with the serious post-war economic problems facing Canada, was telegraphing Borden, telling him of popular unrest and of the grave doubts within the Union cabinet about the dispatch of the force, Borden in London was the same day (November 22) writing to White:

I think we must go on with this as we have agreed to do so and there seems some reason from our own standpoint as well as the common interest why the expedition should proceed. Evidently it is not anticipated that our troops will be called upon to engage in active warfare except perhaps to quell some local disturbances. They will assist in stabilizing conditions and giving needed aid to the recently organized Russian Government in training the newly organized formations of Russian troops. Then it will be of some distinction to have all the British Forces in Siberia under the command of a Canadian Officer. Moreover the Economic Commission which we have sent forward would otherwise be useless and would have to be recalled to our possible detriment in the future.[24]

The following day, November 23, Borden took it upon himself to inform the War Office that, while it was not the intention of Canada

to undertake an offensive campaign in Siberia against the Bolsheviks . . . we attach the greatest importance to maintaining the British and Canadian troops we have already sent, and reinforcing them to the full extent originally contemplated, in order to improve the general situation, to strengthen the hands of the Omsk Government and to assist the organization of the Russian forces now being raised so as to enable them at the earliest possible moment to stand on their own legs and enable our forces to withdraw.[25]

With these largely meaningless reasons for Canadian participation stated to the War Office, Borden wired his colleagues in Ottawa on November 24 urging continuation of the undertaking, since "withdrawal from our deliberate engagement will have [an] extremely unfortunate effect."[26] The ministers visiting London with Borden—Foster, Sifton, and Doherty—agreed with his prognosis.* Borden and his colleagues in London were speaking with one voice and their colleagues in Ottawa with another. White sent a further message to Borden on November 25, stating that,

> ... after hearing many discussions in Council [my own view] is that Canada should, now that the war is over and no necessity exists for the re-establishment of the Eastern front, discontinue further participation and expense. It seems clearly a task for nations more immediately interested in the finances of Russia. There is an extraordinary sentiment in Canada in favour of getting all our men home and at work as soon as possible.[27]

He cited Ballantyne, Calder, Crerar, and Reid as the ministers most strongly opposed.†

This difference had to be resolved at once. Borden's patience with his vacillating cabinet colleagues had worn thin, and on November 25 he sent White a telegram urging continuation of the expeditionary force, which must have crossed with White's telegram to him of the same day. The following day yet another cable arrived from White expressing the implied wish that Borden would reconsider his position, and noting that the Toronto *Globe* "has strong editorial against Canada aiding in interfering in Russian internal affairs and assisting to set up any particular form of Government. . . . question has considerable political importance. . . . "

Borden now realized the impossibility of attempting to reach a consensus by telegram with his sceptical cabinet in Ottawa when he was on the other side of the Atlantic and when his views were so different from those of the majority. He decided

---

* The Right Honourable Sir George Eulas Foster was Minister of Trade and Commerce, the Honourable Arthur Lewis Sifton, Minister of Customs and Inland Revenue, and the Right Honourable Charles Joseph Doherty, Minister of Justice and Attorney General.

† The Honourable Charles Colquhoun Ballantyne was Minister of Marine and Fisheries and Minister of Naval Service, the Honourable James Alexander Calder, Minister of Immigration and Colonization, and the Honourable John Dowsley Reid, Minister of Railways and Canals.

that he himself could do no more to persuade them. He wired curtly on November 27: "We leave question to your own determination." White replied the following day that while, needless to say, the cabinet members in Ottawa wanted to meet his wishes, they hoped that the Allied plans for Siberia would include only those Canadians ready to sail and that they would be able to return by the next summer. Borden sent one more telegram. On November 27 (a day on which he noted wearily in his diary that the "telegrams from White [were as] thick as autumn leaves in Vallombrosa"), Borden informed White that he had again discussed the Siberian force with the Director of Military Operations at the War Office. General Radcliffe had said that if the main body of Canadian troops were not to be sent, the War Office hoped that at least Elmsley, his headquarters staff, and fifty to 100 instructors might be permitted to remain in Siberia. The War Office had already wired Knox and Elmsley that "no British or Canadian troops are to go west of the Urals".* On November 29, White reported that the cabinet had finally reached a consensus to proceed with the dispatch of the Canadian troops as they had originally agreed, on the understanding that any member of the force would be free to request repatriation within one year of the signing of the Armistice agreement (i.e., by November 11, 1919), a suggestion that Elmsley's deputy, General Bickford, had wired to Ottawa the day before.

Borden was gratified to learn of this decision, because he did not want Canada to appear to be going back on its word. With a final position apparently taken, he asked Ottawa on December 1 to communicate direct to the War Office in the future, on Siberian matters. He made a similar request to the War Office

---

* The Chief of the Imperial General Staff warned the Imperial War Cabinet a few days later that operations west of the Urals would increase "demands for personnel, which, in view of the uninstructed state of public opinion as to Russia and the approaching demobilization of the bulk of our forces may meet with much opposition in this country."[28] But east of the Urals was another question. The War Office wired Ottawa: "'We consider that accommodation should be sought in the neighbourhood of Chelyabinsk, where the presence of even a few British troops behind the front would act as a stimulus and an example to the Russian and Siberian troops in training.'"[29]

regarding communications to the Canadian government. Borden's consternation was, therefore, all the greater when he received messages indicating that the cabinet had begun to vacillate again. This time the cabinet's misgivings arose mainly from the possibility of a clash between Japanese and United States interests in the Far East, rather than from doubts about what role the Allied force would play in Siberia now that the war with Germany had been ended. Colonel Lash had reported from Vladivostok on December 3 that the Allies, as represented in Siberia, did not have a common policy and that the Japanese and the Americans could not even agree on the operation of the railway. Canadian sentiment would be with the United States in any quarrel with the Japanese in the Far East. Borden and Ottawa then exchanged yet another series of messages about Siberia.

On December 7, 1918, Mewburn (now back in Ottawa) described to Borden a telegram the Chief of the Canadian General Staff had sent to the War Office that day, inquiring about a report from Lash concerning Japanese support for Cossack insurgents and the continued unwillingness of the United States contingent to move inland. The cabinet in Ottawa had decided that, in these circumstances, while the main body of Canadian troops would be sent as planned, they, like the Americans, would remain in the area of Vladivostok. Furthermore, unless satisfactory clarification of British policy was soon received the Canadians would be withdrawn.[30]

The main problem, as Mewburn commented in his message to Borden, was simply that there was no clear-cut British policy towards Russia after the Armistice. The same day, Borden received a second telegram from Ottawa, in which White contended that there was mounting evidence that Canadian participation in the Allied intervention was an increasingly important factor in the social unrest in Canada. White wired Borden: "There is a good deal of feeling in labour and other quarters here against our continued participation [in Siberia] and my personal view is that a serious political situation may arise later unless some definite statement can be made as to the return of the expedition within a reasonable time."[31]

In his reply the same day, Borden noted briefly that the British government, "with our approval", undertook obligations to "well-disposed persons in Russia with a view to re-establish Eastern Front". With his strong sense of commitment, Borden was in no doubt that obligations had been incurred that had to be honoured, Armistice or no Armistice. On December 9, however, he again and still more emphatically attempted to wash his hands of the whole Siberian problem. Once and for all, Borden wanted to be done with it, so that he could concentrate his attention on the work of the Imperial War Cabinet as it faced the imminent prospect of the Paris Peace Conference, and especially the question of separate Canadian representation.

> Our view is that Canada's military operations in Siberia should b. reduced to a minimum and that troops should be withdrawn as soon as conditions will reasonably permit. Have asked Balfour to advise you regularly as to political and economic conditions. War Office advises you as to military conditions. Canadian political officer at Vladivostock [sic] is in touch with you. Under these circumstances Council is in a better position to judge than we are at this distance and we leave matter entirely to judgment of Council. . . . Please dispose of matter without further reference to us.[32]

Impatient with his colleagues and distant from their worries, Borden apparently believed that he could in such a manner divest himself of further involvement in the deepening dilemma that he had himself largely created. The ministers in Ottawa could not so easily withdraw. And, in Vladivostok, Elmsley was at least as doubtful as they were about what his force was to do in Siberia. On December 17 he formally requested new instructions in the light of the Armistice on the Western Front. This was a wholly reasonable request. Somehow Elmsley had to be answered. What was even more difficult for Ottawa to deal with was a War Office telegram on December 18, stating that the Imperial War Cabinet would shortly consider a proposal to use the Canadian brigade in a "defensive campaign" to help the White Russians hold their lines. But the employment of Canadians in any such campaign would be contrary to the cabinet's recent decision that the men should not leave Vladivostok. The situation was further complicated by the fact that a small detachment of Canadians would soon be *en route* to Omsk to serve as a headquarters staff for the British troops there.

Canada had undertaken to provide the headquarters for the whole brigade. Two of its four infantry battalions were now either in Omsk or on their way there.* In Omsk the 543 "Die-Hards" of the Middlesex Battalion and the 862 men of the Hampshire would require more medical and other support services than they could provide themselves. Three more reasons suggested the need for the Canadian headquarters detachment to go to Omsk. First, if the whole brigade were later to be ordered there, barracks would have to be ready. Second, direct contact with Kolchak and his government would be useful in gaining a clearer picture of what was happening in western Siberia. Finally, the French General Maurice Janin, who commanded all Allied units west of Lake Baikal (basically the two British battalions), was in Omsk.† Janin would be able to discuss the question of accommodation and, more generally, the situation facing Kolchak.

Accordingly, on December 7, Elmsley issued orders to a young lieutenant-colonel, Thomas Sydney Morrisey of Montreal, to proceed at once to Omsk.‡ In addition to carrying out the tasks outlined above, Morrisey was to send his own impressions "in view of the possible move of the main body of the C.E.F. (Siberia) to Omsk". Morrisey was assigned a detachment of seven officers and forty-two other ranks. Three medical

---

* *The Middlesex Battalion was on garrison duty in Omsk from mid October 1918 to May 1919 and the Hampshires were there from January to May 1919 and in Ekaterinburg until August 1919.*

† *The cautious Japanese were unwilling to see Otani involved in any area even remotely near the front line. His command accordingly ended at Lake Baikal and Janin's extended westward from there.*

‡ *Morrisey, a 1911 graduate of the Royal Military College of Canada, had served in France as a regimental officer and a staff officer. He was appointed brigade major of the 8th Canadian Brigade at the time Elmsley commanded it. He helped Elmsley make plans for the Canadian Expeditionary Force (Siberia) in the summer of 1918 in London. He later became the brigade's G.S.O.1.*

officers went to help staff a fifty-bed hospital, the equipment for which was sent on the train with them. Another officer commanded two machine guns, a Canadian-born artillery officer of Ukrainian ancestry acted as interpreter, and the orderly officer was William Mulock.*

The only rail transport available for the long trip was six American-built box-cars that the unit had fitted with rough furniture, insulated, and painted with large Union Jacks on both sides. Into one car went three months' supplies and into others the portable hospital. The 3,800-mile journey to Omsk took twenty days. It was for the most part uneventful except during the stop in Chita when Morrisey received a visit from the Cossack leader Gregori Semenov, a man

> who was told, and believed, that he was a combination of Peter the Great and Napoleon, and through our interpreters we made speeches at each other until we had nothing more to say, and then we had recourse to some of Dewar's pre-war whisky [bought from a Chinese merchant in Harbin]. It appeared that, because of Semenoff's obstructions on the railway, Koltchak had issued an Army Order . . . declaring, among other things, that Semenoff was a traitor to Russia. Considering that Semenoff was the first anti-Bolshevik leader in Siberia, this smarted, and it was impressed upon me that I had an opportunity to perform the greatest service to Russia, to the world even, if I could only persude Koltchak to rescind [the] Order. . . . While this Order stood Semenoff could never see his way to co-operate with the present Government.[33]

Morrisey's interview with Semenov and his subsequent encounters with Kolchak (who, not surprisingly, ignored Semenov's demands) were further evidence of the need for a definitive statement to be made by the Canadian government about what it wanted and did not want the Canadian units to do in Siberia. However, when on December 22, 1918, such a statement was finally made, it was unambiguous and uncompromising. The Chief of the Canadian General Staff was authorized by Mewburn acting on behalf of the cabinet, to inform the War Office that in the view of Canada the situation had

---

* Later Postmaster-General (see footnote, page 147).

... everywhere changed since Canada undertook to furnish Contingent; policy of allied and associated Powers not defined; and public opinion strongly opposed to further participation. Therefore, although despatch of Canadian troops will for present continue, they must all return to Canada next spring.

Meanwhile Dominion Government cannot permit them to engage in military operations nor, without its express consent, to move up country.

No Canadians, other than Morrisey's small detachment, were to go to Omsk. They were to remain in Vladivostok until the Allies agreed on a common program. Thus the basic Canadian policy was at last laid down, only three days before the main body of troops sailed from Victoria.

The following day, in London, Borden supported Lloyd George in a meeting of the Imperial War Cabinet by calling for a halt to any fighting involving Allied troops in Russia, although he considered the Allies had "obligations" to the Czechoslovaks. Would it not be possible to arrange with the Bolsheviks the withdrawal of the Czechs and of the Allied contingents, and the amnesty of those Russians who had co-operated with them? Borden acknowledged that his colleagues in Ottawa had agreed to the Siberian force only after considerable pressure from him. He had come to recognize that Canadians would not tolerate the continuation of the troops in Russia beyond the spring.* At a meeting on December 30, Borden argued forcefully for keeping the British Empire clear of European entanglements and for a determined effort to end the fighting in Russia through negotiation, a necessary concomitant of general peace in Europe.

The War Office was much displeased by these indications of

---

* *The summary records of the Imperial War Cabinet meeting on December 23 imply that Borden may have believed that Vladivostok, like Archangel, was ice-bound during the winter. That Borden had been able to induce his reluctant cabinet colleagues to accede to his approach to intervention is indicative of how, during the course of the war, he came to dominate his government. On February 18, 1918, Foster, the Minister of Trade and Commerce, had noted in his diary: "Government is getting to be too much a one-man Government. . . . There is too much inequality in the Cabinet–the head too dominant and the members too restrained." (PAC, Foster Papers, File 56)*

emerging Canadian policy. In its impatience, it abruptly and without consultation recommended to the British War Cabinet that the participation of the Canadians should be terminated at once. On January 4, 1919, the War Office informed both the Chief of the Canadian General Staff and Elmsley that, since the two Canadian battalions would be limited to service in Vladivostok, it had recommended:

> (1) That the two British Battalions should be withdrawn to Vladivostock.
> (2) That the Canadian Forces should be returned to Canada....
> We suggest, therefore:
> (1) That at any rate no more troops should be sent.
> (2) That if there is no chance of Canadian Government reconsidering decision even those en route ... might be recalled by wireless.[34]

Elmsley was astonished by this sudden reversal in War Office thinking. On January 8 he wired to London (with a copy to Ottawa): "actions suggested by you if concurred in by Canadian Government, may have disastrous effect on a situation already critical and may neutralize any decisions arrived at by Peace Conference for assistance to Russia based on economic, military, or humane grounds."[35] From Omsk, Eliot sent a similar telegram of warning to London.

Given the fact that the British government—and the Allies, generally—had no definite policy towards Bolshevik Russia, the British War Cabinet not surprisingly declined to act on the sudden recommendation of the War Office, pending "decision of Associated Governments as to their general policy in Russia, which is to be discussed forthwith in Paris."[36] The hope that an agreed Allied policy towards Russia would emerge from the Peace Conference remained a vain hope—yet a reason for the Allied powers not to take decisions individually.

The Chief of the Canadian General Staff replied to the War Office that the Canadians *en route* would not be recalled. Furthermore, Elmsley was authorized to go to Omsk to assume command of the two British battalions now there, once Bickford had arrived in Vladivostok. Ottawa's willingness to see

Elmsley—but not the two Canadian battalions—go to Omsk, and not to recall the troops at sea, satisfied the needs of the moment. But it really settled nothing. The basic requirement of the Canadian government for a policy statement by the Allies had still not been met. London had produced nothing. Perhaps Washington might have some insights. Accordingly, on January 5 the Canadian military representative in Washington was asked to inquire exactly what was the current United States thinking about Allied military intervention in Siberia. His reply indicated that, while little thought was being given to Siberia, President Wilson's original decision that American troops would not be used against the Bolsheviks or any other faction in the civil war remained unchanged.

Against this background, Ottawa on January 10, 1919, sent a further telegram to the War Office, this time not first clearing the policy with Borden but, as he had requested, only informing him of it.

> ... Canadian Government feels entitled to be explicitly informed first, as to the present attitude of the American and Japanese Governments with regard to the continued presence of their troops in Siberia, and secondly as to the object which the British Government now has in view in keeping British forces there. . . . Unless withdrawal of Canadian troops will embarrass the British Government the Canadian Government feels, owing to the uncertainty and indefiniteness of the whole situation, that Canadian Forces should be returned to Canada. The Canadian Government is prepared, however, to let matters stand as they are now, provided there is any hope of a very early decision by the Allied and Associated Powers respecting the Siberian problem.[37]

This inquiry went to the heart of the Siberian dilemma, yet the War Office reply of January 12 was only vague and temporizing. It "hoped" that the United States and Japan would soon conform to Anglo-French policy and that the Peace Conference would soon attend to the Russian problem. The War Office concluded with a pious wish to see the Canadian public, like the British, become more concerned about the grave international threat which, in its view, communism posed. The War

Office had deluded itself into believing that "public opinion here [in Britain] is becoming more enlightened regarding Bolshevism and begins to realize it is no longer a Russian domestic problem, but a menace to civilization."

Even the limited role for Canadian troops in Siberia that the cabinet had defined was strongly opposed by many Canadians.* The United Farmers of Ontario, the Vancouver, Winnipeg, Toronto, and Montreal Trades and Labour Councils, and other labour organizations across the country sent resolutions, letters, and appeals to Ottawa calling for an immediate end to Canadian participation. A meeting in Winnipeg, organized by the Socialist Party at the ornate Walker Theatre on December 22 to protest about labour conditions in Canada, was typical of many such gatherings. Given prominence among the resolutions about the living conditions of Canadian workers—some of which pointed to the Winnipeg general strike five months later—was a demand for the withdrawal of all Canadian troops from Russia. Concurrent with such meetings were ominous reports from police and military sources across Canada about unrest and discontent regarding Ottawa's policy towards Russia.

The opposition of radical or left-wing organizations, sometimes manifest in short-lived news-sheets, was consistent and had to a degree been anticipated. Decidedly less easy to disregard was the opposition that appeared increasingly in the editorials of major newspapers as well as in letters to editors.† On

---

* *Nevertheless, there was no interference by labour unions with the sailing of the main body of the contingent or its supplies. On the Vancouver waterfront, only J. S. Woodsworth, the future leader of the Co-operative Commonwealth Federation, gave tangible expression to his opposition. "Of twelve hundred longshoremen on the Vancouver docks, he was the only one to refuse to load munitions destined for the use of the expeditionary force . . . in spite of the double pay offered for the job and his own pressing need for money." (Kenneth McNaught,* A Prophet in Politics, *University of Toronto Press, 1959, pp. 91-2).*

† *Brief contemporary summaries of newspaper and labour union reaction appear in Gordon Grey's "Canada and the Siberian Expedition",* The Nation, *New York, vol. 108, No. 1796, pp. 162-3, February 1, 1919, and in his letter to the editor of the* New Republic, *vol. 17, p. 283, January 4, 1919.*

November 29 the Toronto *Globe*—normally a strong supporter of Borden's Unionist government—contended:

> Were the problem in Russia a simple, clear-cut issue of order or anarchy, there might be a warrant for the despatch of Canadian troops . . . to aid in the restoration of order and to destroy the pro-German group which holds northwestern Russia for Bolshevism. But conditions in Russia are far more complex than they were three months ago, when the Allies determined, with the aid of the Czecho-Slovaks, to reconstitute the Eastern battlefront and prevent Germany from drawing either men or war materials from those parts of Russia overrun by them. . . . Whether Russia adopts a Republican or Monarchist Government is a matter that the Russians have a perfect right to settle for themselves. If a drunken orchestra leader plays "God Save the Czar", he must be disciplined by his own compatriots, not by boys from Ontario and Western Canada who have no interest in the Russian National Anthem and whose rights and liberties as Canadian citizens are not in any way endangered by internal disorganization in Russia. A reconsideration of the Siberian adventure is absolutely necessary.

A fortnight before the departure of the main body of troops, the Hamilton *Daily Times* of December 11 recorded:

> There is considerable dissatisfaction and anxiety all over the country regarding Canada's expedition into Siberia. . . . The original purpose . . . was to prevent Russia from being further exploited by the Germans. The menace is definitely passed; the Germans have enough troubles of their own. What do we propose to do now? Overthrow the Bolshevists? And for what purpose? Are we sacrificing our soldiers . . . to validate Russian bonds held by foreign nations?

Across Canada most newspapers generally greeted the news of the dispatch of the contingent with scepticism, incredulity, or hostility. Another newspaper in Mewburn's home town of Hamilton, the *Herald*, stated on December 13:

> What is going on in Russia is in the nature of a civil war. Outsiders really have no right to interfere. The Bolsheviks are said to be but a fraction of the Russian population. If the vast majority of people are so supine and indifferent as to permit a few rascals to dominate

them, we cannot see why it is the business of Canada or any other nation to sacrifice men and money to save them.

The Toronto *Sun* on December 11 suspected another motive. Canadian participation in the Archangel and Siberian forces was unwelcome evidence of how pre-war ideas of Imperial unity, especially of the "round table" variety, had surprisingly survived the Great War, the *Sun* said; Canadian troops were in Russia because Britain wanted them there, not because Canadian national interests dictated their participation. Noting the widespread opposition, the Toronto *Globe* on December 28 echoed editorials in United States newspapers about American participation when it said, about the Canadian contingent, "sixty to seventy per cent of the men despatched to Siberia went unwillingly because they believed the expedition was one in which Canada had no right to be engaged."

The weekly *Saturday Night* of December 28 was almost alone in supporting intervention. On the same day that the *Globe* was again questioning why Canadian troops were on their way to Siberia, *Saturday Night* pulled together what few arguments it could to substantiate its contention that

> While Bolshevism still remains formidable in Russia there can be no peace, for Bolshevism is an international movement which has declared war against the existing institutions of civilization. . . . a failure to definitely stamp out Bolshevism in its strongholds will cost the world innumerable valuable lives of all nationalities in the future. Duty as well as interest impels support of the Siberian expedition.

Such enthusiasm for intervention was rare in Canada.

One result of the indecision in the cabinet about intervention had been that Elmsley was left to decide, on a day-to-day basis, what he should do. By the latter half of December, he had been in Siberia long enough to gain an insight into the uncertain position in which he had been placed. His first responsibility was the safety of his troops. When he received no reply to his request for new, clear instructions relevant to the post-war circumstances, he had to plan for all possible contingencies. It was conceivable that his whole force would be ordered inland. If it was, he wanted to be sure that it would have a reasonable chance of getting out again. Canadian troops would not themselves be responsible for their own lines of communication. In the hands of others was the security of the Trans-Siberian railway, the vital link if any force in the hinterland were not to become stranded.

In the inter-Allied division of commands, the French General Janin had been assigned western Siberia, the Japanese General Otani eastern Siberia, and the British General Knox the lines of communication and supply. It was to Knox as *Directeur de l'arrière* that Elmsley wrote on December 21. If the day did come when the Canadian government approved the transfer inland of the brigade, Elmsley wanted an assurance from the other Allied representatives in Vladivostok that they would do everything possible to guarantee his brigade's long and exposed line of communication from railhead back to Vladivostok.

> To you, Knox, this demand might appear unreasonable, futile, and non-productive of results. To me it appears reasonable and just, first, because it affects the lives and welfare of my men and, secondly, I am a firm believer that in military matters "he who is not with me is against me".
>
> This last remark does not apply to the Americans—we are of the same blood—and if they cannot be with us, they certainly will not be against us. But hostile Japanese and Russian interests may neutralize your best efforts and mine. . . . [38]

Knox was either unwilling or unable to offer any encouragement about guarantees for the security of the brigade's line of communication. The Allies were so disunited that there could be no hope of obtaining such guarantees. Moreover, Knox bluntly contended that "neither the Americans nor the Japanese wish us to go on, the first because President Wilson is advised by Jews who sympathize with Bolshevism and the second because they want a weak Russia rather than a strong one."[39] Fortunately, the risk to the Canadian line of communications would not, he believed, be great. Knox, who felt intensely about Russia, concluded his letter with an aspersion: "Ottawa seems to have made up its mind to do nothing. If so, why not say so?"

Elmsley, although willing to let the matter of security for his line of communication rest for the moment (probably because he became increasingly convinced that his brigade would never in fact be ordered "up country"), was not prepared to let Knox's scepticism about Ottawa's good faith pass unchallenged. On December 27, he emphasized in another letter to Knox that the lack of any clear policy in London was the basic reason why Canada would not sanction an immediate move inland. He quoted from an agreement reached in London on August 13 between the War Office and the Canadian authorities, when the brigade was first being organized:

> It must be distinctly understood that if the Canadian Force proceeds to Vladivostok that it shall not be committed to any military operations, or subject to the orders of any Officer [other] than General Elmsley, and that the Force receiving his santion and approval and before arriving at a decision a more definite and distinct understanding must be come to and known as to what extent the United States and Japan are committed. Canada will not consent to this Force being committed without positive assurance of the whole policy.[40]

Knox replied the same day that he had never before seen this paragraph and conceded that it explained current Canadian attitudes. But he could not refrain from adding, "I still hope they [Ottawa] will send troops to go the whole hog. If they only think of playing the American-Japanese sitting game ... I honestly don't see much use in their coming at all."[41]

Elmsley was willing to conclude his correspondence with Knox on that note, but he did send copies of the letter to the acting British high commissioner in Vladivostok (Eliot being in Omsk), for his information. Elmsley wanted it on record that he had attempted to obtain a clear statement of the circumstances in which his troops might have to operate if they were ordered inland. After reading the correspondence, the acting high commissioner replied ruefully to Elmsley on December 31: "It requires a clever person to diagnose what any of us are actually supposed to be doing here."

Half-way around the world, the Chief of the Imperial General

Staff marked New Year's Eve with a similar observation in his diary. There was still, General Wilson noted wearily, "*no* policy in our Russian theatre, which at this time of the day after all our discussions for months and months is an absolute *disgrace*."[42] It was against this background of misunderstanding, confusion, and contradictory intentions that the main body of Canadian troops sailed for Siberia during the last days of 1918.

III   *Vladivostok versus Omsk*

Wearing the distinctive purple shoulder patch of the Canadian Expeditionary Force (Siberia), 898 men of the 259th Battalion and a few from the brigade's support services sailed from Victoria for Vladivostok early in the morning on December 22, 1918. Not all of the men were happy to be going. Both during the day preceding embarkation and during the march from the camp to the ship, many of the French-speaking soldiers mutely demonstrated that they did not regard service in Siberia as being within the terms of the conscription act. Following a brief rest halt on Fort Street in Victoria, six declined to march any farther. For their objections, they were promptly arrested and placed on board the ship under guard; later, they were given sentences ranging from ninety days to two years of extra duty.*

It was an inauspicious beginning to the long voyage to Vladivostok. What awaited the battalion on the ship confirmed the gloomy views of the pessimists. One young volunteer, Lance-Corporal Erskine Ireland—a future Toronto lawyer—noted in his diary:

> The evening [of December 21] was spent in the chilly sheds at the wharf. At 11 p.m. we boarded the [British] tramp freighter, "S.S. Teesta". When we proceeded to our quarters below, the natural feeling was one of indescribable disgust, especially when the hammocks were hooked up side by side, as close together as

* *At the suggestion of Elmsley, the sentences were remitted in May, on the departure of the force from Siberia.*

sardines in a tin. . . . The first five days of our voyage were uneventful. Most of the boys had a touch of sea-sickness. . . . Our accommodation is very poor, but the boys seem ready to adapt themselves to nearly all circumstances, and in spite of all hardships, are in good spirits. One of the rules to keep well is to keep away from "down below", but being confined to the front part of the boat and having no place to sit down, you scarcely know what to do with yourself. The meals are good. Sixteen men are placed at each table. . . . On Christmas Day I was on guard, my duty being to keep the men away from the upper decks. I had pity on some of my friends who were standing below in the cold sleet and allowed them to rest on some boxes in a sheltered spot near my post on the upper deck. . . . I was certainly pleased to be on guard, if only to obtain a dry spot to sit down. It did not seem like Christmas to me. My thoughts were back in Canada. . . . The past three days [December 27-29, 1918] have been among the most pleasant of our voyage. . . . On Friday morning when snow was blowing in upon us on the deck, five of us standing together in a little circle spent our time in reading *The Ancient Mariner*. . . . New Year's Day differed only in one respect from other days in that each soldier was given plum pudding for dinner, a bottle of beer, and an apple or orange.[43]

The *Teesta* encountered such rough weather in the north Pacific that a rifleman was killed in falling down a coal chute, a Chinese crewman died in another accident, and several others were injured. Having battled against stormy seas for most of seventeen days, the ship had to put in at Muroran in northern Japan for bunkering. When the 259th Battalion finally disembarked in Vladivostok on January 13 and 14 and marched to the ex-tsarist barracks, which had been readied for them by the advance party, they were immediately paraded for baths, the *Teesta* having been infested with lice.

The 1,808 officers and men of the 260th Battalion and of most of the brigade support units had an even worse passage. They waved good-bye at Gordon Head, near Victoria, on Boxing Day, after a Christmas Day marked by an elaborate dinner and entertainment, paid for partly by the federal government and partly by the Ontario government. It had been a pleasant day, the last one the men were to have for some time. The *Protesliaus*, a British Blue Funnel Line freighter crudely fitted to carry troops, was decidedly not a comfortable ship in which to cross the north Pacific in mid winter. One junior officer later recalled how in the sleeping quarters there lingered the aroma of Chinese labourers the *Protesliaus* had carried to the Western Front. As on the *Teesta*, the *Protesliaus* had closely packed hammocks for the troops, only one small galley, and latrines over the ship's sides.* In a storm beginning the second day out of Victoria, the alley-ways were awash or even deep in ice, lockers came apart, and mess tables were broken. Private Harold Butler was killed and another soldier was injured when a large ice-box tore loose from its deck-mounting and crushed them. It was suggested to the troops that if the ship foundered the men would be better to forget their life-jackets; without them, they would drown more quickly in the freezing sea. After several days of battering, the *Protesliaus* lost her port propeller. By using the starboard propeller in conjunction with the rudder, the captain managed to nurse his battered ship to Vladivostok, where she arrived twenty-one days out of Victoria. Her safe arrival on January 15 was as great a relief to the friends and relatives of the men on board as it was to the hapless passengers. Wireless messages had been received in Canada from another freighter, afire 500 miles to the south, that had been confused with those of the *Protesliaus*.

The arrival in Vladivostok was in keeping with the whole voyage. In temperatures below zero, the ship needed the assistance of two icebreakers to make her way to the Canadian Ordnance Dock. The march to East Barracks through the sub-zero weather was bad enough, but the box-cars that carried the men assigned to the barracks at Second River, about twenty miles from Vladivostok, were even more disagreeable—worse

---

* *A court of inquiry into the conditions on the* Protesliaus *(which was sunk in the Second World War) was assembled on March 27, 1919, and concluded that the ship was overcrowded and the food and accommodation inadequate. As early as August 27, 1918, Borden had written to Charles Ballantyne, his Minister of Fisheries and Naval Service, asking that Canadian Pacific liners be returned to the Pacific to transport the troops. The Admiralty, which had earlier argued strenuously for their assignment to the Atlantic, may have regarded Borden's request as simply a Canadian stratagem to have them returned to the Pacific. It refused to release the liners from Atlantic service in time to carry the main contingent.*

than the infamous "8 chevaux 40 hommes" rail wagons of the Western Front. The distance was short, but it was long enough for there to be several cases of severe frost-bite, since the men were in the boxcars from morning until mid-afternoon. Fortunately, the barracks awaiting the men were happily of sound construction, if only partly restored by the advance party.

Along with the Canadian Trade Commissioner, Dana Wilgress, and the officers of the advance party, three other Canadians were on hand to greet the main contingent on its arrival in Vladivostok: Major James Macintosh Bell, Captain Dennis Stairs, and Lieutenant George MacAllister, all of the British Military Mission.

Bell had served in Vladivostok prior to and during the revolution.* As a consequence of being badly gassed while serving with the Black Watch of Canada on the Western Front, he was no longer fit for active service. His knowledge of Russian, learned before the war while he was a mining engineer in western Siberia, had resulted in an appointment to the British intelligence mission in Russia, from which he was sent in July 1917 to act as Allied Passport Control Officer in Vladivostok. He went back to Canada in January 1918, on leave and for a brief period of service there, and returned to Vladivostok on July 1, 1918, again on behalf of British military intelligence. With him went a Canadian engineer officer, Captain Dennis Stairs of Montreal,

---

* Bell was born in Quebec in 1877. A geology graduate of Queen's and Harvard universities, he joined the Geological Survey of Canada, from which he volunteered to act as the first director of the Geological Survey of New Zealand (where he met his wife, a sister of Katherine Mansfield). During 1911-12 Bell worked for the Spasski Copper Company about 500 miles south of Omsk. While Allied Passport Control Officer in Vladivostok, Bell became the unofficial Allied representative on the left-wing Committee of Public Safety, "which took over from the tsarist authorities the control of the port which was busy with ships either carrying away Russians opposed to socialism and foreigners seeking refuge from the unsettled conditions in Russia or bringing socialists of all varieties anxious to join in the establishment of the workers' republic." After the war, Bell wrote a somewhat disjointed account of his experiences in Vladivostok entitled Side Lights on the Siberian Campaign (Toronto, Ryerson, n.d.), from which the foregoing quotation is taken.

who had been wounded on the Western Front. Stairs later wrote of Bell's assignment:

> He was going to Siberia to collect first hand information on the political and military situation there and to report directly to the Foreign Office in London. The rest of his party consisted of Baron G. Klodt, who had been a captain in the Russian navy in command of a cruiser, a Russian civilian named Dmitri Ahapkin, and Lieutenant [George] MacAllister, an Irishman who had been with Major Bell in the 42nd Battalion, could take shorthand, operate a typewriter and would act as secretary. We were going [disguised] as a party of mining engineers out to acquire mining prospects . . . for a financial group in London.*

It had been anticipated that Bell's group would have to operate in areas controlled by Bolsheviks, but while it was travelling from Japan to Vladivostok the Czechoslovaks seized the city. Nevertheless, throughout the summer of 1918, the group continued to pose as mining engineers. By September, however, when the British Military Mission arrived, it was unnecessary to keep up the pretence any longer. Bell disbanded his group and he, Stairs, and MacAllister formally transferred to the British mission.

After the arrival of their uniforms from Japan, Bell and Stairs were assigned to help establish a training school for Kolchak's officers and NCOs. The school, housed in dilapidated tsarist barracks on Russian Island in Vladivostok harbour, was at first run on British Army lines with small numbers of British troops; later, Canadian troops were provided for demonstration purposes. However, in accordance with the original plan, control of the school was turned over to White Russian officers as the first group of 500 NCOs completed their training. As was frequently the case in Siberia, a promising project soon came to nothing when reactionary officers attempted to reimpose tradi-

---

* Letter of April 16, 1969, from Mr. Stairs to the author. Although their disguise as a group of mining engineers was only a cover for their intelligence activities, Bell and his party were also asked through the British Embassy in Washington to watch for any evidence of alleged platinum deposits in Siberia. (Public Archives of Canada, file MG 27, II, D-13, vol. 17; Rowell Papers, file 71)

tional Russian military practices. Bell, Stairs, and MacAllister watched with dismay during the first weeks of 1919 as control of the school passed into the hands of monarchists who would only alienate the troops. The three Canadians left Vladivostok at the end of January 1919. Perhaps it was as well that they did, for the school they had worked hard to create deteriorated rapidly thereafter. Four months later, on May 24, a British officer passing through Vladivostok noted in his diary:

> Had a look at "Russian Island"; an island in the harbour where the Russian Army is being trained with the help and under the supervision of the British Mission. We are equipping them with uniform complete with bandolier, water bottles, webbing, etc. When this New Army is more or less fitted to take their place in the front line they are pushed up westwards. Unfortunately, very many of them, when they reach the front, walk over to and join the Bolshevik Army.
>
> It is a pity. They are turned out in every detail like our Tommies; it is bad luck on the latter that a shuffling lout should be mistaken for a British soldier. These New Army Russians are to be seen in most towns and public places and gardens slouching about with dirty buttons, caps all on one side . . . or thrust at the back of their heads, and looking perfectly disreputable.[44]

The day before this diary comment was written, Lieutenant-Colonel John Warden of Vancouver had assumed command of the British training unit attached to the school. Warden struggled until September 15 to encourage a greater sense of commitment and military discipline among the pupils, but with singularly little success. He had arrived in Vladivostok in mid April, crossed Siberia to pay a short visit to Omsk, and returned to Vladivostok to assume his appointment on Russian Island. The British staff work—or lack of it—which shunted him around aimlessly for several weeks was, to Warden, reminiscent of Dunsterforce. But worse still was the dissension among the Allies.

> The Canadians are not liked by the British staff here and the British are detested by the Canadians, the same applies to the Americans, Japs and French . . . each branch of the Allies is suspicious of the

other, each is afraid the other will get a little more foothold than he
... there is no semblance of unity ... which augurs very badly.[45]

Well before the two Canadian battalions had sailed into Vladi-
vostok harbour, two United States regiments had come from the
Philippines. Five thousand more Americans had disembarked
from San Francisco on September 1, bringing the total to 8,763.
Japanese units had also already arrived in strength: between
August 3 and 10, more than 12,000 had landed in Vladivostok.
Eventually 70,000 Japanese soldiers were introduced into
Siberia. To the Vladivostok area there also came 2,000 Italians,
1,850 French (mainly Vietnamese), 4,000 Serbs, 4,000 Roman-
ians, and 12,000 Poles.

These soldiers, if they were all sent westward, could constitute
a formidable army against the Bolsheviks. General Knox, having
established the training school on Russian Island, now turned
part of his great energies to inducing the Canadians to go inland
with the two British battalions. Knox had made it clear that he
despised the strictly limited role the United States had decided
to play in Siberia. He was openly contemptuous of the refusal
of the American General Graves to allow his troops to be
employed in any action that could be interpreted as taking sides
in the civil strife. In doing so, however, Graves was acting in
accordance with President Wilson's instructions and with his
orders from the War Department not to place any of his units
west of Lake Baikal (the same limitation the Japanese had placed
on their contingent).

Knox disagreed utterly with Graves that it was folly to try to
fight Russian communism by force of Allied arms. Similarly,
Knox was scornful of Ottawa's reluctance to see Canadian
soldiers involved in the civil conflict. Elmsley, on the other hand,
understood the American government's position. He frequently
urged upon Knox the necessity of working with the Americans,
instead of dismissing them simply as "eye-sores". On more than
one occasion, Elmsley acted as a peace-maker between the
Americans and British, interpreting the point of view of each to
the other. Later, Graves wrote appreciatively of the Canadian
attitude:

As I saw the Canadians, they constituted a conscientious and serious minded force. It is no secret to say they did not believe in the oppressive and repressive measures used by the Kolchak supporters against the people, which measures, if not entirely approved by General Knox and Sir Charles Eliot, were not resented by them. The practices of killing, imprisoning, and beating the people, because they had certain ideas, was repulsive to the Canadians. They could not understand the repeated statements of Governments [i.e., the British and the French] that they did not intend to depart from the traditional policy of non-interference in the internal affairs of the Russian people and, at the same time, act in a manner that would cause ninety-nine and nine-tenths per-cent of the individuals, who were cognizant of these acts, to construe them as interference of the most objectionable kind.[46]

Knox recommended from the beginning that all of the Canadians, including the advance party, should leave for western Siberia as soon as possible after disembarkation. Always eager to do anything that might assist the Whites, Knox had even urged that Elmsley should himself take the initiative in sending most of the advance party to Omsk before any specific orders to the contrary were received from Ottawa. Of course Elmsley had declined. Not only were the men mostly administrative and not fighting troops, but he was fully aware that such a move would be most unwelcome in Ottawa. When he received confirmation of this in a copy of Ottawa's telegram of December 22 to the War Office, ruling out any inland movement of Canadians, he immediately instructed Colonel Morrisey in Omsk to release to Kolchak's forces the barracks he had tentatively reserved.

On the other hand, Colonel John Lash, Mewburn's personal representative, recommended that Canadian troops should garrison the major towns along the rail-line from Irkutsk to Omsk (the Japanese were guarding the line from Vladivostok to Irkutsk). Having recently travelled to Omsk with Eliot and Morrisey, Lash reported to Mewburn on January 13 his conclusion that if Canadian soldiers were placed along the western section of the rail-line "the steadying influence of their presence on the whole area would be prodigious". With the White

Russian forces now on the offensive, Knox regarded this garrison duty as about the minimum the two Canadian battalions should do to help secure the position of the two British battalions already in the Omsk area. Morrisey, too, was won round to this belief and, on February 4, he urged from Omsk that the Canadian battalions be moved "up country".

On January 24, White in Ottawa wired Borden in Paris, noting the widespread uneasiness in Canada about intervention and asking him to attempt to determine whether the Allies intended to declare a common Russian policy. Borden's reply of January 28 was not very optimistic about the likelihood of an early statement, but he did wire that those soldiers who had been sent to British Columbia to reinforce the contingent in Siberia might now be quietly demobilized. Those in Vladivostok were not to move inland. On January 30, even the permission granted to Elmsley to go to Omsk following the arrival of his deputy, Bickford, was rescinded by Ottawa.*

At Omsk, Colonel John Ward of the Middlesex Regiment learned with indignation of the restrictions placed on the movement of the Canadian contingent and commented sourly in his diary on February 3:

> I heard news of general insubordination among the Canadian troops that had just arrived at Vladivostok.† If all the information received could be relied upon, the sooner they were shipped back to Canada the better. There is enough anarchy here now without the British Government dumping more upon us. I can see that it is a great mistake to mix Canadian and British troops in one Brigade. Naturally, British soldiers carry out orders; if other troops do not, then the British troops have to do all the work. The situation produced is that the highest paid soldier does no work and the

* In February, however, Elmsley did obtain permission to transfer Canadian soldiers inland without the prior approval of Ottawa, if in his opinion any British or Canadian soldiers already there were seriously threatened.

† There is no evidence in Canadian army records of the indiscipline and "general insubordination" that Ward alleged to exist among the Canadians in Vladivostok. On the contrary, the discipline seems to have been remarkably good in the unusual circumstances.

lowest paid all the work. It soon percolates to the slowest Sussex brain that discipline does not pay. Nothing but the wonderful sense of order in the make-up of the average Englishman has prevented us from becoming an Anglo-Canadian rabble, dangerous to Bolshevik and Russian alike. I am told that Brigadier Pickford [sic] has done his best to maintain order and discipline in his ranks; that he had been compelled to make very awkward promises to his troops which having been made had to be fulfilled. In all the circumstances it was generally agreed that the proper thing to have done was to send the Canadians home to their farms, and leave the few Britishers who were there to carry on. We had established excellent relations with the Russians which it would have been a thousand pities to spoil.[47]

Some of the Canadians wished to see action on the Omsk front, but most soon became reconciled to remaining in Vladivostok until their return to Canada. An officer of the base depot noted in his unit's war diary (basing himself on his men's outgoing mail which it was his duty to censor):

Letters sent by men show discontent. This is largely due to a lack of definite policy. Might be removed if force were to go up country but this is doubtful as men of Middlesex Regt. returning from Omsk, state that there is nothing doing there except fatigues and guard duty and everything is more uncomfortable than at Vladivostok and accommodation crowded and bad. Everything expensive up country.[48]

White wired Borden on February 6, inquiring whether, in the light of the discussions in Paris, an approximate date might now be set for bringing the troops back from Siberia (where they had arrived three weeks before). In response to a query from Ottawa, the War Office had been unable to say anything more than that Borden was probably in a better position, being in Paris, to provide an answer. In reply to White's telegram, Borden described a letter he had sent to Lloyd George on February 7, saying that, unless he saw good reasons to the contrary, the Canadian troops should be withdrawn as soon as spring came to Vladivostok (i.e., about April). "Russian situation has not recently been under consideration but I am confident that active military intervention is not proposed and will not be continued."[49] Borden was not deterred by the fact that the Canadian contingent had only just arrived in Vladivostok. During their long passage from Victoria, he had moved from the meetings of the Imperial War Cabinet in London to the Paris Peace Conference where he soon became convinced that no common policy towards Russia would emerge at an early date and that there would therefore be no justification for keeping the Canadian troops in Siberia.

Throughout January 1919, the government, especially Rowell and Mewburn, had been pressed continually to justify the assignment of the contingent to Siberia. This had been difficult for them to do. Prior to the Armistice, the cabinet had acceded to the urgings of the Prime Minister from London. Now the fighting in Europe had ended and Borden remained at the Peace Conference across the Atlantic, a distance that greatly hindered the development of a coherent explanation. The dilemma created by the continuation of intervention after the Armistice was a major factor, related to the pressing domestic reasons, in deciding the cabinet to send pleas to Borden to return home immediately to take the lead in dealing with the growing popular dissatisfaction about post-war conditions in Canada.

Cabinet uneasiness mounted daily.* Like most western countries, Canada in 1919 experienced a "Red scare". An exaggerated influence was ascribed to those advocating Marxist solutions to Canada's post-war problems. Dark stories about communist intrigue circulated. Within the cabinet, such stories were given some credence, fuelled to some extent by Borden's reports from London and Paris, transmitting Allied intelligence about suspected communist plots to overthrow western governments.

The cabinet moved uncertainly, being far from unanimous in

---

* By April, the uneasiness in the government about popular discontent had reached such a point that the cabinet appealed to Borden to ask the Royal Navy to detach a cruiser from its China squadron to help still the unrest on the west coast of Canada. Borden's prompt rejection of this anachronistic suggestion did nothing to lessen the growing concern in the cabinet about what many of its members regarded as an explosive situation.

the credence it gave to the reports of communist intrigue and, in any case, aware that the real cure for the turmoil in Canada rested primarily in greater economic growth and in a redistribution of wealth. In such circumstances, two possibilities were open to the government: to respond to public opinion or to attempt to change it.

The *Manitoba Free Press* was typical of many Canadian newspapers—and considerably more restrained than some—when it demanded a full explanation of Canadian intervention, in its editorial of January 8.

> Canadians will not shirk their obligations or fail in their duty to the Empire and their Allies. But they have a perfect right to judge for themselves whether the obligation to proceed with the Siberian expedition, in the new conditions which have supervened, ought still to be regarded as binding. A full and frank exposure of the grounds upon which it is acting will strengthen the hands of the government. An explanation ought to be given without delay in order to remove finally the irritation which undoubtedly exists.

On February 20, the first day of the 1919 session of Parliament, the Member for Brome inquired why Canadian troops had been provided.

> It would have been proper and fitting before this expedition was sent at all that Parliament should have convened in order that the people's representatives might have been consulted. . . . The Government must at the earliest possible moment let the Canadian people know why Canadian boys have been sent there. It has been suggested by someone that they are sent there for the purpose of promoting Canadian trade.

The Member for Brome made it clear what he thought of that idea, which had appealed so strongly to Borden, when he thundered: "I for one would rather that in all the future history of Canada we never sold a single mowing machine or other article of manufacture . . . there than that the blood of a single Canadian lad should be spilled in vain." During the next few days, the Members for North Essex, Laval-les-Deux-Montagnes, and Rimouski joined in the criticism of the government's action. On March 10, following a somewhat disjointed attempt by

Mewburn to explain the government's reason for sending the contingent,* the Member for Ste. Marie (Montreal) reflected the thinking of many French Canadians when he quoted with approval from an article in the Toronto *Sun*,

> Canada committed a national crime in sending to Russia, to participate in a domestic quarrel, men who had no business to interfere with this country's striving after freedom, no matter how blind its efforts may be. The crime is doubly heinous when you think that men who refused to go were nevertheless forced to embark for Siberia. It is a flagrant violation of the law of the country which allows men to be sent beyond the borders of Canada "for the defence of Canada" only. No matter what distortion is made of the phraseology of this clause it can never be claimed that men sent to Siberia to interfere in the quarrels of factions at war with one another are fighting "for the defence of Canada".

All this and much more was bad enough but, in addition, labour unrest, especially in western Canada, was rapidly growing (by May it was to culminate in the Winnipeg General Strike). A temporary recession with rising unemployment gave left-wing agitators fertile ground and the cabinet increasing worries about the appeal of Bolshevism in Canada itself.

Before the Armistice, a determined effort had been made by Ottawa to obtain from the British government a statement of the Allied reasons for intervention, but the effort was in vain. During the last days of 1918, on the eve of his departure for Paris, Borden had hazarded a brief press statement on the post-war European scene including the observation, common to many Allied statesmen, that

---

* In reviewing the reasons for the government's decision, Mewburn stated in the House of Commons: "About the end of June or early July 1918, the Prime Minister was in England. . . . The Imperial War Cabinet discussed the situation with the Canadian ministers who were there, pointed out the whole of the difficulties and the problems which had to be faced and urged that Canada should assist Great Britain in the organization of a small force to go to Siberia. . . . The matter was very carefully considered and all the phases of the situation duly weighed, and it was felt that Canada could not very well refuse to go to the assistance of Great Britain at that period."

in Russia terrorism and anarchy, posing in the guise of liberty, have succeeded for the moment in oppressing a people unable to utilize their new freedom for the purpose of equal opportunity and orderly government. There is the danger that a fanatical spirit thus aroused may spread to those in other nations who look for food and employment. The present disorders in Germany are not without their significance in this respect.[50]

This was, however, clearly inadequate as a basis for a definitive explanation to the Canadian public. In the absence of anything helpful from London or Paris—where the Allied leaders continued to exhibit that they had no clear idea what intervention was to achieve after the Armistice—Rowell, Mewburn, and several of their colleagues attempted to draft a public statement.

Elmsley was invited to send suggestions. In his reply, he attempted a catalogue of reasons, but none was very convincing:

(1) Majority of soldiers here has made no sacrifice in this war compared to their comrades in France.

(2) They represent the whole of Entente interests, both military and economic.

(3) No interference in Russia's internal affairs is intended except to ensure continuance of peace in Europe and Turkestan covering India, which Bolshevicks [sic] are admittedly attempting to destroy.

(4) Without firing definite shot, presence of C.E.F. ensures the protection of thousands of innocent people and millions of pounds of Allied stores.

(5) Withdrawal might wreck whole of Entente policy and leave Japan and America dominating all economic interests; further, it would encourage Bolshevism and precipitate repetition of atrocities under their rule, most appalling of which is the nationalization of women for purposes of sexual intercourse.*

---

* This paragraph was based on a declaration concerning the nationalization of women issued by an anarchist group in Saratov. It was widely quoted by Allied authorities as evidence of the iniquitous nature of communism. It was, for example, cited by Newton Rowell in the House of Commons and again on February 27 when the Member for Algoma East joined in defending the government's decision to send a Canadian contingent to participate in the Allied intervention in Siberia. (A detailed account of the currency given the story in Britain is in Silverlight's The Victors' Dilemma, pp. 192-4).

The Publicity Commission of the Directorate of Public Information in Ottawa was blandly authorized to quote the final paragraph "to any person interested in the subject". Otherwise, Elmsley's terse suggestions were of no assistance to Rowell and Mewburn, who approved the following draft:

> So soon as the Prime Minister arrived in England, he took up with the British Government, the question of whether it was necessary to continue the despatch of Canadian troops in view of the signing of the Armistice. The War Office advised that under existing conditions it was necessary that the troops should be sent, and that their plans had all been made upon the basis of Canada carrying out the arrangement to provide her share of the Force, and upon information furnished to the Prime Minister and his colleagues they all concurred in the view of the War Office that we should continue the despatch of our troops to Vladivostok. The Government has been in constant communication with the British Authorities with reference to the position in Siberia, and as to the policy to be pursued there, and the Government has been assured that it is not the intention to use the troops in offensive action, but solely for the maintenance of law and order. The Canadian troops at Vladivostok will not be sent inland until the Government has more information in reference to the situation. The Prime Minister and his Colleagues will represent Canada when the matter comes up for consideration among the Allied Powers, but until this Allied Conference takes place, it is not possible for the Canadian Government to make any more definite announcement. The Government has already assured the Canadian troops who have gone to Vladivostok, that in any case they will be permitted to return within a year of the date of the signing of the Armistice, if they so desire. The Government hopes that the whole Force may be returned in the early part of the summer.[51]

This statement written early in February, revealing only too clearly the paucity of Allied justifications for the Siberian intervention, was never issued. By February 17, confirmation had been received from Borden that the War Office would make arrangements early in April for the return of the troops. Any thought of attempting to "educate" Canadian public opinion was finally abandoned.

While Ottawa was pursuing its vain efforts, either to obtain from Paris or to prepare, itself, a definitive public statement on intervention, Elmsley was becoming increasingly pessimistic about the course of events in Russia, despite the fact that during the first months of 1919 the fortunes of the White Russian forces appeared to be improving, following their successful offensive that had resulted in the capture of Perm, a city closer to Moscow than Knox had believed the ill-equipped White forces should venture.

Nonetheless, Elmsley remained sceptical about the long-term chances of Kolchak. "In Siberia, public feeling is slow but sure [moving away] from Kolchak Government, which is looked upon as representing, or at least typical of, Old Monarchy Régime."[52] After almost five months in Vladivostok, Elmsley had become convinced of the bankruptcy of Allied interventionist policy. On February 6, in a cable to his old friend at the War Office, General Radcliffe,* Elmsley put his finger on a basic weakness by pointing out that, in fact, two conflicting policies were being pursued by the Allies in Siberia: the Anglo-French, on the one hand, and the American, Czechoslovak, Japanese, and Canadian, on the other. The former wished to intervene more actively in the internal affairs of Russia; the latter, for various reasons, did not. Somehow, Elmsley urged, this basic conflict must be reconciled. The ambivalent and, at worst, aggressive policies that Britain and France had adopted were wrong and would only lead to further trouble.

> The past has shown that neither you nor the French can take an unduly prominent part in Russia's affairs without danger of having the brand of Imperialism placed upon your actions and thereby giving our home Bolsheviks material for . . . initiating industrial unrest. . . . Adopt a more conciliatory attitude towards America, Japan and Canada. Modern nations can be led but not driven.[53]

Elmsley further developed his thesis in a long personal letter

---

* Elmsley and Radcliffe had known each other well on the Western Front where the former had commanded the 8th Infantry Brigade while the latter was Brigadier-General, General Staff, Canadian Corps.

to Radcliffe five days later.[54] The letter reveals much more of Elmsley's thinking, particularly about Anglo-French policy in Russia, than any of his official communications. It is worth examining at length, for it is a candid and perceptive analysis of why military intervention was bound to fail. In his letter to Radcliffe, Elmsley defined immediately one of the basic weaknesses in the Allied intervention. The French and British had originally undertaken the venture in the hope of reopening an eastern front. The Japanese, on the other hand, had seen intervention as an opportunity to establish their political and economic hegemony in eastern Siberia. The Americans, for their part, had announced that they were going to Vladivostok to help the Czechoslovaks depart safely and to guard the Allied stores there. How could unity of action be expected when there was so little unity of purpose?

> Following the signing of the Armistice, America, Japan and Canada . . . became inactive and the Czechs adopted the same attitude, as they too stated in no uncertain manner that they were willing to fight Germans but not Russian Bolsheviks, and that Russia's internal affairs were no concern of theirs. Thus, America, Japan, Canada and the Czechs were in accord and understood each other's attitude, and furthermore awaited some reconstructed policy which, known and agreed to by all, would meet the new situation created by the signing of the Armistice.[55]

Britain and France, in contrast, had no scruples about attempting to suppress Bolshevism, Elmsley said, even if this were to be interpreted as intervention in the internal affairs of Russia. They went "bald-headed" for the Bolsheviks, associating themselves with all anti-Bolsheviks, particularly Kolchak—a policy never explained to their Allies and never fully understood by Russians. Many of those whom the British and French supported were reactionaries. The Bolsheviks, accordingly, had little difficulty in presenting themselves as the real champions of the workers, the poor, and the oppressed. As a further complication, the Japanese, who were supplying the greatest number of soldiers, were eager to penetrate eastern Siberia with both people and money. Yet they were being alienated by the

Franco-British support for a strong Russia able to exclude such penetration and to undertake its debt payments.

Britain and France, Elmsley contended, had gone after the wrong goals. Even now it might be possible to reverse this futile policy by three steps. First, the Allies should endeavour in every way possible to end the civil war by peaceful means. All factions in Russia should be encouraged to consult on free elections on the basis of universal suffrage. Any government elected in such a manner should be assisted freely and generously by the Allies in restoring the Russian economy. Only if any faction fighting in the civil war was unwilling to recognize the freely elected government, and only "if it is considered that peace in Russia is essential to the peace of the world", would Allied military intervention be justified. But, if intervention were then to be undertaken, it should be on such a scale as to be decisive. It would have to involve fully the Japanese, even to the extent of agreeing to all their terms. If on such terms intervention was unpalatable to the Allies, they should withdraw from Russia.

Much of what Elmsley said in his letter to Radcliffe was similar to the thinking, during late January and February, of Borden in Paris and his colleagues in Ottawa. Borden had taken an active part at the Peace Conference in calling for an appeal to all elements in the Russian civil war to meet under Allied aegis to discuss their differences.* The Bolsheviks had sent a temporizing reply. The White Russians, despite the weaknesses inherent in their situation, took advantage of Allied differences to reject indignantly a proposal that would have had them sit down at the same table as communists. The failure of the "Prinkipo Proposal"—so called after the Island in the Black Sea where the meeting was to take place—was the final factor in convincing Borden that no further purpose would be served by leaving Canadians in Siberia.

Lloyd George did not reply until February 16 to Borden's letter of February 7 requesting the withdrawal of the Canadian contingent from Siberia. The British Prime Minister, who had blown hot and cold on the issue of what support, if any, should

* See pages 245-52.

be given to the White armies, on this occasion simply suggested that Borden discuss the matter with Winston Churchill (who was in Paris appealing to the "Council of Ten" for support for the Whites), since "the decision to withdraw the Canadians from Siberia is . . . a very important one, and may have considerable bearing upon our Russian policy."[56] Both Churchill and Arthur Balfour immediately pressed on Borden a number of reasons why the Canadian brigade should remain in Siberia.* But Borden knew that Lloyd George would offer no opposition to his decision and, in any case, he had made up his mind. At a meeting of the British Empire delegation on February 17, he announced that the Canadian units would withdraw from Siberia in April. Borden's report of the meetings to his cabinet is illuminating:

> I adhered absolutely to my determination that Canadian troops must be withdrawn in April. . . . Balfour and Churchill agree that opinion in Great Britain and United States is practically same as that which I urged on behalf of Canada but they submit following considerations as to consequences of withdrawing troops and discontinuing military effort in aid of anti-Bolshevist Governments.
> First. Bolshevists will over-run and control all Russia.
> Second. If present Allied forces remain in Russia for some months Bolshevist power will probably crumble.

---

* Borden also heard strong pro-intervention arguments from Honorary Lieutenant-Colonel J. W. Boyle (1867-1923) "of Yukon fame" who, in interviews in London in December 1918 and in Paris in February 1919, stated that his recent experience in Russia had convinced him that the "triumph of Bolshevism in Russia means that it will overrun Germany [an opinion in which Lenin and Trotsky would have readily concurred] and that Germany and Russia will overrun the world or reduce organized society to anarchy" (Borden, Memoirs, vol. II, p. 888). Borden remained unmoved. He wrote to Kemp from Paris on February 5, 1919: "Colonel Boyle called on me yesterday morning and offered some suggestions with regard to conditions in Russia. He mentioned also that a number of Canadians in the Machine Gun Brigade would be willing to volunteer for service in Russia for instructional purposes, and he believed that 250 men could be obtained in this way who would be very useful if attached to General Denikin's Army. He inquired whether or not such a force would be financed and maintained by Canada. I told him that there was no probability whatever that we would entertain any such proposal." Boyle's adventures against the Bolsheviks in Romania and Russia are described at length in William Rodney, Joe Boyle, King of the Klondike (Toronto: McGraw-Hill Ryerson, 1974).

Third. Bolshevist Government will combine with German Government who will reap enormous fruit therefrom and become stronger than ever.

Fourth. The military power of Germany and Russia combined will in that case menace the world and especially the British Empire exposed to attack in India and elsewhere.

I replied that these considerations would not carry judgment of Canadian people in favour of further military effort. Russia must work out her own salvation which may take years. If Bolshevist power crumbles other Governments will probably fight each other for some time to come. Bolshevists no more likely to combine with Germany than any other Russian Government. Moreover Bolshevist policy and actions are becoming more moderate. I promised however to suggest to you [i.e., the cabinet] desirability of postponing as long as possible any public statement as to withdrawal [of the Canadian troops].[57]

Churchill was unhappy about this blow to his interventionist policy, especially at a time when Kolchak's armies were engaged in a major offensive in the western Urals, but he recognized that he would be unable to alter Borden's decision. That night General Wilson noted in his diary, "Much talk about Russia and of course nothing settled. Borden plainly said that he was going to withdraw his Canadians from Vladivostok leaving our two poor battalions in the lurch at Omsk."

By early March, Churchill began to implement the War Cabinet's decisions to withdraw British troops from northern Russia and from Omsk, but he remained profoundly apprehensive about what this could mean for the security of Britain and France. He feared most of all a Russo-German *rapprochement*. With regard to Canadian withdrawal, he wrote somewhat archly to Borden on March 17: "The War Office have no option but to acquiesce, as they have felt it impossible to continue to urge the Dominion Government to share, against its will, in a task of much difficulty and anxiety."[58]

On March 10, Elmsley reported that Eliot and Knox were both much discouraged by Borden's decision and hoped that it might yet be changed. Elmsley confirmed to Knox that the Canadians would not move from Vladivostok before they embarked for Vancouver, but Knox was determined on one last attempt to move the Canadians inland. On March 30, Elmsley sent an especially stiff letter to Knox, protesting about a telegram Knox had sent to the War Office without reference to him, urging once again the deployment of Canadian troops in helping to protect the railway.[59]

On March 12, the Japanese informed the British and French that they had reason to expect an uprising by the Bolsheviks in Vladivostok. When the Japanese had passed this information to General Graves, he had replied that no United States troops would be made available to help suppress such an uprising. Always suspicious of Japanese motives, Graves was convinced that any such act would, by constituting interference in the internal affairs of Russia, contravene his orders. Brigadier-General J. M. Blair, the deputy head of the British Military Mission, cabled the War Office:" . . . attitude of the Americans is ridiculous and is likely to place the other Allied troops in an impossible position should any rising actually take place. . . . The American representatives here are making absolute fools of themselves and it is becoming quite impossible to work with them."[60]

Sir Charles Eliot decided that, given the threat of a possible uprising in Vladivostok, he should ascertain where Elmsley stood on the employment of Canadian troops. On March 14, in response to a request Eliot had made during a conversation the previous evening, Elmsley stated in writing that he was prepared to co-operate with the other Allies in the maintenance of order in Vladivostok but that he was unwilling to place his troops unreservedly at the disposal of General Otani. Eliot in turn replied that he believed that the Japanese should be informed that the Canadians would be available for keeping order, but "not to suppress political movements except in so far as such movements may interfere with safety and freedom."[61] Elmsley was ready to concur in this definition of the role of his force, but he continued to worry about Anglo-American differences. He wrote candidly to Eliot on March 15:

> If there is no unity amongst the Allies in Vladivostok regarding the suppression of an uprising, then the chief danger of this uprising will be that the Allies themselves will come into armed conflict, a

situation we must avoid at any cost. To be frank, I consider that both you and General Blair have misrepresented General Graves and that he is anxious and willing to protect the lives and property of all Russians, irrespective of their political leanings.[62]

The same day, Elmsley called on Graves in an effort to learn what exactly the role of the Americans might be in the event of an uprising. As Elmsley stated in a telegram to London and Ottawa on March 18: " . . . feelings between Americans, Japanese and Russians are far from friendly. My officers and men are in sympathy with the Americans and their viewpoint. I cannot guarantee their neutrality in any disagreement between the Americans and the Japanese or Russians"[63] To this the War Office, echoing Knox, simply replied that it regarded the Americans as the only discordant element among the Allies in Siberia and urged Elmsley to move his troops away from any possible point of friction between the Japanese and the Americans.

The disagreement between Americans like Graves who hoped to remain impartial and Britishers like Knox who actively opposed the Bolsheviks was never entirely resolved. Elmsley, however, anticipated the "honest broker" role of a later generation of Canadian diplomats by attempting to formulate a minimum statement on which all could agree. At his initiative, the generals commanding the contingents in Vladivostok met on March 28 and agreed to announce publicly that they would insist on the maintenance of order in the city. If necessary, all Allied forces would be placed at the disposal of Otani, "it being distinctly understood that these forces are not employed either to support or suppress any political party or individual unless the activities of these parties are illegal and endanger life and property".[64] Both Knox and Graves having agreed to this statement, the Allies in Vladivostok for once, and in a very limited respect, took on a semblance of unity.

IV *The Canadians in Vladivostok*

The single operation in which Canadian troops in Siberia were involved, and it was a very small one, was undertaken in April

1919. General Otani requested Canadian troops to serve in a small Allied column to be sent against an irregular Bolshevik force centred on the village of Shkotova, thirty miles north of the city, at the junction of the Trans-Siberian railway and a branch line to the Suchan mines. One hundred and ninety-two men, mostly from "B" Company of the 259th Battalion, joined with French, Japanese, Italian, and Chinese troops in the advance on the village which, not surprisingly, they found deserted. The Bolshevik force was nowhere in evidence. It had simply melted back into the rest of the populace. With their mission accomplished without having fired a shot, and after camping at Shkotova for six days, the Allied troops returned to Vladivostok. There, the Canadians received, as a mark of appreciation from Otani, ninety-six bottles of wine, eighteen bottles of whisky, and three casks of sake.

Canadians, with soldiers drawn from other Allied contingents, guarded banks, the rail station, and the vast quantities of stores on the docks, in the overflowing warehouses, and on the barges along the shore. Pilfering was common. Efforts to steal on a large scale for the benefit of Bolshevik forces were not unknown.

Beginning on December 10, two dozen return trips to Omsk of almost 4,000 miles and as much as two months each were made by volunteer platoons sent as escorts for trains carrying supplies to Kolchak's wavering forces. The trains, occasionally shot at during the day, sometimes stopped on sidings at night and, like a wagon train in the wild west of America, readied themselves for possible attack.* The journeys were always hazardous; sabotage was frequent with rail lines or bridges demolished.

Elmsley's chief practical problem was to find ways of occupying his men. Their morale remained high, partly because he kept them busy. From the first, the contingent continued the training it had begun in Victoria. Exercises on company, battalion, and

---

* A graphic description of the difficulties encountered on these hazardous journeys is in the diary of Captain Harold Vernon Ardagh of the 259th Battalion; in March 1919 he commanded a train carrying clothing and ammunition to Omsk. (PAC, MG 30, G134)

even brigade scale took the troops over the bare, frozen ground
of the surrounding hills and along the deserted beaches. Calis-
thenics were also a daily routine, as well as camp guard and
other regular duties such as carrying water from the wells to the
barracks wash-places. At least once a week the men marched to
a central bath-house for a hot shower. Their winter clothing and
their food were generally good, both in quality and in quantity.
All food left over from each meal was given to needy refugee
children who eagerly collected it daily.

The Y.M.C.A. assigned several of its representatives to the
contingent, and they, from the beginning, organized entertain-
ments and other diversions. With their help, the Canadian
officers announced their arrival in Vladivostok by giving a dance
at the Vladivostok Commercial School, to which they invited a
large number of Allied officers. To help the men fill their off-
duty hours and to avoid the temptations of Vladivostok, the
Y.M.C.A. and the Knights of Columbus established canteen huts
in all three Canadian barracks areas. The Y.M.C.A. also opened
cinemas in each camp, calling the large one, at the Second River
Barracks, British Columbia Hall. Enough ice hockey equipment
had been provided for an eight-team league. In addition, the
Y.M.C.A. renovated a dilapidated theatre known as the Casino,
near the East Barracks. There, from March 3, concerts, lectures,
boxing matches, church services, and three film shows a week
were held.

The concerts sometimes featured talented Russian refugees
eager to earn a little money, but more often Canadian soldiers,
sometimes assisted by Mrs. Ross Owen, the wife of the local
Canadian Pacific Railway representative, were the performers.
The "Roadhouse Minstrels" were particularly popular.
"Salome's Dance" by a young artillery officer named Raymond
Massey so impressed visiting United States officers that they
invited him to perform at their own theatre—the first of many
American audiences whose acclaim Massey was to win. The
newspaper of the United States 31st Infantry Regiment (*Here and
There with the 31st*) reported on February 22 that the officers of
the regiment had been given "the opportunity to see the best
Allied show yet produced in Siberia. Special mention must be

made of Raymond Massey, as end man and as a dancer. His interpretation of 'Salome's Dance' would make Ruth St. Denis turn green with envy. And his solo poker game was one of the hits of the evening. In fact, the exhibition so impressed the American officers that they promptly extended him an invitation." In the spring, the Y.M.C.A. opened a club in the centre of Vladivostok, near the post office, and called it the Maple Leaf Café and Cinema. It proved popular with the troops despite the fact that, unlike the American canteen, it was not staffed by girls from home. The British commercial community still in Vladivostok was small, but it also contributed to the entertainment of the troops.

Among the soldiers were a number of typesetters and others experienced in newspaper work. On March 6 there appeared the first issue of *The Siberian Bugle*, published by the 259th Battalion, and sporadically there also appeared the tabloid *Canadian Sapper*, published by the 16th Field Company, Canadian Engineers. Both were informal and gossipy, commenting on the local scene and particularly on events within the Allied force. They contained few stories about Canada since no news services were available and the newspapers from Canada came but slowly and infrequently.

Back in Canada, on the other hand, something was known about the life of the troops in Siberia and political events there as a result of the dispatches of Honorary Captain Wilfred Ernest Playfair of Playfair, Ontario, the official correspondent with the force. Playfair's articles were sent direct to newspapers in Vancouver, Winnipeg, Toronto, and Montreal.* They were generally mildly favourable to Kolchak, but for the most part were restricted to descriptions of life of the soldiers in Vladivostok, the nature of the city and the surrounding countryside, and the happy relations of Canadians with other Allied soldiers,

---

* *On September 17, 1918, Newton Rowell wrote to Lord Beaverbrook at the British Ministry of Information to ask whether a cameraman might be assigned to the force to make films "for Empire use". There is no indication in the Canadian archives that this proposal was acted upon.*

particularly the Americans and Czechoslovaks.* Similar scenes were also recorded in paint or chalk by Lieutenant Louis Keene of the 20th Machine Gun Company, a former art student in his native London and a cartoonist with the Montreal *Herald* after his emigration to Canada.† A.Y. Jackson had been asked to go to Siberia as official war artist, but the decision to withdraw was taken before arrangements could be made for his departure. ‡

Aside from the recreation provided by the Y.M.C.A. or by personal hobbies and pursuits, some of the men passed their leisure time in wandering through the barren hills or along the deserted beach, watching the small Japanese and Korean boats fishing off shore. Saturday afternoons and Sundays—and in the spring, Wednesday afternoons—were free for excursions into Vladivostok for those willing to walk the several miles to the end of the city tram-line. The trams were, however, infrequent and always crowded. Often the men, in heavy army boots and an extra pair of woollen socks, would walk the ten miles into the

---

* *Playfair went to Omsk in April to interview Kolchak (who spoke good English). Kolchak explained to him at some length why he was convinced that his military régime was the only Russian government that could hope to defeat the Bolsheviks.*[65] *His strategy was to vanquish the Red armies in the field, rather than to attempt the immediate capture of Petrograd or Moscow. After their defeat and the subsequent capture of the major cities, Kolchak envisaged—somewhat vaguely—free elections and a liberal form of government. In reviewing the various Allies who had intervened in the civil war, Kolchak praised the British and French but criticized the Americans for "supporting, at times very strongly, the Bolshevik Government". Kolchak concluded the interview by remarking: "I am working my hardest for the good of Russia and I hope to be successful. But if I should fail, I am willing to go under for the sake of my work, and it will be proof that Russia has not yet reached the stage of lawful self-government."*

† *Fourteen Siberian scenes by Keene are in the War Collection of the National Gallery of Canada, Ottawa.*

‡ *Jackson wrote in his autobiography: "I received twenty-four hours' notice to go to Siberia with the expeditionary force which was being organized to support the White Russians, and [in a short time] we found ourselves back in Canada receiving instructions and getting information about extra equipment. The Armistice was signed while I was in Canada and the Siberian affair collapsed. All I got out of it was twenty tubes of white paint. It was probably this paint that was responsible for my becoming a snow painter as I had to find some use for it."* (A Painter's Country, Toronto, Clarke, Irwin, 1958, p. 42)

city and back, so as to be able to visit the shops, markets, churches, or Allied warships in the harbour. Lance-Corporal Ireland noted in his diary:

> We spent considerable time walking up and down the main street which was crowded with people of many nationalities and of a variety of costumes. Japanese, Chinese, American, Czechoslovak and Canadian soldiers were mingled in the moving mass of strange-looking people. Although the streets were thronged, there was little traffic on the roads. Occasionally you would see a Russian endeavouring to encourage the movement of his pony and little cart, or perhaps a large and costly motor car would whiz past, conveying Russian or Japanese officers. Frequently along the gutter, Manchurians or Russians would pass, carrying heavy burdens on their backs by means of a wooden attachment. We certainly enjoyed watching the various types of humanity to be seen on the streets.[66]

There were cases of misbehaviour by Canadian troops in Vladivostok but they were few. An international military police unit, under the command of an American major, included a Canadian detachment and did an excellent job of keeping order among the troops. Most Russians kept off the streets at night, uncertain of their safety. The Canadians laughed at a report in the Toronto *Globe* of January 25 that they had every afternoon and evening free to wallow in the fleshpots of the port where vodka flowed endlessly. Vodka was illegally sold near the gates of the camps, but the incidence of drunkenness or of venereal diseases was not high, despite the fact that both afflictions were readily attainable in the city. Not far from one Canadian barracks were Japanese brothels, but these were reserved for Japanese soldiers, a restriction enforced by armed guards.

The Canadians in Siberia had a better record for discipline and good behaviour than the more numerous United States troops who were more frequently embroiled in fights and trouble over women. There was an abundance of prostitutes as well as of vodka in Vladivostok. Overcrowded with refugees and a mecca for speculators and all types of social parasites, the port was a centre of corruption and despair—and a constant temptation to underemployed United States soldiers, who, unlike the

Canadians, had their barracks in the city. Some began to accost women indiscriminately, being convinced that almost all were prostitutes. The better record of the Canadians was not, of course, due to any moral superiority but rather to the fact that, stationed fifteen miles out of the city, temptation confronted them less frequently.

Little effort was made to explain to the soldiers why they were in Siberia, either before or after they arrived. One of the few attempts to offer an explanation was made in a brief series of lectures by Sir Bernard Pares, a leading British student of Russian history who had served in various liaison capacities with the Russian forces during the war. If we can judge by the reaction of one Canadian soldier, Sir Bernard's audience was not convinced by his explanations of why it was necessary to have Allied troops in Russia. Lance-Corporal Ireland noted in his diary:

> I have come to the conclusion now that it should rest with the Russians to settle her own internal affairs. . . . Sir Bernard Pears [sic], in his speech delivered at "The Casino" the other night, said, "We are here for the building up of democratic Russia. There must be a Russia. It must live a united, free, democratic Russia." This assertion may be true, but there is the subsequent question to be answered—"Why should we be here for the reconstruction of Russia?" To me there appears only one course for the Allies to adopt. If it has been decided that the outside Powers should intervene, then the intervention should be on a large scale, and not insignificant as it has been during the past four months. But such an effort to suppress Bolshevism and establish a stable government in Russia would involve tremendous casualties for the Allies, and sacrifices which I cannot conscientiously feel that we should bear. Therefore, I maintain that our policy should be one of non-intervention. The colossal population of Russia, consisting of peoples of diverse nationalities, cannot be moulded into a sane and democratic nation in a day. It is something that must be created by the inhabitants of Russia themselves; and before there is a free, united Russia, the process of evolution from the deplorable conditions there existing, must be painful and long.*

* Ireland, Diary, pp. 118-19. Pares gave his lectures in Vladivostok in mid March. He reached Siberia by crossing Canada and sailing in February with Canadian troops aboard the Monteagle. (Pares, My Russian Memoirs, chapter XXIV)

The weather in Vladivostok during the winter and spring of 1919 was remarkably good; the cold and clear days reminded the eastern Canadians of winter at home. When the days began to lengthen in the spring, a baseball league was organized, with the Americans sometimes participating, and soccer games were played on the still-frozen ground. The British cruiser H.M.S. *Kent* anchored offshore near the barracks during the first week of April to allow members of its crew several soccer matches with the Canadians, and to ride the R.N.W.M.P. horses. McIntyre, a black Canadian (there were twelve from Nova Scotia in the 260th Battalion), became the light heavyweight champion of the Allied forces and a tug-of-war team under a Lieutenant Martin of Halifax defeated all opponents. The main event of the spring was a gymkhana and sports day on May 1, organized partly for the entertainment of the local people. A musical ride and a march past by the R.N.W.M.P. was the main attraction, but bucking contests, tent-pegging (mainly for Albertans), and jumping supplemented the track and field competition organized by Captain Lewis Scholes of Toronto.

The Canadian Red Cross joined the Y.M.C.A. in providing the troops with various amenities such as new socks and underwear (partly as an anti-typhus measure). But it did much more. It helped to equip the five small hospitals of the brigade in the Vladivostok area. To Omsk, it sent six car-loads of medicines and "comforts" to British, Czechoslovak, and White Russian units. Even more important were its efforts to combat epidemics and to assist the neglected prisoners-of-war from Germany and Austria in whose plight few others took any interest. At a cost of more than $20,000, the Canadian Red Cross equipped an anti-epidemic train, under the command of Captain F.A. Dallyn of Toronto, and sent it across Siberia to help counter the epidemics of typhus and other infectious diseases.

In March, Colonel John Dennis, the quiet and determined commissioner of the Canadian Red Cross in Siberia, proposed to Ottawa and to London a much more ambitious project. He suggested that the Canadian Red Cross should assume responsibility for the welfare of all former prisoners-of-war in western Siberia, whether Russian, German, or Austrian. He estimated that there were probably 200,000 prisoners from the Central Powers stranded in Russia and 300,000 returning Russian prisoners-of-war. No one considered himself responsible for these half-million men. Dennis accordingly urged that Canada, with British support, should attempt to provide the food and medicine desperately needed to overcome the diseases that malnutrition and unsanitary conditions were spawning. He did not suggest any changes in the responsibility for relief in eastern Siberia, which the United States and Japanese Red Cross shared. Nor did he propose that the United States Red Cross should in any way curtail the modest activities it had already undertaken in western Siberia. But he did believe that one agency should immediately assume the responsibility for the undernourished and often diseased men for whom no one cared. Dennis sketched an outline of a hierarchy of officials to administer the relief program, which he estimated would cost, initially, $10 million. Any Canadian soldier in Vladivostok willing to volunteer should be assigned to the Red Cross, along with surplus military stores. They would work under his general supervision with the assistance of his deputy commissioner, Lieutenant-Colonel Douglas Young, and his Chief Medical Officer, a Captain Brook of Toronto.

Nothing came of Dennis's ambitious suggestion. By the time his proposal had arrived in Ottawa, the Canadian government had already decided to withdraw its force from Siberia. The Canadian Red Cross Society did not consider it advisable for its representatives to remain there after the departure of the Canadian contingent. This decision was received with dismay in Vladivostok where the work of the Canadian Red Cross had earned a solid reputation in a very short time. Perhaps the greatest tribute to its work was a telegram sent to the War Office by the deputy head of the British Military Mission.

> I most strongly recommend that authority be obtained for this
> organization to remain and work in conjunction with this mission
> as it is of very great service to us. I further request you will press
> the British Red Cross Society to support this organization with
> funds and stores. No better organization could be found for their

support, it is doing real work and amongst conditions which must be seen to be appreciated.[67]

General Radcliffe in turn appealed for Borden's support and, from Paris, Borden passed on the recommendations to Ottawa. But the Canadian Red Cross Society, anxious about the safety of its representatives in Siberia, declined to let them remain after the departure of the Canadian contingent.

V   *Canadian Withdrawal*

In March, Churchill had appealed to Borden to keep the Canadian units in Siberia. In April, Churchill still had not surrendered his belief that Kolchak might yet defeat the Bolsheviks. Since Canada held the key to intervention on a larger scale by the British Empire, Churchill was determined to make one final appeal.

On May 1, 1919, although the first Canadians had already sailed from Vladivostok, he addressed a last plea to Borden, despite the fact that he knew the Canadian headquarters in London had been pressing for the withdrawal of all Canadians from northern Russia and that there was little real prospect of continued Canadian participation in Siberia. It was a skilful letter. Churchill began by recalling the "assistance" Borden had given him during the navy estimates debate of 1913,* and then proceeded to present an optimistic interpretation of Kolchak's chances.

> I cannot help being sorry that Canada has not been able a little to help us in bringing about these good results. I of course agreed to your wish to withdraw the Canadians from Vladivostock [sic]. If they were not allowed to go beyond Vladivostock, there was not much use in their taking up the limited accommodation available.

---

* *A reference to Borden's visit to England in 1912 when he indicated to Churchill, then First Lord of the Admiralty, the willingness of his government to consider a cash contribution to the Royal Navy for the construction of dreadnoughts.*

But is it not possible for us to have a few volunteers from the Canadian Forces to co-operate with the volunteer detachments which compose our various missions to the loyal Russian armies?

Last night at the dinner of the Canadian Cavalry Brigade numbers of officers spoke to me on [sic] their desire to volunteer for service in Russia against the Bolsheviks, but they complained that the Canadian military authorities would force them to quit the Canadian service before joining any special unit of this character. Surely this is a little hard and falls somewhat short of all the splendid help we have had from Canada throughout this perilous struggle. Even a few hundred Canadian volunteers would be of great assistance and would make a name for themselves in this most righteous crusade.

The Russians have lost faith in the Allied Powers one after another. Japan they always feared and distrusted. America has made herself indescribably hated in Siberia. The French have lost all credit at Odessa and in the Crimea. But Britain has never failed. Tied down as we have been and unable to use our strength and resources with full effect, we have nevertheless given real help, and in every theatre where we have assumed any degree of responsibility, the Russians are either holding their own or prospering.

It may well be that our future friendly relations with a regenerated Russian State, with all its immense commercial and military possibilities, may depend on action taken now.

I no longer feel that I am asking you to share in a failure. The hopes of success are sufficient to justify me in appealing to you to participate in a hopeful and prosperous policy. Will you not encourage volunteering of Canadian officers and men to provide a small contingent for action both in relieving our men in North Russia and in participating in our mission to Admiral Kolchak? Will you not facilitate this? I am sure there would be a good response. ... If Canada takes the lead, Australia will be bound to follow.[68]

Largely in response to this appeal, Ottawa granted permission for any officer or other rank to take his discharge in Siberia for the purpose of serving with the Canadian Red Cross, or with the White Russian or another Allied force, or to transfer to the British Military Mission. Only a few volunteered. In England, the 1st Canadian Tank Battalion, then awaiting shipment home, had indicated an eagerness to serve in Siberia, but Borden had agreed only to the transfer of Canadians already in Siberia.

Those transferring to the British Military Mission were not required to take their formal discharge. Fifty-three Canadians volunteered (at Canadian rates of pay) to serve for up to six months with the British Military Mission or with the Railway Mission. Another twenty volunteered to work as civilians for the Canadian Red Cross before its decision to withdraw from Siberia. One American citizen transferred to the American Red Cross and the French-Canadian chaplain agreed to stay on as chaplain to the French contingent. One Russian citizen in the brigade enrolled in the White Russian officers' training school, while six others deserted, whether to join the Bolsheviks or Kolchak's army was not ascertained.

The withdrawal of the Canadian headquarters staff from Omsk was particularly opposed by the War Office. Elmsley, in response to a British request, asked Ottawa whether the fifty-seven Canadians of the headquarters staff might be left at Omsk to help provide essential services for the Middlesex and Hampshire battalions. The reply was a flat no. *All* Canadian troops had to be withdrawn. Colonel Lash left Omsk late in February. Colonel Morrisey, ill with influenza and recurrent malaria, departed early in March. Lieutenant-Colonel J. T. Brooke replaced Morrisey until the withdrawal from Omsk of the major part of the Canadian detachment on April 13. The last Canadians from Omsk, a small medical unit, arrived in Vladivostok on May 23.

On April 21, to the music of the band of the 31st United States Infantry, the first major Canadian detachment of 1,076 (including 168 sick) embarked in Vladivostok for Vancouver. The *Monteagle* was a comfortable and commodious ship in comparison to the two dirty, overcrowded steamers that had brought the main body of the contingent to Siberia. On May 9, a further 766 Canadians sailed for Vancouver on the *Empress of Japan*; on May 19, another 1,524 on the *Empress of Russia* (who were held in quarantine for a fortnight upon arrival, as a result of a smallpox scare), and on June 5 General Elmsley and the remaining 653 troops on the *Monteagle* (which also carried five Russian stowaways).* According to a British embarkation officer, the kit-bags of some of the soldiers of the 260th Battalion on the *Empress of Japan* contained communist propaganda in English intended for distribution in Canada and the United States. Much equipment, including the eighteen-pounders of the 85th Battery,† and the surviving 164 riding horses of the R.N.W.M.P. were turned over to the British Military Mission for disposal.‡ "The decision to leave the horses behind was not a popular one with the members of 'B' Squadron. They had grown attached to their mounts [sic]. Some of them had ridden the same horse on detachment duty back on the prairies."[69] Six volunteers, led by Farrier Sergeant J. E. Margetts, crossed Siberia by train in May–June 1919 to deliver the horses to White Russian cavalry in Ekaterinburg. Severe sabotage on the rail line resulted in a westward journey of thirty-eight days. The six "Mounties" arrived back in Canada only in late August, six weeks after the main body of "B" Squadron. In the words of the Commissioner of the R.N.W.M.P., "B" Squadron had become "conspicuous for its efficiency and good conduct, and although it had not the good fortune to see active service, it reached a high state of efficiency".[70]

Nineteen Canadians did not return. Three had died in accidents and sixteen from disease.§

* *One stowaway was a young Russian, Nicholai Demotrovich ("Nick Samson"), whom Sergeant Charleston helped to hide aboard the* Monteagle. *The boy was raised by Charleston and his wife in Brandon, Manitoba, and later became director of the Metro-Goldwyn-Mayer property department in Hollywood.*

† *Among those in the British Military Mission responsible for the transfer of such* matériel *to the White Russians at Omsk and, later, along the Trans-Siberian railway were five Canadian officers under the direction of Lieutenant J. G. Rycroft. They had left Halifax in January 1919 for Siberia, where they served until September.*

‡ *One of the horses later assisted–along with an abandoned Cadillac automobile–in the overland escape of a British officer cut off in western Siberia. (P. Hodges,* Britmis, *London, Cape, 1931, p. 138)*

§ *Typhus, influenza, and spinal meningitis were the most common fatal diseases. A lieutenant in the 260th Battalion, apparently depressed as a result of a number of war wounds, was a suicide.*

Early in June, before departing from Vladivostok, Elmsley compiled a long and able final report on the situation in Siberia as he saw it after eight months there. Comments on British, French, Japanese, and American policies in Siberia bear clearly the mark of Elmsley's own pen, while other sections were prepared by his staff. In appendixes, the general attached, *inter alia*, copies of Playfair's interview with Kolchak; a perceptive Czechoslovak study of the current state of Siberia; notes on the railway problem; United States Army reports on atrocities by both Whites and Reds; and a copy of his own outspoken letter to General Radcliffe of February 11.

Elmsley had not changed his mind since writing that letter. In June, as in February, he was convinced that the French and British had followed a misguided and even dangerous policy of intervention in the internal affairs of Russia. He noted that Balfour, in telegrams to Ironside and Eliot on December 7, had explicitly denied that Britain had any intention of intervening in Russia (although Balfour had added, paradoxically, that Britain was committed to support anti-Bolshevik forces which had grown up under her shelter). Yet, in fact, the non-interference policy even as outlined by Balfour had been ignored or modified. The British in Omsk and Vladivostok were actively working with Kolchak in his efforts to suppress Bolshevism. In doing so, they were not acting in concert with their Allies. Furthermore, while Kolchak might be a man of moderately liberal views, those around him clearly were not. The peasants simply did not support his government. They would be against any government, Elmsley contended, unless that government would take steps to guarantee their liberty and "to give the ignorant man an inkling as to the reasons for the seemingly drastic laws and enforce them in a humane and lawful way as judged by the standards of modern civilizations". The Bolsheviks were no less guilty of crimes and atrocities.

> Whatever may be the abstract merits of this extreme form of socialism, the facts have abundantly proved that an attempt violently and suddenly to transform the social order does result and only can result in misery and chaos. The fact that the creed inculcates class hatred, that it offers so much that is attractive to

poorer and more ignorant classes of humanity makes it easy of acceptance and consequently all the more dangerous.

What in these circumstances should the Allies do? It was a case of choosing the lesser of two evils.

It is true that [the Kolchak] Government represents autocracy and militarism and every undesirable factor that we have been fighting in Europe during the last four and half years. Nevertheless, the recognition of Kolchak's Government is now the only alternative if peace in Russia is to be secured.

To remove chances of stigma being attached to this Allied recognition of Kolchak, the following conditions, dependent upon this recognition, should be imposed:

(a) That when Bolshevism is suppressed and peace assured, then Kolchak must resign in favour of whatever form of government the Russian people desire as a whole;

(b) That the people must now be guaranteed their liberties under the Kolchak Government and in accordance with modern ideas of liberty and justice until the All Russian Government is established;

(c) That the despotic and medieval customs and practices now employed by Kolchak's supporters should be abolished;

(d) That no unlawful reprisals be permitted against captured Bolsheviks.

I feel certain that if the above reservations were made that American antagonism towards Kolchak would cease and they would be willing to give him their full support if he would adhere to both the spirit and the letter of the above agreement.

Elmsley's advice was sound, but events had already rendered it irrelevant. The Allies were not, however, ready to give up. At the moment when the Canadian contingent was being withdrawn, the Allied governments were moving towards recognition of the government of Admiral Kolchak. After prolonged debate, and in the light of impressive advances made during April and early May, the Allies formally extended to the Admiral on June 11 the support (although not, strictly speaking, recognition) they had been giving to him informaliy since his assumption of power six months before. Churchill later inquired in *The Aftermath* why this formal pledge of support was extended in June, when it was too late to do Kolchak any good whereas in January it might have been of use to his hard-pressed forces. There is no simple answer. The basic explanation for this ill-considered decision (as in the case of so many mistakes harassed Allied leaders made whenever they turned their attention to Russia) was simply the absence of any consistent policy and the *ad hoc* and hurried nature of their decisions.

Over the summer of 1919, all Allied contingents withdrew both from northern Russia and, in the case of the Canadians and British, from Siberia.* For a while, some White Russians fought on.† From mid May 1919, Kolchak's disintegrating armies were driven eastward, ever deeper into Siberia. His supply system, if it could be called that, collapsed during the winter of 1919-20 and his armies faded away. A British officer recorded in his diary a graphic example of what was happening to Kolchak's army as early as July 1919:‡

> We saw a battalion of troops come up to the Front the other day, and to-day we hear that they walked *en masse* over to the Bolsheviks. These men are conscripted from villages which do not know what Bolshevism means; they know that the Bolsheviks are advancing, and as a safeguard, therefore, the men join the Bolsheviks, so that when the Reds arrive at their respective villages, no pillaging takes

* *The withdrawal of the Canadian troops did not mark the end of the Canadian army's interest in events in Russia. In September 1918, a section of the Directorate of Military Operations had been established in the War Office in London to deal with Russian affairs. A Canadian staff officer was attached to it (as G.S.O. 2) from November 1919 until May 1920, keeping a channel open for British information about the fortunes of the White Russians and the role of the United States and Japanese contingents still in Siberia.*

† *The two British battalions withdrew from Omsk to Vladivostok early in the summer. The* Middlesex *sailed from Vladivostok on September 8 and the* Hampshires *on November 1, 1919. (The latter returned to England by crossing Canada from Vancouver to Montreal.)*

‡ *First-hand accounts by the British officer of the collapse of Kolchak's armies, the corruption of many of his followers, and the incredible cruelty of both sides are contained in Hodges,* Britmis, *1931; Horrocks,* A Full Life, *1960 (pp. 40-63); and Vining,* Held by the Bolsheviks, *1924.*

place. Besides which, the Bolsheviks pay their soldiers infinitely better than the Russian Army do.[71]

Kolchak himself was captured by the Bolsheviks at Irkutsk in January and executed on February 7, 1920. The United States and Japanese contingents, each suspicious of the other, lingered on east of Lake Baikal with no clear idea of what to do. The United States finally withdrew all of its troops by April 1, 1920. The last of the Czechoslovaks, who had played so important a part in influencing President Wilson in favour of the partici- pation of American troops, finally sailed from Vladivostok for Vancouver in September.* The Japanese, however, stayed on, still hopeful that they could salvage some permanent advantages from the wreck of the Russian Empire. It was not until October 25, 1922, that the Japanese government, largely at the insistence of the United States, finally withdrew its last troops from Vladi- vostok and the Bolsheviks took over the city.

Lloyd George, in his *War Memoirs*, put the best possible face on intervention when he wrote, long after the event:

> As parts of the military effort of the Allies during the Great War, the expeditions to Murmansk and Archangel, to Siberia and to the Caucusus, played their part in strengthening opposition to what at one time appeared to be a very real and terrible danger of Prussian imperial expansion in Russia and across Asia. They barred the road to the Arctic and Pacific Oceans, to the cornfields of Southern Russia, to the minerals of Siberia and the oil of the Caspian. They enabled us to bring to safety scores of thousands of Czecho-Slovaks and Serbians, and a large number of refugees stranded in a country where law and order had temporarily vanished.

---

* *During the spring of 1920, the British government undertook to repatriate from Siberia 54,000 Czechoslovaks, 11,000 Poles, 3,000 Serbs, and 4,000 others, mainly Romanians and Letts. Many of the Czechoslovaks crossed Canada during June 1920. The Canadian Pacific Railway and the Immigration Department joined to induce some to spend the summer working on the railway (a few remained in Canada permanently). Before sailing for Europe, the Czech Legion gathered at Camp Valcartier, Quebec, where they held a parade on July 1 to express their thanks to the government of Canada for co-operating in their repatriation and to honour the Canadian contingent with which they had served in Siberia.*

The final word on the attitude of the Canadian troops involved in these various ventures may perhaps be given to a Calgary librarian who had served in the 260th Battalion. Upon his return from Vladivostok, he wrote in the *Albertan* of August 1, 1919:

> The Canadian soldier . . . very soon became obsessed with one idea—that [he] had no business in Russia, that it was Russia's business to settle her own troubles, that the Russians were a hopeless lot anyway, and that he was only prolonging the muddle by staying there. . . . However much one may deprecate the Bolshevik methods, we Canadians in Siberia could neither see nor hear anything which inspired in us any confidence in the Kolchak Government . . . there came to our ears stories of the workings of that government which savoured more of Caesar Borgia than of the 20th century democracy . . . the Canadian soldiers' solution still seems to me the only solution of the Russian problem—let Russia put her own home in order.

This was a judgment that carried the support of most Canadians. There had at first been widespread sympathy in Canada, as in Britain and the United States, for the overthrow of the Tsar's autocratic régime. When civil war followed and the situation in Russia became increasingly complex, there was still no enthusiasm for Allied intervention. If the decision to dispatch Canadian troops had not coincided with the final hectic months of the Great War, they would never have been sent. Once the war was ended, pressures for the recall of the troops found reinforcement in the new social thinking that was leading to widespread unrest in Canada, culminating in the Winnipeg General Strike. But opposition to the presence of Canadian troops in Russia was by no means restricted to those of left-wing persuasion. Throughout Canada there was a general inclination to look upon the whole enterprise as misguided and ill-judged, a blunder to be brought to an early end. Henri-Severin Béland, the Member of Parliament for Beauce, who had spent the War in a German internment camp, asked in the House of Commons on June 10:

> We are confronted with the bare, cold and shocking fact that

Canadian troops, after a contribution of men unexampled in this country, after the sacrifice of 50,000 lives, after casualties that have reached a total of over 100,000, after an outlay in money of about $1,000,000,000, are despatched . . . to fight whom? Nobody knows. This expedition was a political error, a military mistake, and a wanton extravagance. Are the people of Canada responsible? Is Parliament responsible? The people of Canada and Parliament were not consulted. Who, then, is responsible? The Government is responsible. A few weeks ago, when this subject was broached in Parliament, the President of the Privy Council (Mr. Rowell) and the Minister of Militia and Defence (Mr. Mewburn), in their eagerness to exonerate the Government, answered that the expedition to Siberia had been asked for by the Imperial Government. Either the representatives of Canada in the [Imperial] War Cabinet have agreed to this or they have dissented from it. If they have approved the scheme, then they have shown a disposition to yield that is lamentable and that will be so considered by the country at large. If they opposed the idea, their opposition was disregarded; they were out-voted. If that be the case, I ask: What becomes of Canadian autonomy?

In the few months between July 1918 and February 1919, Borden had moved progressively from forceful advocacy of Canadian participation to a desire to transfer the whole question to his cabinet, and finally to adamant opposition to the continued presence of Canadian troops in Russia. It was not, all in all, a policy of much consistency. Borden's role was, however, in large part only a reflection of the confused, harried, and erratic days in which the Siberian venture unfolded. They were not days that left time for cool decisions or reasoned judgments. What can be said for Borden is that he changed his policy rapidly when it became obvious that it was wrong, and that there was no pot of gold at the end of the economic rainbow he had seen stretching from Vancouver to Vladivostok. His instincts for political survival were certainly acute enough to sense, even across the Atlantic, that the policy he had done so much to initiate was increasingly unpopular at home.

To Borden's credit, once he was convinced that the various Russian factions would not negotiate, he concluded that continued Allied intervention would serve no purpose. He became forceful and persistent in saying so. He was not prepared to sacrifice Canadian interests for what some British statesmen regarded as overriding Imperial considerations. As we shall see, Borden took a leading role both in London and in Paris in urging Allied withdrawal. He helped to set the pace of that withdrawal by his prompt removal of the Canadian troops both from northern Russia and from Siberia.

PART FOUR

Sir Robert Borden and Russia

I Three-way Involvement

During the winter of 1918-19, Sir Robert Borden became increasingly involved in matters concerning Russia and the Allied military intervention there, especially in Siberia. His initial support for Canadian participation in the intervention arose largely from his acceptance of the strategic argument that an eastern front must somehow be reopened. But the strategic argument was the occasion, rather than the motive, in his decision to send Canadians to Russia.

There were two principal reasons for his support of Canadian participation. First, he regarded the provision of a Canadian contingent for Siberia as a proof of Canada's commitment to join in the implementation of Imperial—or Commonwealth—policies that had been agreed upon in advance. Second, he hoped that the expected slump in the post-war economy of Canada might be less severe if Canadian business could gain access to the great markets of Siberia.

Also, his interest in Russia having been thus aroused, he was moved to play a leading role in an effort at the Paris Peace Conference to bring the warring Russian factions together. Compromise is not a dirty word in the Canadian political vocabulary. Borden sought, in a typically Canadian way, to create a forum where Reds and Whites might reach a compromise settlement.

What follows is an examination of these three major facets of Borden's involvement with Russia in the period immediately after the revolution.

II Canada and Imperial Policy

The history of the Canadian contribution in the First World War is, in a sense, the story of how Canada gradually asserted control over its own military forces. As early as 1914, when a British general was appointed to command the First Canadian Division, Borden's government made it clear that he would be expected to communicate directly with Ottawa, and not via the Colonial Office. From that starting point, Canadian control over Canadian units was gradually extended to cover all aspects of their service. As the military and economic wartime effort of Canada came to surpass anything originally envisaged, a Canadian general was eventually appointed to command the Canadian Corps. A Ministry of Overseas Military Forces of Canada was established in London. Later, an Overseas Military Council and a Canadian section at the British headquarters in France were added (although over-all operational responsibility remained throughout the war with the British general commanding on the Western front).

The case of Siberia, where a Canadian general would command not only Canadian but also British troops, represented for Borden, who was intent upon winning a distinctive place for Canada in the post-war world, a new high point in the wartime evolution of Canada's status within the Empire. It was with satisfaction that Borden informed his cabinet colleagues in Ottawa: "It will be of some distinction to have all the British forces in Siberia under the command of a Canadian officer."[1] Here was tangible recognition of his long-standing concept of Canada's place in the Empire as being "a greater part in a greater whole".

Before the war, Borden had sought a voice for Canada in the determination of the foreign policy of the British Empire in so far as it might affect Canada. In 1912, for example, while urging upon the House of Commons his dual policy of an immediate cash contribution by Canada to help strengthen the Royal Navy and a longer-term plan to create a Canadian naval service, he had contended that the cash contribution to Imperial defence would entitle Canada to participate in the formulation of certain aspects of Imperial foreign policy. Earlier, Sir Wilfrid Laurier had stated: "We should have the right to say to Great Britain: if you want us to help you, call us to your councils." Echoing Laurier, Borden told an audience in London in 1912:

> Those who are or who become responsible for . . . Empire defence must, in the very nature of things, have some voice in that policy which shapes the issues of peace and of war. . . . Canada does not propose to be an "adjunct" even of the British Empire, but . . . to be a greater part in a greater whole.[2]

For Borden, as for Laurier before him, there was a mutual obligation in this evolving relationship within the Empire. For their part, the Dominions would assume a greater share of the total Imperial defence burden. Britain would in turn open the way for the Dominions to join in formulating the foreign policy of the Empire.

Recognition by the British government of this evolving mutual obligation was reflected to a limited extent by the establishment in 1912 of the Committee of Imperial Defence to which Dominion ministers were invited. "A very marked advance," Borden noted with satisfaction. The Great War soon revealed, however, that this initial step towards closer Imperial consultation on defence and foreign policy was not enough. From the very first days of the war, Canada had, in Borden's view, promptly met its obligations to help defend the Empire. Canadians had rushed to volunteer to fight alongside the troops of the "Old Country". In battle, their quality as soldiers was soon evident and, in Borden's view, it far surpassed that of the British generals under whom they had the misfortune to serve. Canada was meeting its

obligations to the Empire by providing men and *matériel* in hitherto unimagined quantities. Was Britain meeting its parallel obligation to provide Canada and the other Dominions with an opportunity to help formulate the grand strategies of the Empire?

Under Herbert Asquith, the answer was clearly no. From the
early days of the war, Borden became increasingly unhappy over
the dearth of information from London about what was actually
happening on the Western Front, as well as in the highest Allied
councils. His growing feeling was that while Canada, for its size
and numbers, was making a major sacrifice for the Allied cause,
Britain was not recognizing its obligation to inform and consult
Canada and the other Dominions. When Borden visited London
in July 1915, the pre-war Committee on Imperial Defence was
virtually defunct and there was no ready vehicle for discussions
between Britain and the Dominions. In December 1916,
however, David Lloyd George became prime minister. In him
Borden found a willing collaborator in his search for a new
status for the Dominions. Both prime ministers shared a low
opinion of British generalship. Both were committed to pursuing
the war more vigorously and imaginatively. Lloyd George
valued Borden's support in his struggle with the British military
establishment. The Dominions, in any case, were making an
enormous contribution to the Allied effort and consequently had
every right to be consulted.

Upon becoming prime minister, Lloyd George had immediately created the War Cabinet of five members for the purpose
of "initiating policy and for the work of co-ordinating the great
Departments of State". To an Imperial War Conference and to
special meetings of his War Cabinet he invited the Dominion
premiers, "in order to consider questions affecting the prosecu-
tion of the War, the possible conditions in which we could
assent to its termination and the problems which will then
immediately arise". What soon came to be known as the Imperial War Cabinet—that is, the British War Cabinet plus a few
additional British ministers and the Dominion prime ministers
or their representatives—first met on March 20, 1917. Lloyd
George also created the Committee of Prime Ministers, which

met much less frequently and was intended to discuss only the most confidential matters.

Borden later stated that he went to London in March 1917 with the "fixed purpose to set forth in terms that could not be misunderstood and by authority that must be respected a new conception of the status of the Dominions in their relation to the governance of the Empire".[3] Concurrent with the meetings of the Imperial War Cabinet, there was held an Imperial War Conference, with representatives of the Dominions meeting with certain British ministers to discuss Imperial questions of both war and peace. In this Imperial War Conference, Borden achieved recognition of a new status for the Dominions through the unanimous adoption of a resolution calling for "an adequate voice in foreign policy and foreign relations" for the Dominions and "effective arrangements for continuous consultation in all matters of common Imperial concern".

The constitutional theory having been attended to in the Imperial War Conference, Borden gained what he sought in practice through meetings of the Imperial War Cabinet and, later, in the Committee of Prime Ministers established by the Imperial War Cabinet in June 1918. There, he was afforded every opportunity by Lloyd George to speak his mind. Borden, a purposeful man of strong principles, believed that his presence in the highest councils of the Empire obligated Canada to join in the Empire's military undertakings. In addition, there was a parallel obligation for Canada to speak candidly about strategy and foreign policy. In doing so, Borden displayed little regard for the Imperial General Staff and even less for ambiguous or futile military ventures.

The minutes of the Imperial War Cabinet reflect the respect with which Borden was heard. During the many inconclusive meetings held concerning Russia, Borden's was generally a moderate voice, urging realism and restraint. Nevertheless, Borden subscribed to the conventional Allied wisdom that the reopening of the Eastern Front was an essential element in the grand strategy to defeat the Central Powers. In London he had participated in the reviews of how best to bring this about. He

responded by fulfilling what he regarded as his part of the
mutual obligation. On behalf of Canada, he undertook to
provide troops for intervention in Russia, but making certain
that he would have a voice in the policies determining their
deployment.

Like most Allied people, Canadians were profoundly weary of
war when the Armistice was finally announced. Thereafter, it
soon became evident through newspaper reports and editorials,
letters sent to Members of Parliament, and the tenor of public
meetings and demonstrations that the attitude of the great
majority of Canadians towards the idea of Canadian troops
fighting the Bolsheviks in Russia ranged from scepticism to
outright hostility. Not long before, the overthrow of the Tsar had
been welcomed enthusiastically. For most Canadians, the
Russian Empire had been a remote and strange land in the grip
of a despotic ruler, his infamous secret police, a repressive
political system, and brutal pogroms. As in the United States
and Britain, many headlines and editorials in Canada had hailed
the end of an undemocratic régime.
    Although sharing these views, Borden was also hostile to
communism. It was contrary to his belief in the limited role the
state should play in society, and the inviolability of private
property. For Borden, the right to private property was the
primary guarantee of individualism. Private property provided
an assurance of political and economic independence, which the
individual must have in order that his consent to be governed
was fully given. A Red revolution would violate this contract and
could only lead to misery and chaos. Borden was fully aware of
the role communists might play in the mounting social unrest
in Canada after the Armistice. He took the Soviet leaders at their
word, that the new Russia was to be the centre of world revolution. In December 1918, for example, he wired his cabinet
colleagues in Ottawa that Bolshevik propaganda was making
headway in Britain, being heavily subsidized from Moscow.
There was a similar danger for Canada. In March 1919, he
warned that a "careful watch should be kept in Canada for

Bolshevist emissaries who are exceedingly clever and skilful and are supplied with an abundance of funds".[4]

Yet Borden, although clearly not unaffected by the widespread "Red scare" of 1918-19, never regarded the Canadian troops in Russia as forming part of an Allied crusade to wipe communism from the face of the earth. He was never so irrational as to become fanatical in his opposition to communism, or as single-minded as Churchill, who worked consistently for the eradication of communism in Russia, as well as for its exclusion from Britain.

Borden was prepared to defend the Allied intervention in the Russian civil war as long as the demands of Allied strategy appeared to require it, or pending a decision about a concerted Allied policy. But when the strategic requirement was removed by the Armistice, and the subsequent discussions at the Paris Peace Conference made it evident that the formulation of a concerted Allied policy towards Russia was most unlikely, Borden withdrew the Canadian troops, ending that particular complaint of agitators and meeting the more general demand to "bring the boys home". In retrospect, it is easy to point to errors of judgment committed by Borden. He was hasty in acquiescing in the original British requests for Canadian troops to go to Russia. But, to his credit, he was equally prompt in demanding their return once the original justifications for their presence had either vanished or proved fallacious.

The course of Allied intervention in the Caspian Sea area and, initially, in northern Russia was determined entirely by the British. But once it became clear that the Allies were incapable of agreeing on a policy towards Russia, Borden successfully demanded the withdrawal of the Canadian soldiers from Murmansk and Archangel. In Siberia, his policy was even more distinctive. It was not the British who decided upon the course of Imperial policy there. In a major way, it was Borden. It was he who had ensured that a Canadian general would command the joint Anglo-Canadian force and that Ottawa, not London, would have the final voice in the disposition of that force. When, after the Armistice, Allied thinking became even more confused about what military intervention in Russia was intended to accomplish, Borden flatly rejected War Office proposals to move the Canadian brigade across Siberia in direct support of the White Russians. Lloyd George was reaching similar general conclusions about the futility of the intervention in Siberia, but its course, although probably not its outcome, might have been markedly different if the Canadian government had permitted its troops to fight the Bolsheviks in the Urals as the War Office had envisaged. Instead, Borden made certain that the Canadians remained in Vladivostok, along with the Americans and Japanese, pending the clarification of Allied policy towards Russia. The Canadians, moreover, sided with the Americans in their suspicions about why the Japanese were in Siberia. Here, too, Canada pursued a policy different from that of Britain. In Vladivostok and in London, Canadians worked constantly to reduce the friction between the aggressive British and the passive Americans. For Canada, good relations with its neighbour were coming to take precedence over more distant Imperial interests.

III   *The Economic Commission to Siberia*

Manufacturing in Canada expanded rapidly in response to wartime demands. Borden and his colleagues were dissatisfied during much of the war about how few British and other Allied contracts went to Canada, compared with the number that went to the United States, and they took every occasion to press the claims of Canada for more war work. Gradually the demand for Canadian products grew, thanks in large part to the efforts of the Ottawa-based Imperial Munitions Board. By 1917, aware of growing social unrest and uncertain about the implications for Canadian industry of the complex adjustment to peacetime conditions, Borden and other members of his government redoubled their efforts to find new markets for Canadian products.* Borden was eager to avoid the widespread unemployment

---

* *Underestimating the pent-up purchasing power in Canada as well as in other Allied countries, the Canadian government eventually dispatched missions to Romania, France, Belgium, and Greece to explore the trading possibilities that were expected to result from offers to each of those countries of credits of $25 million for the purchase of Canadian products.*

that many considered inevitable once the soldiers came home, and he was convinced that one outlet for the productive capacity of Canadian factories, swollen by wartime demand, might be a rehabilitated Russia or, at least, Siberia.

As early as 1915, Canadian trade opportunities in Siberia were discussed in articles and editorials in *Industrial Canada*, the monthly publication of the Canadian Manufacturers' Association. Promising reports from the Canadian trade commissioners in Petrograd and Omsk were published in the *Weekly Bulletin* of the Department of Trade and Commerce. Borden was not alone in believing that Siberia might provide an answer to the anticipated post-war dilemma. In 1916 and 1917, the Sherbrooke and Trois Rivières Boards of Trade urged him to send trade missions to Russia. The revolution was even welcomed by some Canadians as providing an opportunity to strengthen trade. On March 15, 1917, for example, the Toronto *Star* was rhapsodical about the possibilities offered by the revolution. "Under free institutions," the *Star* said, "we may expect swift development of the huge area of Asiatic Russia. . . . We are witnessing not only political revolution but the opening of a new world."

Borden, when he was urging Canadian participation in the Siberian intervention upon his colleagues in Ottawa, emphasized the trading opportunities that he was convinced awaited Canadian businessmen in Siberia. As we have seen, Leopold Amery, one of the secretaries of the Imperial War Cabinet and a close friend of Borden's, had urged on him the case for a Canadian military contribution to the Allied intervention in Siberia. As part of his argument, Amery had portrayed the prospect of great new markets. Borden was an eager listener. A vast area with great natural resources, Siberia would be able to produce minerals, furs, foodstuffs, and timber in abundance and Siberia could become a market for Canadian machinery to exploit its abundant natural resources, as well as for Canadian-made consumer goods. Sir George Foster, the Minister of Trade and Commerce, shared with Borden and a number of Canadian entrepreneurs a conviction that Russia, and especially Siberia, represented a challenging new trade possibility. If troops were sent, it was argued, trade would follow the flag.

Part of the sudden allure of the Russian market arose from the simple fact that its needs appeared to be gratifyingly large. This conviction arose partly from an ignorance of what the Russian market really offered. There was very limited knowledge in Ottawa about Russia. Before the war, Canadian and Russian interests had only occasionally touched: even then it was the Foreign Office in London and the British Embassy in St. Petersburg that dealt with such questions of common interest as territorial waters and the regulation of pelagic seal hunting. Few immigrants from Russia had reached Canadian shores (the majority of Ukrainians had come from the Austro-Hungarian Empire), except for the short-lived influx of Doukhobors. The annual flow of Russian immigrants into Canada had increased slowly until in 1914 it exceeded 24,000, but this was only a small fraction of the total pre-war flood of settlers. The Russians were too few to have much influence, beyond encouraging the impression that tsarist Russia was a land of oppression utterly opposed to democratic ideals.

What did gradually bring the Russian Empire more to the minds of influential Canadians was the rapid growth in trade. From a mere $16,000 in 1896, Canadian exports to Russia grew to $4.9 million in 1916, making Russia the seventh most important market for Canadian goods. Admittedly, Russia had used Allied loans and credits to pay for some of its wartime purchases, but the new market seemed promising to those in Ottawa who were concerned with promoting Canadian exports. One of the leading proponents of trade with Siberia was Conradin F. Just, who had been dispatched during the summer of 1915 on an exploratory visit to Russia, and had sent back favourable reports on trade prospects (some of which were published in the Department of Trade and Commerce's *Weekly Bulletin*). Partly on the basis of Just's reports, the government decided the following year to appoint him trade commissioner in Petrograd. Another trade commissioner was assigned to Omsk and, after much prompting from Ottawa, a Russian purchasing mission was established in Canada (a Russian consul-general had for some years been based in Montreal and there were honorary consuls in Halifax and Vancouver).

Even after the revolution, Just remained convinced that there would be enormous opportunities for Canadian exporters in Russia, once a stable and friendly government had been established.* But in the unsettled conditions following the Bolshevik seizure of Petrograd, there had been nothing for Just to do but close his office and go to Ottawa. There, he began to urge on the receptive Sir George Foster—a brilliant man in many ways but an overly ambitious minister whose judgment Borden doubted—that a concerted effort must be made by Canada to open trade between Vancouver and Vladivostok and to join in the exploitation of the abundant natural resources of Siberia.[5]

The economic possibilities of Siberia were present in the mind of General Mewburn when, in his first letter (July 12) to Borden about the proposed Siberian expeditionary force, he noted: "It has been suggested that the trade conditions in this territory will be a vital factor, looking to the future, and it might be advisable to have some Canadian representative accompany this force."[6] Not surprisingly, Borden agreed. On August 8, he cabled from London urging his cabinet colleagues to follow the precedent of Britain and the United States in sending economic missions to Vladivostok concurrently with their military forces. In response, the cabinet approved in principle the dispatch of an economic mission, but it deferred the question of its composition until Borden's return to Ottawa.

Foster received a long memorandum from Just examining specific sectors of the Siberian economy where he believed Canada could find major markets. Just noted that several

---

* As has been noted, the tsarist government had placed major orders in Canada for war supplies, at first mainly through the Russian consul-general in Montreal. In the spring of 1917, in response to a request Borden had made as early as June 1915, and which had been supported by a mission the Imperial Munitions Board had sent to Petrograd, a Russian purchasing commission was established in Montreal with an agent in Ottawa. Its work, however, was short-lived. At the request of the British Treasury, all shipments from Canada to Russia were suspended on November 30, 1917 (PAC Borden Papers, file OC 244(1)). At the end of 1917, when it became clear that Siberia had not fallen to the Bolsheviks, a final shipment of railway and agricultural equipment—some of it financed by United States credits—was sent to Vladivostok from Vancouver.

thousand box-cars had been built in Canada earlier in the war for the Siberian railways. This might provide Canada with a peg on which to hang further sales. The shipyards in British Columbia were capable of producing the types of river barge and coastal steamer required in eastern Siberia. Canadian farming and dairy equipment had already penetrated the Siberian market before the war and the merits of Canadian farm and grain-handling machinery were also well known there. After stable conditions had been secured, the demand for such products should be enormous. Wartime food shortages had given canned salmon unprecedented popularity throughout the Allied countries. For Siberian fishermen to exploit this new world-wide market, additional canning machinery would be required. Canadians themselves might seek permission to enjoy the same fishing rights in Russian territorial waters as had been granted to Japan (rights that Just himself had already provisionally obtained for Canada from the tsarist government). A unit of the Canadian Forestry Corps (which had worked with such distinction in Britain and France) might be sent to teach Canadian logging practices, as had already been arranged for northern Russia.[7] Stretches of the Amur River were rich in placer gold deposits, similar to those in the Klondike. Canadian miners might also help to develop the large coal areas near Vladivostok (which had hitherto been exploited only in a very limited way).

At first, barter trade might have to be envisaged, Just conceded, since in the unsettled conditions of Siberia credit was scarce. At the same time that Just was submitting his proposals to Foster about trade with Siberia, Lord Shaughnessy, President of the Canadian Pacific Railway Company, was painting encouraging pictures about trade opportunities at public meetings in western Canada. The C.P.R. was not the only Canadian company eyeing the Siberian market: Massey-Harris had exported there for many years. Foster also received encouraging reports from a large company that had conducted business throughout Russia before and during the war; R. Martens and Company, with offices in New York and Paris as well as in Britain and Russia, was eager to revive its once-flourishing business in Russia. In July, Martens had called on Borden, Rowell, and Ballantyne in London, outlining his expectations about Siberian trade. At the end of that month, Martens had sent to Borden—who forwarded them to Foster—fifty-nine maps illustrating the economic life of Russia, maps that Borden said he found "exceedingly interesting and instructive".[8] At the suggestion of Colonel John Staughton Dennis of the British and Canadian Recruiting Mission in the United States, Martens on October 8 described to Foster his ideas about the nature, scope, and activities of a proposed Canadian economic commission.

Having swallowed the idea of a military force to Siberia and having listened to the Prime Minister's hopeful review of the supposed trading opportunities, the cabinet soon approved Foster's formal recommendation for the establishment of a Canadian economic mission to Siberia. On October 21, 1918, an order-in-council authorized a commission to be composed initially of John Dennis, A. Ross Owen, Dana Wilgress, and Conradin Just. John Dennis, who had spent much of his early life as a surveyor and engineer for the Hudson's Bay Company and for the Canadian Pacific Railway Company, was thought to have the necessary qualifications for evaluating the economic potential of an underdeveloped area like Siberia. He was, in any case, going to Siberia on General Elmsley's staff as representative of the Canadian Red Cross.

A. Ross Owen, the general manager in Siberia for the Canadian Pacific Railway Company, was to be available when his regular duties permitted. Like Dennis (who was paid by the army), Owen received no salary from the Department of Trade and Commerce for his work.

Dana Wilgress, a graduate of the University of Toronto, had been appointed Trade Commissioner in Omsk at the same time that Just had been sent to Petrograd. He had served in Omsk from July 1916 to April 1918, learning Russian and travelling extensively on business throughout Siberia.* At the time of the order-in-council, he was Trade Commissioner in Vladivostok.

---

* Wilgress (1898-1969) described his Omsk experiences in his Memoirs, Toronto, Ryerson, 1967. Following his service in Siberia, Wilgress had a long and distinguished career in the Canadian public service.

Provision was also made in the order-in-council to increase the commission "by the addition of four members representing respectively the Agricultural, the Mining, the Banking and Manufacturing interests of Canada, who should proceed to Vladivostock early in the year 1919." Although eight commissioners were thus originally envisaged, only one more was in fact added to the original four. The President of the Canadian Bankers' Association nominated a recently retired assistant general manager of the Bank of Montreal, A. D. Braithwaite, who was appointed vice-chairman of the commission. Several groups in British Columbia pressed to have a representative from that province. By that time, however, Foster had already begun to have second thoughts about the value of the commission. From London on January 8, he wired the acting minister of trade and commerce, recommending that no further members be sent "for the time being".

Louis Kon, an employee of the United Grain Growers Securities Company in Winnipeg, was assigned to the commission as secretary (he was not a commissioner). Born in the Polish part of Russia in 1882, Kon at the age of twenty-three had participated in the abortive revolution of 1905. He emigrated to Canada two years later, and became a Canadian citizen in 1910. Before joining the United Grain Growers, he was employed in the immigration department of the Grand Trunk Pacific Railway in Winnipeg.

With the addition of Kon, the political spectrum of the Commission was complete: Just had a very low opinion of communists from his service in Petrograd; Dennis and Owen were more or less neutral; Kon was openly sympathetic.

The order-in-council of October 21 authorizing the commission, despite its ponderous language characteristic of so many official documents, was fairly precise about what the commission should do. This passage appears to have been drafted by Just:

> It should be the duty of the Commission to make a careful study of local conditions, both economic and social; to enquire into the facilities for transportation, both by land and water, and the equipment needs of the same; to ascertain the wants of the farming

community in respect to agricultural machinery, tools and equipment of all kinds; to note the possible improvement in methods of handling grain and in mining, forestry and fishing operations and equipment therefor, and to examine into the barter basis of trade in connection with co-operative associations, municipal bodies and trading corporations. They shall also enquire into the current financial conditions and the arrangements of credits in connection therewith which are necessary to a successful exchange of commodities and generally to investigate the opportunities, present and prospective, for increasing commercial interchanges between Russia and Canada and the particular lines along which Canadian experience and industry might best contribute to the rehabilitation of Russian business activities and the development of her vast natural resources. The Commission should from time to time report the information thus gathered and its recommendations as to the nature of the commodities to be supplied and the organization for transport and sale thereof.

With these instructions, Just, Dennis, and Kon made their way in early December to Vancouver where they were to embark for Vladivostok.

From Vancouver, Dennis and Just sent a preliminary report to the Minister of Trade and Commerce, outlining the commission's prospects as they foresaw them. Between the order-in-council of October 21 appointing the commission and the submission of this first report on December 9, the Armistice had been declared on the Western Front. This the commissioners rightly regarded as an event requiring a re-thinking of their assignment. "The dramatic suddenness with which peace has arrived has altered, in the opinion of your Commissioners, the whole conditions under which they will now have to work, and that the situation will call for a speeding up of their own activities, and that of quick decisions and rapid action in Canada." Accordingly, the two commissioners made three specific proposals:

(a) That the additional four members of the Commission, representing respectively the agricultural, mining, manufacturing and banking interests of Canada, be appointed at once . . .

(b) That immediate steps be taken to organize a Siberia Supply

Commission, through which the goods [required in Siberia] can
be provided for shipment. . . .

(c) That a sum of not less than $100,000 be immediately expended
in the purchase of the boots, food and clothing [for distribution
by] the Canadian Red Cross Commissioner in Vladivostock . . . 9

This last suggestion was not entirely an altruistic one, the
commissioners being convinced that "this action will have the
effect of laying a strong foundation upon which to develop
Canadian trade later on." With these practical recommendations
mailed to Ottawa, Just and Kon embarked with the troops on
the *Teesta*. The twenty-day voyage from Victoria was stormy,
and a blizzard and temperatures below zero awaited their arrival
in Vladivostok in January 12, 1919. "This fact coupled with the
overcrowding of the ship made the whole passage . . . a most
unpleasant and trying experience from the effects of which it has
taken Mr. Kon and myself some days to recover."10 Wilgress
had been overcome by the cold on the dockside while waiting
for the ship to arrive, but Owen had remained on hand to drive
Just and Kon from the Canadian Ordnance Dock to the centre
of the city.

The other members of the commission gradually congregated
in Vladivostok. Dennis had an easier passage on the *Madras*,
arriving on February 3. Before Braithwaite sailed from
Vancouver on the *Empress of Japan* on February 12, he travelled
to New York to discuss with officials of the branch of the
Moscow-Narodny Bank their understanding of the financial
conditions in Siberia. Braithwaite finally arrived in Valdivostok
on March 2. He was to remain in Siberia for less than three
months.

At first, when the whole commission had finally assembled
in Vladivostok, "very frequent meetings were held at which all
the questions delegated to the commission were aggressively
undertaken."11 Early in February, the commission resolved itself
into three study groups: transport (Dennis and Owen); markets
and supplies (Just and Wilgress); and financial conditions and
credits (Braithwaite and Just). In addition, Dennis, assisted by
Wilgress, kept in close touch with Sir Charles Eliot and his large
staff. Partly on the basis of his close friendship with Eliot,

Dennis sent occasional political commentaries to Ottawa along with his commercial reports.

From the beginning, the commission was discouraged by the chaos in the port of Vladivostok and the breakdown of the Russian transport system. On January 20, only eight days after his arrival, Just wrote to the Deputy Minister of Trade and Commerce in Ottawa:

> According to Mr. Owen and others in a position to know, the congestion in Vladivostok both in regard to living accommodation and for the storage of goods can hardly go further. The town has now three times the population that was here in 1914, and no building operations have been undertaken during the war. Every warehouse is overflowing with goods, and the open spaces at the docks and along the shores of the harbour are piled high with goods, for a great part of which all records are missing.

It did not take Dennis long to make the same observation and draw the logical conclusion. On February 16, Dennis stated in an interview that the paralysis of the railroad, the congestion in the port, and the absence of credit combined to prevent any early opportunities for trade. The commission was, accordingly, "confining its efforts at present to securing data as to the character of goods that will be needed in the country and the possible methods of distributing them when they have been received."[12]

The commission was soon convinced that if only a dependable way could be found for moving Canadian products inland, a great demand for them would exist among the 15,000,000 inhabitants of Siberia. But because of the congestion in the port of Vladivostok and on the railway, "the sale of goods to Siberia on any extended scale is not regarded as feasible for the present and is not to be encouraged." Wilgress later recalled:

> It was not long before Colonel Dennis began to realize that there was one key problem which had to be solved before other plans could be considered. This was the situation on the railway. . . . Other countries realized this too and there had been appointed American, Japanese, British and French railway commissions, charged with the attempt of bringing order out of chaos. Colonel Dennis soon commenced to devote his main attention to this basic

problem. He established intimate relations with Colonel Jack, the head of the British Railway Commission, who had been in charge of the United Railways of Havana in Cuba and knew thoroughly the technique of operating railways. The chief difficulty was that no country would allow another to assume responsibility for reorganizing the railway. To a large degree this reflected the jealousy between the Americans and the Japanese, each of whom suspected the other of territorial ambitions in the Far East.[13]

The Japanese were deeply suspicious of the real motives of the United States railway experts who strove valiantly but vainly to create order in the confusion. The United States was equally suspicious about Japanese motives. It did what it could to prevent Japan—or its puppet, Semenov—from gaining too great a hold on the railway.

> The Japanese-American struggle for control of the railways constituted the basic economic aspect of the Allied intervention in Siberia. In the end it proved also to be the decisive phase of the Japanese efforts to control Eastern Siberia. The next phase—the attempt to strangle the economic life of Siberia by control of railway terminals and strategic harbors and rivers—came too late to achieve the conquest for which Japan hoped. By this time the Soviet Government had survived the main force of civil war and intervention. . . . In the long run, therefore, the Japanese-American duel for the railway proved as decisive for the future of the Soviet Far East as the Allied victory on the Western Front had [for] the success of the Bolshevik Revolution.[14]

Japan was convinced—wrongly—that a weak administration in Siberia would give it an opportunity to draw on Siberian natural resources and sell its own manufactured goods on an unparalleled scale. This latter-day manifestation of the mercantile theory of trade had its origins in the post-war plight facing Japanese industries. The war had brought unprecedented prosperity to Japan. Her industries had been greatly stimulated by new opportunities in the markets of Asia, Africa, and the Americas, where the supply of European products had dwindled. While Japan profited greatly from new and expanding markets, raw materials from traditional suppliers were sometimes difficult to obtain. Great new sources of raw materials as well as new markets for manufactured goods were seen in Siberia. As the end of the war approached, Japanese businessmen and government officials became increasingly worried about the return of western competitors. Not even neighbouring Siberia would be immune from their resurgent commercial activities.

Borden had looked upon the participation of Canadian troops in the Allied expeditionary force as a means of ensuring that a share of the Siberian market would go to Canada. The Japanese were unscrupulous in the way they used their military forces to try to achieve an exclusive place in Siberia for Japanese entrepreneurs. By 1919, Japan had increased its exports to Siberia to the point where they were five times those of the United States and her imports sixteen times as large. But Japan was, in fact, building on sand. By seeking to prevent the establishment of a strong local government, it was in fact creating conditions that in the longer run could benefit only the communists.

One luckless shoe merchant from Calgary was among the many businessmen from Allied countries who learned the hard way about conditions in Vladivostok. After reading newspaper accounts by an American correspondent on the shortage of footwear in Omsk, he sold his shop in Calgary and bought a large number of shoes to send to Vladivostok. He went to Vancouver with the shoes, and arranged for them—and himself—to be taken on the *Empress of Japan* to Vladivostok. There, however, the inefficiency and corruption was such that he was unable to receive any assurance that his shoes, even if they were landed, would be carried to inland markets. The Calgarian was not a man to be discouraged easily. While his ship was still in the harbour, he sought the assistance of the Canadian Economic Commission and tried manfully to make a satisfactory arrangement to rid himself of his unwanted footwear. He finally had to dispose of the shoes, at a considerable loss, to a British speculator who sent them on to Shanghai.

Economic recovery in Siberia, however inevitable in the long run it might appear to members of the commission, would not, they recognized, be easy. The dislocations caused by war and revolution had been profound. Pending the stabilization of the rouble—an obviously distant prospect—and the re-establishment of normal commercial practices, the commission recommended in its preliminary report of December 1918, and again in its final report of June 1919, that trade by barter should be seriously considered.

On March 15, 1919, the commission held a meeting in Vladivostok with representatives of a number of co-operatives. The Canadians found them as keen to trade as they were themselves, and were impressed by the widespread organization they administered. With over two million members, the Siberian co-operatives promoted the dairy industry in particular, but they also interested themselves in the standards of schools and in the expansion of what popular education there was. They were, in a sense, as essential to the health of the Siberian economy as the Trans-Siberian railroad.

But no matter how eager the officials of the co-operatives were to extend their operations and trade with Canada, the obstacles in the way of Siberian-Canadian commerce, even on the rudimentary level of barter, remained. Railway and port dislocation stifled trade and contributed to the debasement of the several currencies employed in Siberia. Few exports could find their way to the sea to pay, whether by barter or by earning foreign exchange, for the much-needed imports. To rectify the monetary chaos, the commissioners proposed far-reaching steps, steps that transcended the question of clearing the rail-lines and the port.

By the spring of 1919, the Allies had pinned their main hopes for a non-communist Russia on Admiral Kolchak. So did the commissioners. They urged the recognition of his Omsk directorate which, they hoped, would soon be changed into a "constitutional government". It should then be "in a position to pledge its various assets as a security, both for internal currency issued and for external loans". Having recommended that Canada join with other Allies in formally recognizing the Omsk régime as the government controlling Siberia, the commissioners, somewhat inconsistently, proceeded to recommend that the Allies themselves fulfil some of the tasks that are the prerogatives of a sovereign government. All financial affairs, they urged, should be placed in the hands of an Allied advisory council and, under its aegis, a new state bank of Siberia created that would be the only bank empowered to issue currency.

Whether Braithwaite, the financial expert on the commission, went so far as to discuss such far-reaching ideas when he paid a visit to Omsk is doubtful. Braithwaite, with the agreement of Dennis, left on March 16 for Omsk, only a fortnight after his arrival in Vladivostok. After covering 3,500 miles by rail, he arrived in Omsk nine days later. There, he stayed with the Canadians who provided the headquarters staff for the 25th Battalion of the Middlesex Regiment. During his short visit, he called on Kolchak and his ministers of trade and of finance.

Upon his return to Vladivostok, Braithwaite was cautious in his recommendations. But he had evidently been influenced by the political ideas then common among many Allied officers and other officials in Omsk.

> It appears to me that the first step must be for the Allies to acknowledge and support the Siberian (Kolchak) Government, if the various powers interested feel that their interests and investments are of sufficient importance to justify such action. Should the Allies not take the steps necessary to that end, Siberia politically, financially and commercially must fall under the dominance of Germany, China and Japan, and in time it would naturally follow that European or older Russia would come under the same influence.
>
> The second step I would advise would be to create Siberia into a separate Province, drawing the boundary line at the Ural Mountains. It would not, I gather, be a very difficult task to restore law and order in Siberia, as apart from the Western part of Russia. Then, if thought advisable, the parts could again come together, making a United Russia.
>
> The only reason I have touched on the political side of the question is because, following recognition, it would be necessary for the Allies to make loans to the recognized Siberian Government, and with a stable Government, properly supported by the Allies, such loans could be adequately secured.

Long before the members of the commission had sailed for Siberia, even before the Canadian government had decided to send an economic mission there, the British government adopted a different approach to the commercial possibilities of Siberia.

It was fully aware of the disruption of trade. It recognized the difficulties individual British firms would encounter in trying to penetrate the market. So the British government agreed to the establishment of a controlling monopoly, the Siberian Supply Company, under the direction of Leslie Urquhart, whose family had large business interests in Russia (principally the Russo-Asiatic Corporation).* On September 25, 1918, the British government appointed Urquhart to head the company it would both finance and guarantee, agreeing to remunerate him personally at the rate of one-half of one per cent of the value of the total trade.

Wilgress, from Vladivostok, described the consternation of the British businessmen there when they learned of this new arrangement. They believed that it would virtually exclude them from what appeared to be a promising market. More detailed information about the new organization arrived in Ottawa from London, but the Canadian government showed no interest in this monopolistic venture as a possible alternative to sending its own commission. The commission itself was to recommend the ways in which Canada might best conduct its Siberian trade.

Several factors gradually changed the Canadian attitude about the British project. Scepticism gave way to increasing enthusiasm for direct participation. Foster went with Borden to London in November 1918. There, he began to hear much more about what the British expected from the establishment of a single company to trade with Siberia. With Foster's concurrence, the Vladivostok director of the new company, the Honourable Raymond E. Hubbard, arrived in Canada in late January, visiting Ottawa and the major cities and describing enthusiastically what he hoped the company would achieve.

Certainly, the British, and perhaps Foster, were convinced that the addition of Canadian resources to the British company would place it in such a strong position in the Siberian market that it would be able to do more than all the individual companies or entrepreneurs together. But the consideration that seems

* Urquhart was a friend of Kolchak. The Russian who was managing director of Urquhart's Irtysh and Tanalyk Corporation was a close adviser of Kolchak in Omsk.

to have been uppermost in Foster's mind was his understanding that the British government would take all the roubles earned by the company and pay exporters in Britain—or Canada—in sterling. Here was a solution to the problem of the rapidly declining value of Siberian currencies. Dennis had joined many others in reporting that trade was almost at a standstill partly because of the instability of the currencies in Siberia. Now the British government, it seemed, was ready to convert all roubles resulting from Canadian trade into a hard currency. This was enough to convince Foster.

An order-in-council of February 20, 1919, authorized a Canadian agreement with the Siberian Supply Company. It goes far in explaining Foster's motives and places special emphasis on the arrangement for the exchange of roubles for sterling.

> . . . the British Government had constituted a Trading Company known as the Siberian Supply Company, Limited, to which it will give its financial backing. This Company will purchase goods in the United Kingdom, pay transport charges thereon and sell them in Siberia. Strict supervision of prices will be maintained, thus preventing speculation and extravagant charges upon the buyers. The company is to look after all matters of credit and exchange, and the profits in the aggregate will go to the British Government. . . . [After careful study it would appear] in the best interests of Canada, that the facilities offered by this Company be availed of . . . [15]

This far-reaching decision reached Dennis and his colleagues like a bombshell. Since their appointment, they had been led to believe that their recommendations would determine how Canada would trade with Siberia. On February 12, Dennis telegraphed a strong protest to Ottawa, contending that the decision undercut both his commission and Canadian entrepreneurs.

Dennis followed up his telegram with a letter twelve days later that F. C. T. O'Hara, the Deputy Minister of Trade and Commerce, did not receive until April 10. Dennis contended that the contract the government had undertaken would simply place Canada in the same bad light in which the British government already stood in the eyes of both British and Russian entrepreneurs. One justification advanced for the contract was that it would prevent exploitation of the Siberian peasants by unscrupulous businessmen. Yet the Siberian Supply Company, without a whole network of agencies, could no more control the final price to the consumer than a private firm. The only organizations capable of doing this were the Siberian co-operative societies. There could be no opportunity for individual initiative by Canadian businessmen when the Canadian Trade Commission in Ottawa had been designated the sole purchaser of Canadian goods ordered by the Siberian Supply Company. In these circumstances, Dennis concluded, there could be little or no use for the continuation of his commission, as the whole matter of supply of, and demand for, Canadian goods would be decided by the Siberian Supply Company.

Having by March 1 received no satisfactory reply to his telegram, Dennis reminded Ottawa that under the terms of the order-in-council appointing the commission he and his colleagues were responsible for reporting on the character of the Canadian goods desired and the best ways in which they might be shipped to Siberia and sold there. Yet, without awaiting a report from the commission, the Canadian government had entered into a contract with the Siberian Supply Company. This, moreover, was done in the face of adverse comments from Wilgress about the company and the protests of reputable British and Russian firms about their virtual exclusion from Siberian trade. Finally, and perhaps most important, it seemed to Dennis that it was most unlikely that the British government would direct towards Canadians many of the contracts it expected to get from Siberia.

Having still not received any satisfactory explanation from Ottawa as to why the agreement had been made, Dennis sent a brief telegram to Ottawa on March 11. "Commission has decided close work here and return Canada at early date. . . . "[16] Dennis, Braithwaite, and Owen were not employees of the Canadian government; they received no remuneration beyond their expenses, and they felt free to depart. They believed that their usefulness in Siberia had ended. Just and Wilgress could hardly oppose their decision. Wilgress, as Canadian Trade

Commissioner, remained in Vladivostok, but he did not comment on the commissioners' action. In a telegram on March 21 to Ottawa, he simply observed that the commission had decided that, given the terms of the agreement with the Siberian Supply Company, there would be no further role for it. The chaotic transport system was not, in any case, expected to improve for several months at the earliest. On April 8, Wilgress again touched on the new arrangements that had been made for Canadian-Siberian trade. While avoiding any comment on the decision of the commission to withdraw, he noted that the agreement with the Siberian Supply Company failed to answer a fundamental question that had exercised the commissioners. How far was the Canadian government prepared to go in underwriting the risks involved in Canadian sales in Siberia? Then Wilgress added, almost casually, that the British government had not, in fact, guaranteed the value of the roubles the Siberian Supply Company would accumulate in its transactions.

In providing this incidental information, Wilgress unknowingly removed the very foundation for Foster's recommendation to his cabinet colleagues that the contract with the Siberian Supply Company should be signed. Foster had hoped to render immune from inflation the roubles that Canadian exporters might earn. Now it was obvious that the company could do no more than the commission to overcome one of the principal barriers of trade.

Convinced that there was no further useful work to be done, Dennis crossed from Vladivostok to Yokohama during the last week of March, less than a month after the arrival of Braithwaite (who in the meantime had left for Omsk).* Dennis arrived back in Canada late in April; Just, Braithwaite, and Kon got home in May. None had spent more than four months in Siberia.

No record of the reactions of Foster or O'Hara to the commission's decision to disband is to be found in the files of the Department of Trade and Commerce. There was nothing they could do to keep the commissioners in Siberia. Their attention was, in any case, largely taken up with other events in the after-

* Dennis and Braithwaite were together for only a fortnight in Siberia.

math of the European war, especially the serious economic and labour problems facing Canada.

On July 12, after having reassembled in Canada, the commissioners (less Wilgress, who remained *en poste* in Vladivostok) sent their final report to Foster. If the port and railway could once be cleared, some order imposed on the monetary system, and Allied credits extended, the commissioners were convinced, the trade opportunities between Canada and Siberia would be enormous.

From everything they had been able to learn, many practices—forestry, for example—were primitive compared to those in western Canada. This was amply borne out by their own investigations and by a meeting on March 12 that the Russo-American Association had arranged for them with the Forestry Department and "the timber interests" of the Maritime and Amur provinces. A representative of the Russian Timber Association had been dispatched to North America to study saw-mill operations. The commission quickly arranged for him to be met in Vancouver and to be given "every opportunity of examining our Canadian system of work in British Columbia and elsewhere". Any hospitality Canada showed him would be well repaid, the commission urged, if a Canadian forestry engineer were later to visit Siberia. Early trade of a significant volume or immediate Canadian investment in saw- or paper-mills was impossible. An engineer could, however, survey prospects and recommend the best way for immediate entry into the market, once this became feasible.

The commissioners also found the Siberian fishing industry to be in its infancy and potentially almost equally attractive to Canadian salesmen and investors as the lumber industry. Much useful information was available, both from the superintendent of the Russian Far Eastern Fisheries and from a report on the Amur River Fisheries, prepared in 1916 by the United States consul in Vladivostok.*

* *Fisheries managers from Canada were not unknown in Siberia. In February 1919, John Fried, a Canadian who was manager of one of the largest fisheries on the Amur River, was killed by the Bolsheviks for being a "counter-revolutionary".*

Until the establishment of sufficient stability in Siberia to permit exploitation of these promising openings, the commissioners recommended to Foster the following steps:

a) The continuance of a Canadian government trade office at Vladivostok and the appointment of "commercial correspondents" at Irkutsk, Harbin, and Nikolayevsk.
b) The establishment of a Canadian samples warehouse at Vladivostok by the government . . .
c) The wide distribution of a carefully prepared and illustrated pamphlet in Russian describing Canada and her resources.*
d) The production of a series of silent films on Canadian life and industries for use in local government, co-operative, school, and other organizations.
e) The invitation to Canada of twenty Russian agriculturalists to familiarize them with the industrial and social life of farming communities in the Canadian Northwest.

Thus the work of the commission ended. Dennis, Just, Braithwaite, and Kon returned to their homes in Canada, leaving Wilgress and a few representatives of the Royal Bank of Canada as the only Canadians in Vladivostok still attempting to develop trade possibilities.

The Department of Trade and Commerce, in addition to organizing the Economic Commission, had encouraged Canadian companies and banks to send representatives to Siberia. The Royal Bank of Canada decided in November 1918 to establish a small office in Vladivostok. It selected a branch manager in Toronto, David C. Rae, and a junior staff member in Winnipeg, Roy A. East, to open the new office. With them went Gustav Grenier of Montreal who, as the result of pre-war work in Russia, spoke fluent Russian (in addition to English and French). They arrived in Vladivostok on December 18, 1918. Their new office was not officially opened until March 1919.

It never did much business. Trade failed to materialize and

* Such a pamphlet had already been prepared in draft before Dennis, Just, and Kon left Ottawa. But it was never printed, being replaced by a small leaflet printed in Vladivostok.

the business from the Canadian troops never amounted to much. Banking in Vladivostok was a risky undertaking not only from a commercial point of view. Criminals were common in the city. The bank office was constantly guarded by eight Canadian soldiers and, after the departure of the Canadian contingent, by British and American.

By the spring of 1919, seven foreign banks (including the Royal Bank) and eleven Russian banks had branch offices in Vladivostok. Their efforts were in vain. The Royal Bank office remained open for seven and one-half months only, closing on October 15, 1919. The lack of co-operation from local Russian officials, the falling value of the rouble, and the monetary and underlying economic problems of Siberia, as well as the with-drawal of the Canadian military contingent, at last decided the bank to cut its losses and close its unprofitable office, leaving only Roy East in Vladivostok as agent.

Wilgress also remained in Vladivostok throughout the spring and summer of 1919, doing whatever he could to advance Canadian trading interests. Together with the Vladivostok representative of the Siberian Supply Company, he worked to secure the speedy shipment from Canada of seeds urgently needed by the peasants in the surrounding area. Wilgress later recalled:

> After the impracticable efforts of the Canadian Economic
> Commission to Siberia, it was a pleasure to be dealing with less
> ambitious plans. However, even these more modest efforts soon
> proved to be too difficult to realize. The forces of Admiral Kolchak
> commenced to suffer reverses, as the communist armies became
> reorganized.[17]

The seeds were shipped from Canada but they arrived in the middle of May instead of April 1, the date for which they had been ordered. They were, therefore, too late for planting in 1919. Two other small shipments sent from Canada on order for the Siberian Supply Company were equally badly handled by the shippers. Spare parts for agricultural machinery left Canada only on May 24, too late to be of much use during the summer. Army blankets and utensils were sent without adequate prior notification. Yet despite this bungling, the Canadian Trade Commission in Ottawa was eventually paid for all three shipments (whether the payment was in convertible currency is unrecorded).

In June, with Roy East as his best man, Wilgress married the daughter of a Swiss engineer who had played a leading role before the war in the development of the Trans-Siberian railway. Wilgress closed the commission's office and departed for a honeymoon in Japan. Upon his return to Vladivostok, he opened a smaller office opposite the railway station. With the further disintegration of the White forces and no trade prospects in sight, he was granted leave in Canada. His departure, fourteen months after his arrival in Vladivostok, marked the end of the Canadian Trade Commissioner's office there.

The British government had become just as disillusioned with the trade prospects in Siberia as the Canadian government. The closing of the office of the Canadian Trade Commissioner in Vladivostok almost coincided with the termination by the British government of its agreement with the Siberian Supply Company. On October 22, 1919, the Secretary of State for the Colonies informed the Governor General of Canada that the agreement was to be ended. By then, no one in Ottawa believed any longer in an economic rainbow stretching from Vancouver to Vladivostok.

James Mavor, a professor of political economy at the University of Toronto, a friend of Tolstoy and of the Doukhobors, and the author of a respected two-volume *Economic History of Russia*, publicly attacked the government for wasting the taxpayers' money in such a worthless venture.

But the commission never attracted much attention. Agitation and pressure in Canada were directed towards getting the Canadian soldiers home from Siberia. As in the case of the troops sent to Siberia, the dispatch of the commission had not been carefully considered. At first glance, the possibilities of trade seemed significant. In the conventional wisdom of the nineteenth century, trade would follow the flag. That was regarded by Borden, Foster, and others in Ottawa as sufficient reason, in the rush of the final days of the war and the first days of the uncertain peace, for undertaking the gamble. More advance consideration would probably have shown that it was likely to fail.

IV   *The Prinkipo Proposal*

In the summary of the meeting of the Imperial War Cabinet in London on December 30, 1918, Borden is recorded as having indicated that

> ... he did not see how the war could be regarded as terminated if we left the Peace Conference with five or six nations and Governments still fighting in Russia. There were only two alternatives: one was to go and forcibly intervene in Russia itself; the other, which he preferred, was to induce the Governments of the various States in Russia to send representatives to Paris for conference with the Allied and associate nations. These could then bring pressure, if necessary, upon them to restrain and control aggression, and to bring about conditions of stable government under the power and influence of the League of Nations.*

In that way was conceived the embryo of what came to be known as the Prinkipo Proposal, the idea of an intra-Russian conference under Allied aegis on the island of Prinkipo in the Bosphorus.

The Armistice in November 1918 had at first brought enormous relief to Europe. But disillusionment soon followed. The energies and emotions that for more than four years had been directed at the enemy were now splintered into various resentments, fatigue, and a profound revulsion against war. The world was in a state of great flux, but there was no interest in Allied countries in any further war, any crusade against communism. From the Bolsheviks had come protestations of peaceful intentions and a call to the Allies for negotiations to end all fighting in Russia. Such appeals played skilfully on the war-weariness of the Allies, thereby contributing to the attitudes that encouraged Borden to take a lead in proposing a negotiated end to the Russian civil war.

The day after Borden's statement to the Imperial War Cabinet,

---

* *Unless otherwise identified, quotations on pages 245-58 are from the minutes of the meetings of the Imperial War Cabinet or the British delegation to the Peace Conference.*

On December 5, more than three full weeks before Borden, H. A. L. Fisher, the British Minister of Education, had called for an all-Russian conference in a paper which he circulated to his British cabinet colleagues.

New Year's Eve, 1918, George Barnes, a minister without portfolio in the British government, a self-styled spokesman for the Labour Party, and a plenipotentiary of Britain to the Paris Peace Conference, warmly supported Borden's proposal. "It was no use merely poking with sticks into the kennel to infuriate the dog." But the decisive support came at the end of the meeting. Winston Churchill had urged that if the Russians themselves would not "come together", force should be used to establish a democratic government in Russia. Lloyd George, with whom Borden had developed a certain rapport, rehearsed the various telling arguments against military intervention:

> He felt that we had never yet arrived at any satisfactory decision.
> He himself had found himself frequently leaning first in one
> direction, and then in another, owing to the absolute contradiction
> between the information supplied from Russia by men of equally
> good authority.
> ... he hoped that the Cabinet would agree to support him in
> refusing to countenance any military intervention, and in inviting
> the representatives of all sections of Russia to appear before the
> Peace Conference, as Sir Robert Borden had suggested, with a view
> to their composing their differences.

The meeting agreed to the proposal of Lloyd George for an All-Russian Conference, after the Australian Minister of the Navy had likened the idea to "walling off a fire in a mine". With this general proposal agreed upon—along with a multitude of other decisions about the peace settlement—the Imperial War Cabinet transformed itself into the British Empire delegation and left for the Peace Conference in Paris.

Borden's idea was not carefully thought out. Paris in January 1919 was not a place where it was easy to make well-considered proposals. Lloyd George later described to the House of Commons the confused atmosphere in which the participants at the Peace Conference found themselves.

> We had to ... work crowded hours, long and late, because, whilst
> we were trying to build we saw in many lands the foundations of
> society crumbling into dust and we had to make haste ... I am
> doubtful whether any body of men with a difficult task have

worked under greater difficulties—stones clattering on the roof and crashing through the windows, and sometimes wild men screaming through the keyholes.[18]

In such circumstances, it is hardly surprising that Borden's idea was so inchoate. There was, furthermore, no time to reflect on it at leisure and Lloyd George acted promptly in attempting to implement it. He saw in it not only a possibly unique opportunity to bring peace to Russia, but also an occasion, unlikely otherwise to occur, when the Allies and the Bolsheviks could begin the task of settling the differences between them. On January 2, the Foreign Office dispatched notes to the principal participants in the Peace Conference, proposing a meeting of all Russian factions. To each note was attached a draft message addressed to the combatants, to be sent if the other Allies deemed it useful. The draft was not written in impartial language—it had a distinct anti-Bolshevik tone—and in a major respect it departed from Borden's original idea that a principal subject for discussion would be how the fighting might be terminated. The Foreign Office draft message called for a cease-fire first, then consultations. Since the Red Army was beginning to gain momentum, this proposal, too, appeared to have anti-Bolshevik implications.

It came as a surprise to none that Clemenceau strongly opposed the idea of a Russian conference. He repeated his statement of the previous month that France was unalterably hostile to any suggestion that a Bolshevik delegation should come to Paris. As Balfour noted at a meeting of the British Empire delegation on January 20, 1919: "Nothing would induce the French Government to alter their decision. Ministers and members of the Chamber were unanimously opposed to the Bolshevists coming here, and M. Clemenceau had said that if the Conference forced that course upon him he would have to resign." That ended any thought of a Russian conference in Paris under the aegis of the Allies. It did not mean, however, that a conference could not be held elsewhere.

The French government favoured a simple policy of military intervention to drive the Bolsheviks from power. But France did not itself have the men, the resources or the will to carry out such a colossal undertaking. Wilson indicated that the United States would not provide troops. At the British Empire delegation meeting on January 20, Lloyd George, Borden, and W.M. Hughes, the Prime Minister of Australia, all made it clear that they would not supply soldiers. Borden repeated the basic position that he had first outlined at the meeting of the Imperial War Cabinet in London three weeks before:

> ... the Bolshevist forces were rapidly increasing in numbers. They were in control of affairs, and we were bound to negotiate with them, whatever their opinions might be. [The Allies] could not go back from the Peace Conference leaving five or six governments fighting amongst themselves in Russia.

The British Empire delegation had concluded its review of the Russian problem with an agreement that Lloyd George and Balfour should convey to the other Allies the information that the British Empire forces currently in Russia would not be withdrawn immediately if some effort was made to bring the contending factions together in some such place as Salonika or Lemnos.

Thereafter, events moved more quickly. At a meeting of the Peace Conference the next day, January 21, President Wilson strongly supported the idea of a negotiated settlement. Faced with Anglo-American unity and recognizing that no Allied nation had the will to intervene decisively, Clemenceau compromised. He reluctantly agreed with Wilson and Lloyd George that a proposal for a conference should be addressed to all factions in the Russian civil war. Wilson undertook to prepare a suitable message himself. To Lenin, Kolchak, Denikin, de Miller, and all other warring elements in what had been the Russian Empire went the same invitation.

> Great Friendly Powers call upon all the governments, parties and peoples in the States and Territories in question to abstain from further aggressions, hostilities and reprisals and require them to keep peace both at home and with their neighbours.

They were invited to gather by February 15 on Prinkipo

(Prince's) Island in the Sea of Marmora, thirteen miles south of Constantinople (partly so that no Bolshevik need be allowed to cross an Allied country *en route*).* There they could settle on peace terms and on the future government of Russia. The discussions with the Allies would be carried on

> ... in the freest and frankest way, with a view to ascertaining the wishes of all sections of the Russian people, and bringing about, if possible, some understanding and agreement by which Russia may work out her purposes and happy co-operative relations be established between her people and the other peoples of the world.

At the meeting of the British Empire delegation on January 23, Lloyd George announced that each of the five Allies would appoint two representatives to attend the Prinkipo conference. He nominated Borden as the chief British Empire delegate, "as the original suggestion for the meeting had come from him."†

Borden told Lloyd George that he could hardly refuse "to undertake any duty which it was thought I could fulfil but that I must consult my colleagues." Accordingly, on January 23 he wired White, asking for his comments about undertaking "this highly important duty". White, preoccupied with the increasing unrest in Canada, where unemployment and social upheaval were everywhere felt, immediately urged Borden to decline the offer and to return to Canada as soon as feasible. "Political situation in West developing seriously again through persistent agitation systematically carried on." Moreover, the reason why Borden was in Europe—if he had to be in Europe—was to lend

---

* *Churchill later observed that "very near to Prinkipo lay another island to which the Young Turks before the war had exiled all the pariah dogs which had formerly infested the streets of Constantinople. These dogs, shipped there in tens of thousands, were left to devour one another and ultimately to starve. . . . To Bolshevik sympathizers the place seemed oddly chosen for a Peace Conference. To their opponents, it seemed not altogether unsuitable."* (The World Crisis, *p. 170)*

† *The day before, Lloyd George had offered the post to Lord Hardinge, the Permanent Under-Secretary at the Foreign Office, who, in declining, recommended Lord Robert Cecil, Parliamentary Under-Secretary at the Foreign Office, but he also declined (Lord Hardinge,* Old Diplomacy, London, Murray, 1947, *p. 235).*

the prestige of his office to the Canadian representation at the Peace Conference, not to absent himself on the distant shores of the Sea of Marmora.

During Borden's absences abroad, his cabinet frequently found it difficult to reach a common position. The Prinkipo invitation was no exception. White had to wire Borden on January 24 that the cabinet had been unable to agree on a common position: "You must decide personally." To which Borden promptly replied: "If I remain here I see no ground on which I can refuse. . . . It is a choice between undertaking that duty and returning [to Canada] at once. Therefore I have said I would accept. It is however very doubtful whether the Conference will take place."*

That Borden never had to pack his bags for Turkey to undertake the difficult—if not impossible—task of helping in the attempt to reconcile the Reds and Whites was largely due to the refusal of the Whites to negotiate with the Reds. The Bolsheviks broadcast a reply to the Allied invitation that was both long and, to some Allied statesmen, insulting. But it did explicitly accept the invitation. One historian of the Allied intervention has aptly noted:

> All that [the Soviet] Note did was to irritate the American President and the British Prime Minister. The episode, indeed, aptly illustrates the almost complete inability of the two sides [i.e., Allied and Bolshevik] to communicate. Wilson and Lloyd George quite failed to realize that to good Marxists it was merely logical, not offensive, to take for granted that any move by a capitalist politician would have an economic motive. For their part . . . the Bolsheviks rarely seem to have been aware of the divisions within the Allied camp. . . . [They] could not have known of all the hard work by Lloyd George and Wilson and the angry confrontations that had gone into getting the Allies to accept the Prinkipo proposal.[19]

---

* *Despite White's telegram leaving the decision to Borden, Calder wired separately on January 24, strongly urging the Prime Minister to keep himself available in Paris. Borden then asked Lloyd George to make the arrangements for the British Empire representation at Prinkipo Island in such a way as to permit his immediate withdrawal in case of an emergency (letter of January 25, 1919, to Newton Rowell).*

The rejection by the various White Russian factions was categorical and, in large part, emotional. That the call for a conference failed was not, however, simply due to the intransigence of the Whites. Their refusal to sit at the same table as Bolsheviks could presumably have been overcome if the Allies had put pressure on them. The important point is that the Allies were themselves not united in their policy towards Russia. The British ambassador in Paris noted his impression sourly in his diary:

> I suppose that Clemenceau found it advisable to make a concession to the inexperience of President Wilson and to the obstinacy of Lloyd George, in the expectation that, even if the Soviet Government accept the invitation and terms, they will not observe the conditions of the invitation.[20]

However, it was not the Soviet government that aborted the Prinkipo Proposal. The White Russians were fully aware, from secret messages conveyed to them, that the French were no more enthusiastic about the idea than they were. Even Lloyd George could not apply all the pressure that might have been expected of him. The right-wing Conservatives in his own coalition government and the *Daily Telegraph* were increasingly restless about his Russian policy and were, in the future, to prevent the revival by him of the Prinkipo approach.

The Whites' indignant rejection of the Prinkipo Proposal was basically irrational. It ignored the fact that, after the Armistice, they could not hope for any massive Allied military assistance. After their rejection of the Prinkipo idea, they could not even hope for limited direct support for very long, whatever the promises of the French. Lloyd George and Borden thereafter refused to countenance any prolongation of the British intervention in northern Russia or Siberia. Churchill was to continue for months to urge more, not less, Allied involvement, but he and to a lesser extent Balfour were virtually alone among British leaders in doing so.*

* *Maurice Hankey, the Secretary of the British War Cabinet, noted in his diary that Churchill "is quite barmy in his enthusiasm for the anti-Bolshevists" (quoted in Roskill, Hankey, vol. II, p. 115). Churchill was to remain throughout the post-war period the most vocal of the pro-interventionists. Hankey recorded in his diary on*

Following the rejection of his Prinkipo Proposal, Borden responded more energetically to the pleas from Ottawa for either withdrawal or, at the least, restrictions on the Canadian intervention in Siberia. He agreed to the demobilization of the troops still awaiting transport in Vancouver and he informed Churchill and Lloyd George on February 7 of his intention to withdraw all Canadians from Russia in April or as soon after that as it was feasible to do so.

Borden's initiative in attempting to bring together the warring factions in Russia was generally welcomed by Canadians when they became aware of it. William Kennedy, the Member of Parliament for North Essex, was in a small minority when he expressed in the House his regret that the "Earl of Prinkipo had appeared to be opening communications with [the Bolsheviks] and inviting them to meet decent people."

V   A Concept of Canada

Following the rejection of the Prinkipo idea by the indignant Whites, Borden began to take steps to withdraw the Canadian troops from Russia, a policy that was popular at home. At a meeting of the British Empire delegation on February 17, 1919, he made his policy of withdrawal clear. Balfour had given a somewhat enigmatic review of his own thinking about Russia, ending with a statement implying a belief in some sort of moral commitment to help the White Russians and the various new

---

February 8, 1918, the conventional Tory reaction to Lloyd George's efforts to respond to the Russian Revolution with something other than bullets: "Ll.G., who is half a Bolshevist himself, wants to get into closer relations with them, and seems to have forgotten that they have shamefully broken Russia's solemn treaty with us, repudiated the enormous sums we have lent Russia, seized our property, allowed the guns we supplied to fall into the enemy's hands, and that they are engaged in a war against all civilized institutions. Cecil [Lord Robert Cecil, Parliamentary Under-Secretary for Foreign Affairs] on the other hand is too much anti-Bolshevik. Balfour [Foreign Secretary], as usual, rather on the hedge between these" (quoted in Roskill, Hankey, vol. I, pp. 493-4).

border states. Churchill had then made a long exposition in which he noted the difficulties of using conscripts in a major intervention in Russia, and, accordingly, urged that supplies and volunteers be provided to the White Russian forces, as the only alternative to leaving Russia to "stew in her own juice". Churchill is recorded as stating:

> It ought to be possible for our military experts to explore this proposal and determine, within a week or ten days, whether, within these limits, some active policy towards Russia was feasible and likely to be effective. He had therefore pressed for the institution of an Inter-Allied Military Commission for this purpose.

Borden followed immediately with what was to be his last major statement on Allied policy towards Russia. The following is from the minutes of the meeting:

> There was much strong feeling on the subject in Canada. It was with great difficulty that he [Borden] had been able, after the Armistice, to secure the agreement of his Government to go on sending troops to Siberia. The Canadian Parliament would open on the 20th of the present month, and there would undoubtedly be demands to know what purpose these troops were serving in Russia and how long it was proposed to keep them there. Canadian public opinion had not yet been convinced that it was necessary to send troops to Russia, and he was absolutely certain that public opinion would never sanction the use of the Military Service Act for the purpose of military operations in Russia. He appreciated the view-point expressed by the Secretary of State for War, but there were other considerations to be borne in mind. The telegrams and papers received on the subject invariably disclosed that the anti-Bolsheviks in Russia themselves admitted that they could not fight alone. That meant that if we should embark upon any active operations against Russia, however limited, we might inevitably be drawn into a course whose consequences it was impossible to foresee. Public opinion would certainly not sanction our embarking upon such a hazard. As for the policy of waiting on the chance that the Bolsheviks might weaken, there was little to give confidence in that direction and there was much to indicate its extreme peril.
> His conclusions on the whole were that the Russian pot would simply have to boil, that Russia would have to work out her own

salvation. At first he had been dismayed at the thought of the Peace Conference adjourning without the Russian question being settled, but he remembered that France, at her Revolution, had suffered for over a decade and that what we were seeing in Russia to-day was doubtless the result of long years of slavery and misery in Russia under the pre-revolutionary autocracy. It might even be an open question whether Russia's present misery was really worse than her former state. Further, it ought to be considered whether there was not some indication that Bolshevism was becoming more moderate, or, if that was not yet so, whether, if Russia were left to herself, Bolshevism might not tend in the direction of moderation through the influence of those Russians who would then, having no other alternative, be driven to join the Bolshevik ranks.

At all events, even if there was no hope in this direction, and even if it were necessary to face the possibility that Germany might gain a dominant position in Russia, he felt that the case had been so presented to the world, or had so presented itself, that it would be impossible to persuade the Canadian Parliament to undertake any active operations however limited, and it was, therefore, necessary for him to say to the Imperial War Cabinet that the Canadian troops would have to be withdrawn in the spring, or, at the latest, in the early summer.

While Borden made it abundantly clear that Canada would not participate further in any Allied intervention in Russia, he did not oppose the decision of the British Empire delegation to press on the other Allies Churchill's somewhat vague suggestion for an Inter-Allied Military Commission. It was, however, received coolly and proved to be still-born. As the periodic report of the Canadian delegation to the Canadian cabinet noted tersely on February 22, "Thus the question of future policy in Russia is still undetermined."

During the three months between his long statement of February 17 and his final departure from Paris for Ottawa on May 14, Borden did not again participate actively in the dwindling debate on what to do about the Russian enigma. He was, however, as conscious as anyone at the Peace Conference of the fundamental threat communism posed to the established institutions of the West. Unrest and agitation in Canada about post-war conditions were growing, but the situation was far more severe in Europe. The Peace Conference appeared to be making little progress, while the flood of communism seemed to be moving daily farther westward. On March 20 Borden wrote to Lloyd George: "Every hour's delay in arranging the preliminaries of peace is fraught with the possibility of evil and even of disaster." Later, he opposed the severe measures against Germany that some urged, since impossible demands might encourage the rise of Bolshevism in Germany and create there a dangerous inclination to co-operate with Russia.

Five months after Borden returned to Canada, Lloyd George gave his Guildhall speech of November 8 in which he stated flatly his government's conviction that Britain had given the Russian people "the opportunity, if Russia wished to be liberated, of equipping her sons in order to free themselves . . . we cannot, of course, afford to continue so costly an intervention in an interminable civil war." That stated, Lloyd George moved decisively, if sometimes deviously, to place the relations of Russia and Britain on a more normal footing. (Within eight months a trade agreement would be reached and *de facto* recognition accorded.)

On December 16, 1919, Lloyd George wired Borden about the final stage of the Peace Conference's intermittent consideration of the Russian question. During the previous days, Lloyd George noted, the Allies had agreed among themselves that none would enter into further commitments in Russia, although missions either to governments or to military forces might continue. Siberia was disposed of by the simple statement that it was "to be dealt with by agreement between the United States and Japan. Conference was agreed that no useful purpose could be served by summoning a general conference of anti-Bolshevik communities at the present time." The Peace Conference had never been able to deal effectively with the problems that Soviet Russia posed. The conference's final disposition of the subject was a suitably inconclusive end to its long and inconclusive discussions.

Months before, Borden had clearly stated his ideas about the

Russian problem in meetings of the British Empire delegation to the Peace Conference. Having become convinced of the futility of military intervention after the Armistice, he took the lead in the Imperial War Cabinet and in the British Empire delegation in urging an Allied-sponsored, all-Russian peace conference. His idealistic proposal had appeared naïve to some, in the light of the bitter animosities the civil war had aroused, but it represented a significant excursion by Canada into international affairs beyond the hitherto traditional bounds of the North Atlantic. When his idea failed to win wide support and was rejected by the Whites, Borden promptly demanded the withdrawal of the Canadian troops in Russia. He was not deterred by the consideration that, without them, two British battalions already in Siberia would be deprived of essential support services. He knew that they, too, would have to be withdrawn. It was Borden who took the practical steps to terminate intervention by the British Empire in Siberia.

A student of Canada's Imperial attitudes has written:

> Many factors limited and curtailed the appeal of imperialism [in Canada]: the First World War killed it. Military co-operation between the dominions and Great Britain encouraged some hope in the early stages of that conflict that permanent means of union would soon be formalized. . . . Such expectations quickly vanished as the early enthusiasm for participation in the war changed to disenchantment and disillusionment. By 1918 fifty thousand Canadians were dead in Europe and that fact overshadowed and dominated all discussions of Empire, imperialism, and Canadian nationality.[21]

At the end of the war, Borden noted in his diary that the time had come for Canada to assume full sovereignty, externally as well as internally. He won the support of the Imperial War Cabinet for separate Canadian representation at the Paris Peace Conference and later obtained international recognition of the sovereign status of Canada within the Empire through separate membership in the League of Nations and the International Labour Organization. But to say this is not to say that Borden was set on a course of demonstrating to the world Canada's independence of Britain. Nor, on the other hand, was he a convert to the "Round Table" theories of British imperialism; he was as sceptical of schemes for Imperial federation as Laurier had been before him. He did not seek an Imperial parliament or council to direct Imperial foreign policy. What he did seek was an assurance that Canada's voice would be heard in the councils of a co-operative Empire. Each autonomous dominion would then decide on the responsibilities it would assume in the context of the Imperial co-operation of like-minded states.

In each of the three areas of Russia—north, south, and east— where Canadian troops served, Borden personally sanctioned their assignment because he believed that Canada had an obligation to the Empire when Britain first consulted the Dominions, as it had done in the Imperial War Cabinet. This was a fundamentally different attitude from the one Mackenzie King was to exhibit during the Chanak crisis of 1922, when Churchill sought Canadian support for armed resistance to a Turkish advance into an international neutral zone on the Bosphorus. On that occasion, King looked for a confirmation of Canadian autonomy, rather than for an opportunity to review mutual obligations within a co-operative Commonwealth.

Borden did not discern any basic conflict between Canadian nationalism and the interests of the British Empire. As he defined it, British imperialism was an expression of Canadian nationalism. The constitutional relationship between the dominions and the Empire was for Borden a dynamic relationship requiring constant redefinition. For those Canadians who survived the fighting on the Caspian, the rigours of the subarctic winter, or the boredom of Vladivostok, the evolution of constitutional arrangements within the Empire was hardly of first concern. Canadian participation in the Allied intervention in the Russian civil war was nevertheless an occasion for the clarification and resolution of some of the ambiguities that the Great War had revealed in the relationship between Britain and Canada.

During the war, Borden developed a concept of Canada as a state having full sovereignty under the Crown, consulting with Britain and with the other dominions that shared a common heritage. It was a creative, imaginative concept, and from it arose—among other things—the duty of Canada to participate in the Allied intervention in Russia. And Borden was never a man to shirk what he conceived to be his duty—or that of his country.

Canadian Airmen with the Volunteer Army

Canadians served in the Caspian and White Sea areas and in Siberia with the express agreement of the Canadian government. In the north and in Siberia, Ottawa took a mounting interest in the welfare and role of the Canadian troops. However, there was another group of Canadians in Russia, more numerous than those with Dunsterforce, who were ignored by Ottawa, since they were members of the Royal Air Force and not in any way connected with the Canadian forces. All were volunteers and all were entirely under the orders of London.

They were the last Canadians to leave Russia (in March 1920) and their adventures were, in many ways, the most bizarre of all of the estimated 6,000 Canadians who participated in the Allied military intervention. No account of Canadian involvement in the Russian civil war is complete without a description of their service.

In the great plains to the north of the Black Sea, there had been formed, by 1918, a "Volunteer Army" composed of White Russian forces led first by Generals Alekseyev and Kornilov and, after their deaths, by General Anton Denikin. Making common cause with the Volunteer Army, although suspicious of the real intentions of its officers, were the Kuban and Don Cossacks, who were primarily concerned about protecting their lands from non-Cossack people. "Denikin was no great strategist, but he had patience and utter integrity and under him the Volunteer Army developed into the most formidable single military challenge to the Soviet regime in the whole Civil War."[1]

By the summer of 1919, its strength had grown to a point where Denikin hazarded a drive northward on Moscow, an offensive that was intended to be related—in some ill-defined way—to Kolchak's westward advance from Siberia. The British War Office again demonstrated its eagerness to aid any promising White Russian force, in this case despite an obvious lack of support from the workers and peasants of southern Russia, who rightly suspected the leaders of the Volunteer Army of reactionary views. Major-General F. C. Poole, after his transfer from Archangel, was one of a group of British liaison officers at Denikin's headquarters who successfully recommended to London the provision of money, munitions, equipment, and training staff, including flying and tank instructors.*

The Royal Air Force instructional unit, well supplied with two-seater aircraft and other equipment, initially restricted itself to establishing a training school at Ekaterinodar (Krasnodar), about sixty miles from the Black Sea. But training was only of long-term assistance. It could not, of course, immediately render Denikin's forces immune to attack by Bolshevik pilots or by the few ex-German air force pilots who flew with them. It was equally obvious that air support would be of vital importance in open warfare across the steppes towards Moscow.

No. 47 Squadron of the R.A.F. was assigned to Denikin's operational command, in theory until such time as the White Russians were ready to take to the air. During 1918, the squadron had served with distinction against the Bulgars in Macedonia. In April and May 1919, after overhauling its aircraft,

---

* Poole was at the headquarters of Denikin (1872-1947) from November 1918 to February 1919. From the beginning of 1919, Britain supplied to Denikin's forces more than 500 artillery pieces, 250,000 rifles, thirty tanks, 1,500,000 shells, and 160,000,000 rounds of ammunition. The United States and France also sent sizeable shipments of surplus matériel. Some of the British tank instructors, like the pilot instructors, were soon in action.

the squadron moved from Salonika to Novorossiisk on the Black Sea, and from there flew its first sorties against the Red Army.*

Over the open plains north of the Black Sea, the squadron soon proved itself a potent weapon against the Red Army. The senior R.A.F. officer in southern Russia was able to report prompt and significant results—and also to note a possible dividend for British aviation if the Whites should regain control of Russia:

> The moral influence of British flying units at the Front has been tremendous and the prestige of Great Britain has been still further enhanced. The result has also been to put the future of commercial aviation in this country completely at the will of Great Britain in view of the unique opportunity that will be offered here for commercial aviation. This is no small matter.[2]

Most of the men of No. 47 Squadron who had served in the Balkans were to be demobilized. A new commanding officer was appointed who visited R.A.F. stations in Britain, selecting replacements from among the many volunteers. More than 200 officers and men, mostly veterans from the Western Front, crossed France in a special train and in Italy boarded a steamer bound for Constantinople. From there they made their way across the Black Sea to Novorossiisk.

The new commanding officer was only twenty-six, and he wore the ribbons of the D.S.O., D.S.C., D.F.C., Croix de Guerre, and several other decorations on his tunic. A brilliant leader, Major Raymond Collishaw was a top Allied "ace" of the war, with sixty German aircraft to his credit. His home was in Nanaimo, British Columbia.† He was one of a small number of

---

* An account of the Squadron's first months in Russia as well as its earlier service in the Macedonian theatre is in H. A. Jones, Over the Balkans (London: Arnold, 1923). At the same time that No. 47 Squadron was assigned to Ekaterinador, No. 221 Squadron and "A" Flight of No. 17 Squadron were sent to Batum where it co-operated with the Royal Navy in driving Bolshevik shipping from the Caspian Sea. Some of the pilots from these two squadrons later joined No. 47 Squadron in the Black Sea area.

† Collishaw had served for seven years in Pacific fisheries patrol vessels of the Department of Naval Service before joining the Royal Naval Air Service in 1915.

wartime fliers who had been offered permanent commissions in the R.A.F. at the end of the war. Upon returning to England from leave in Canada, he was appointed to command No. 47 Squadron. "I now was a career RAF officer; what I had thus far heard about the Bolshies led me to believe that they were a thoroughly bad lot, and I accepted [the command of No. 47 Squadron] without hesitation."[3]

By June 18, 1919, when Collishaw and his 265 volunteers from England had congregated in Novorossiisk, they were joined by others from R.A.F. units in the Middle East, as well as from No. 47 Squadron itself. Collishaw's party included "many famous pilots and mechanics who were keen for hard work and adventure. They were, before the campaign ended, to need all their skill and faith and courage."[4] Their aircraft (mainly well-worn De Havilland 9s) arrived from Malta and from several Middle East bases where they had been flown against the Turks. Both men and machines were in such ample supply that Collishaw soon found himself commanding a unit as big as three standard R.A.F. squadrons. All R.A.F. personnel in southern Russia came under Lieutenant-Colonel (Acting Brigadier-General) A. C. Maund, who had been in Russia from early 1917 on an air training mission. Maund had been in Canada at the outbreak of war, had enlisted as a private in the Canadian army, and had flown with the Royal Flying Corps since early 1916.

The fighting that awaited Collishaw and his pilots and observers—among whom were about twenty Canadians—was totally unlike that on the Western Front. There was little aerial combat, because the Bolsheviks had few aircraft. On the ground, the stagnant life of trench warfare was unknown. Great distances were often covered in a short time, especially by the cavalry. Ground support work was constantly demanded of the fliers as Denikin's forces began to move rapidly northward from the Black Sea. There could be no question of No. 47 Squadron supporting them from fixed bases. The rail-line did, however, enable the airmen to more or less keep pace with the cavalry. Four special trains of fifty cars each were assigned to Collishaw's squadron, one for each of its three flights and one for its headquarters staff. Each train was equipped with workshops, mess-cars, and flat-cars for carrying the DH 9s. The trains were self-contained so that they could support the flights from sidings on the rail-line, near improvised airfields.

Three days before Collishaw officially assumed command of his nomadic squadron on June 13, the first of its three flights left Novorossiisk to support the right sector of Denikin's widespread army. There, from June 23, "A" Flight carried out daily bombing and strafing raids, whenever heavy rains permitted, to assist Baron Wrangel's force advancing on Czaritsyn.* One raid over Czaritsyn particularly pleased Denikin: a 112-pound bomb was dropped on a plenary session of the local Soviet, killing thirty-nine of its forty-one members. Collishaw himself was forced by the great amount of administrative work to remain at Novorossiisk and at his headquarters at Ekaterinodar from his arrival on June 8 until September 14.

At the end of June, after Wrangel's capture of Czaritsyn, "A" Flight moved on to Beketovka, where two Canadian aircrew were soon killed in a landing accident. "A" Flight was replaced by "C" Flight, which joined in the increasingly frequent encounters with enemy Fokkers, Spads, and Nieuports, some reportedly flown by German airmen. On July 30, a Canadian pilot and three other members of his flight on reconnaisance had a narrow escape. Collishaw wrote to a friend in Toronto,

> . . . we were out on a show attacking a flock of Red Cavalry, and one of my chaps named Elliott, flying at 500 feet, was shot down about six miles beyond the line. Neither he nor his observer was hurt. The observer kept the cavalry off with his Lewis gun until the pilot set the machine on fire. Then, carrying the Lewis gun, the two started away, keeping the cavalry at a respectful distance.
> Captain Anderson, another Canadian,† landed nearby amid the

---

* Subsequently Stalingrad (1925) and Volgagrad (1962).

† Captain Walter Fraser Anderson was the son of a Toronto clergyman. He was constantly in action and was wounded by machine-gun fire while on a strafing mission in October 1919. In late November, upon recovering from his wounds, he was appointed to command one of the flights. Anderson was killed in an accident in 1936 while chief pilot with British Airways.

enemy cavalry, he and his observer [John Mitchell] scattering them with their machine gun fire.

Elliott and his observer then set off to join the second pair, clearing the way with their Lewis gun. The Bolshies immediately surrounded the burning machine just as six Cooper bombs went off in it.

In the meantime, a Red bullet had punctured the gas tank of the rescue machine, so the observer climbed out on the wings, and held both holes on each side of the tank with his thumbs. Elliott and his observer got into the observer's seat, and away they went, four aboard the machine, and got home safely.[5]

Elliott and Mitchell were fortunate not to be captured. The Red Army, without many aircraft to protect itself, was highly vulnerable to air attack. Its threats of reprisal if an R.A.F. airman ever fell into its hands were vicious. He would be nailed to a tree by his testicles and disembowelled alive before being slashed to death by sabres. Fortunately, no R.A.F. pilot was ever captured, but by October, four airmen—including the two Canadians—had died in flying accidents and Captain J. L. McLennan of Montreal had died in combat.

While "C" Flight continued its operations over the Volga front, Collishaw and the remaining members of the squadron at Ekaterinodar readied "B" Flight. Stolen, lost, or damaged equipment delayed the deployment of its ex-Royal Navy Sopwith Camels, but Collishaw was satisfied that "B" Flight would finally be able to join "C" Flight by the end of September. Collishaw went into action himself on September 15, leaving to his headquarters staff the time-consuming task of trying to find enough serviceable equipment and parts to complete "B" Flight's equipment and to make "A" Flight operational.

From mid September, Collishaw flew at least once daily with "C" Flight. Before illness stopped him early in October (by which time he had already made thirty-seven sorties), he led the flight from the pilot's seat of a DH 9, bombing and strafing munition and other supply dumps, troop concentrations, and the river gunboats which had gathered on the Volga to attempt the recapture of Czaritsyn, and occasionally tangling with whatever aircraft the Red Army was able to send up.

While Collishaw had been readying the flights for action ("B" Flight joined "C" at the end of September), the pressures in Britain for the termination of intervention in Russia had intensified. Collishaw's unit was, however, neither withdrawn nor, as had been first proposed by the Air Ministry, changed into a purely instructional unit. Its R.A.F. squadron number was, however, dropped on October 1, 1919, when it was simply designated "A" Squadron of the R.A.F. Training Mission to Denikin. General Maund had protested to the War Office: "The value of this squadron, the damage it has done to the Bolsheviks, and the moral effect it has had on the Volunteer Army, are so great that to withdraw it will have a most deplorable effect. They are worth as much as the whole White Russian Air Force put together."[6]

On October 8 Maund informed Collishaw of the success of his appeal—and the conditions the Air Ministry had set in accepting it:

> Very expressive orders have been received . . . that 47 Squadron as a combat unit is to be disbanded by 1st October.
>
> However, they granted me a free hand as to the employment of your personnel from that date. You are, therefore, officially volunteering for service in Denikin's army at present. This state of affairs will continue until winter sets in. Of course, you will be unable to retain anybody who objects to serving in this manner as no grounds must be given for any public complaints in England later as to our policy in Russia. Therefore, I must be able to state that all of your unit have volunteered for service under that condition. . . .
>
> When winter sets in it is proposed that gradually Russian officers and men be drafted to you and instructed, and gradually take over the work of your unit. I should like your opinion on this suggestion because in view of the political situation at home it is impossible to maintain officially . . . any active service units and certainly none next year.[7]

Collishaw readily agreed with Maund's plans, since most of his men had volunteered to stay on and since he was himself convinced of the military value of the work they were doing. "Our attacks on Red Cavalry on the open steppes, as well as on infantry, caused the Bolsheviks serious losses and there is no doubt that the advance of the White Armies owed much to the work done by my detachment."[8] The Camels of "B" Flight were particularly effective in their support of White cavalry.

> Troop concentrations, transports, artillery, armoured trains and other targets were dive-bombed and strafed. . . . Many of their strikes—some of which I participated in myself, flying one of the Camels—were flown in co-operation with the Cossack General Ulayai, who commanded Wrangel's cavalry corps. The Camels would go in first, bombing and strafing the enemy, and Ulayai would then follow up with a wild cavalry charge, sabres flashing as the White horsemen descended on the by-now disorganized Reds. Ulayai's forces came from different parts of South Russia, some wearing the traditional Cossack garb and others sporting even more picturesque uniforms. Some came from Moslem areas and galloped into battle with their green banners, enscribed with sayings from the Koran, streaming overhead. Watching one of these cavalry charges from the cockpit of a Camel was an exhilarating but odd sensation, almost as if one had suddenly turned the controls of some Wellsian time machine and was watching a battle that had taken place a hundred years or more before.[9]

The change in their squadron designation meant little to Collishaw and his men. Joined by DH 9s of "A" Flight early in October, they made sorties almost daily. Collishaw's personal involvement in combat came to a temporary end during the second week of October, shortly after he had shot down an Albatros D-V.

Fever prostrated Collishaw. The R.A.F. medical officer quickly diagnosed a suspected case of typhus, a disease fast becoming epidemic in southern Russia. He was placed on a train for Ekaterinodar, under the care of two sick airmen who became immobilized *en route* with dysentery. In the small village of Verikourarjjevskaya where the train stopped, an elderly refugee countess chanced to hear of the plight of the now-delirious Collishaw and asked that he be carried to her hut so that she might care for him. Through several weeks of near-fatal illness, the old woman nursed Collishaw. "Anyone who has any conception of typhus," Collishaw later wrote, "will be able to imagine what she must have endured as an act of grace in nursing a strange, unconscious man for several weeks in a one-room cabin."[10] General Maund soon learned where Collishaw was, but he could do little to help him, since to move him would be more dangerous than to leave him in the village. Maund had to content himself with sending Collishaw a case of champagne, the traditional British army stimulant for convalescents.

When Collishaw was finally well enough to resume command of his squadron on November 27, the Volunteer Army had already succeeded in reaching Orel, less than 250 miles south of Moscow, capturing almost a quarter of a million prisoners during the offensive. It had been a daring advance, but it soon proved a precarious one. The Volunteer Army was rife with political disputes, strategic controversy, and disease. Weak supply lines were impossibly strained, with the result that Denikin's exhausted troops had had neither the will nor the equipment to hold the Red Army when White reverses on other fronts permitted the reinforcing of the southern front during mid October.

Collishaw ascribed the White reverse to another factor. He shared with many Canadians who served in Russia a decidedly low opinion of the White officers.

> The officers were a mixed bag. Some were charming and energetic persons, highly dedicated to their cause. Others were merely charming and some lacked even this trait, being good for little more than gracing the sidewalk cafés of Ekaterinodar with their immaculately turned out persons . We were very close to RAF Training Mission, whose job it was to teach the Russians to fly and to help them in forming squadrons from the RE8's and equipment provided by the British. . . . Many of their students were hopelessly inept and others resented taking instruction from officers of lesser rank than themselves.
>
> . . . I recall seeing infantry regiments leaving for the front, the feet of most of the men wrapped in rags. Not because there were no boots—they had been supplied by the British—but because someone had simply not taken the trouble or was not able to have them issued from the stores depot to the regiment. Special trains rolled over the tracks, filled with the entourage and possessions of

senior officers while combat units at the front went short of
desperately needed ammunition and supplies.[11]

After the Bolsheviks recaptured Orel, the over-extended front
of the Volunteer Army crumbled quickly. Denikin had staked
everything on his gamble to be in Moscow by Christmas. He had
failed. And gradually the support of the Cossacks had waned.
Once the Bolsheviks had been driven from their homeland,
differences between the Cossack leaders and Denikin's tsarist
officers reappeared and became even more acute. Others in the
Volunteer Army were discouraged by the reactionary ideas
advocated by many of its officers. On the eve of an anticipated
triumphant entry into Moscow, Denikin alienated many of his
followers or potential supporters by increasingly reactionary
statements, further undermining the already shaky coalition he
led. The Red Army, in contrast, was growing in strength and
confidence. As Winston Churchill noted with regret at the time,

> ... the Bolsheviks succeeded in gradually developing their armies.
> These armies were far weaker than the forces potentially opposed
> to them; but, as they lay in the centre of the circle, and could,
> subject to the limits of their transportation, throw their weight from
> one part of its circumference to the other, they have been able to
> attack in detail and in many cases to overwhelm the forces opposed
> to them. Thus, while Denikin was getting on his feet Koltchak [sic]
> was broken and defeated. ... During the last three months the very
> large numbers of men which the Bolsheviks were able to transfer
> from in front of Koltchak, from in front of the Poles, and from in
> front of the Baltic States ... have given them a large superiority of
> numbers over Denikin. His army ... spread out in practically a
> single line on a front of more than 1,200 miles, has now been
> thrown back everywhere by these superior forces.[12]

Against this background of White squabbling and Red victory,
all three R.A.F. flights were ordered to Kharkov to help hold
the Bolshevik advance there. "A" and "B" flights reached the
Kharkov front, but "C" Flight was unable to leave before the
pressure of another Bolshevik advance made it imperative that
it remain on the Volga front. After arrival in Kharkov in early

December, the RE 8s, Camels, and DH 9s of "A" and "B" flights were unable to fly more than a few sorties. The White retreat was so rapid that the aircraft had to be dismantled and placed back aboard the trains almost as soon as they had been assembled. "B" Flight's Camels were in any case so in need of a re-fit that they had to be withdrawn to Taganrog on the Sea of Azov. They saw no more action. Denikin's forces, plagued by dissension and disease, and encountering the worst winter in forty years, collapsed so quickly that several aircraft and quantities of supplies had to be destroyed to prevent them from falling into the hands of the advancing Red Army.

On the Kharkov front, Collishaw provided what air support he could for the retreating Volunteer Army. His RE 8s of "C" Flight and of "Z" Flight, hurriedly formed from among the remaining members of the R.A.F. instructional mission, fought constantly as they fell back along the rail-line. One of Collishaw's officers later described their fighting retreat amidst the chaos of the White collapse:

> ... the method adopted was ... to start up the aircraft and fly down
> the line a distance of 20 to 50 miles ... it was the duty of the senior
> pilot to pick a flat piece of ground with a railway siding near it,
> land, and stop the train when it arrived, which might be hours or
> even days. The train was put in the siding and operations would
> begin. If the weather was too bad for the aircraft to be flown and
> it was imperative to move at once, they had to be partially
> dismantled and loaded onto flat trucks. With practice this operation
> could be carried out very rapidly.[13]

The weather deteriorated as White discipline and resistance collapsed. Snow prevented further flights against the Bolsheviks. The aircraft were loaded aboard the trains which then made their way toward Rostov, the only rail-bridge crossing of the Don. The White retreat was rapidly becoming a rout as the terrible winter deepened. "Z" Flight managed to cross the river at Rostov, but "A" Flight and Collishaw's headquarters train were so delayed by refugees clogging the line that they had to abandon any plans for further operations and make instead for Denikin's last stronghold in the Crimea. Collishaw wrote later:

Conditions on the railways were almost indescribable. There was neither fuel nor water for the locomotives. The people along the route had become intensely hostile and anxious to welcome the Reds. Forces of hostile irregulars were operating freely across the lines of communication. There were no trains going in the direction of the enemy—all were making their way as fast as they could in the other direction. The R.A.F. train was armed with aircraft machine gun turrets mounted on the roofs of some of the cars. The normal train crews had gone over to the Reds and airmen served as engineers and firemen on the two locomotives that pulled our train. As an act of mercy we had taken aboard several hundred Russian officers' wives and children and they now became a source of embarrassment to us. Typhus had broken out and they hid their dead on the train, rather than throw the corpses on to the edge of the right of way as I had ordered. This was perhaps a brutal order but it was necessary, for we could not afford to stop and dig graves in the hard-frozen ground.[14]

As Collishaw's train began its slow trip southward, Rostov fell to Red cavalry. A Red armoured train soon was on the heels of the R.A.F. train, but, despite such obstacles as tracks torn up by hostile peasants, Collishaw was able to keep just out of the range of its heavy gun. At Bolshoi-Tomak, about 100 miles north of the Black Sea, where Collishaw's train had stopped for fuel, the Bolsheviks jammed open the throttle of a locomotive and sent it crashing into the rear of the R.A.F. train. "Our train was turned into a shambles," Collishaw recalled. "The wooden trucks were telescoped but the steel coaches withstood the shock. Herculean efforts were required to thrust the smashed trucks off the rails and to join up the surviving steel coaches. Somehow it was done and the remnants of our train moved off towards the Crimea."[15]

At a speed of no more than ten miles an hour—and often much less—Collishaw's train made its way southward, through hordes of refugees carrying with them the typhus that decimated them as they struggled towards Ekaterinodar and the Crimea. The horror of the journey later became the background for a dramatic novel written by one of Collishaw's pilots, a young flyer from California,* but there was no exaggeration in his descriptions of the danger in which the R.A.F. and the Whites found themselves.

On January 4, 1920, the nightmare journey of the flyers came to an end as their train crossed into the Crimea. Where the Perekop peninsula joins the Crimea to the mainland, and where the guns of British warships could prevent a final Red advance, Denikin attempted to re-form his rapidly dwindling army. At Sevastopol, Collishaw obtained enough coal from a British warship to take his train to Simferopol, where there was a small White Russian aircraft repair base. There Collishaw assembled and repaired his DH 9As, along with a number of DH 9s that had been given to the White Russians. In mid February, the flights moved on to Djankoi, a town on the rail-line in the northern Crimea. From there, Collishaw flew reconnaissance sorties over the Bolshevik lines, personally choosing targets for his aircraft. "C" and "Z" flights were also in the air, flying from Ekaterinodar.

But it was to no avail. It was everywhere evident that Denikin was fighting a lost cause. Time was clearly on the side of the Bolsheviks. Dissension, the lack of supplies, sickness, and low morale had undermined the White forces. Collishaw himself became involved in the omnipresent squabbling when a new Cossack leader at Simferopol suddenly and inexplicably announced his intention to expel the R.A.F. from Russia. Equally promptly Collishaw threw the Cossack leader and his immediate followers into jail, only to find that the next White Russian general assigned to the command was both an alcoholic and a drug addict. Nevertheless, the R.A.F. flights fought on through March, Collishaw alone making seventeen sorties, strafing and bombing Red targets, while Denikin reorganized his beleaguered forces in the Crimea.

The Red Army no longer encountered much real resistance. It captured Ekaterinodar, from where "C" and "Z" flights escaped in the chaotic evacuation through the port of Novoros-

* *Marion Aten,* Last Train over Rostov Bridge *(New York: Messner, 1961).*

siisk, the same bleak port in which they had disembarked almost a year before.* Richard Ullman, in the third volume of his definitive study of Anglo-Soviet relations following the revolution, has well described the final chaos and terror:

> After 9 March . . . all thought of serious resistance was abandoned; now there was only a race to reach the sea at Novorossiisk before the Red Army could get there. Fighting sporadic rearguard actions, often more a rabble than a disciplined military force, the remnants of the Volunteer Army and the Don Cossacks (who had mostly remained loyal to Denikin) made their way, together with hordes of civilian fugitives, towards the fuelless, typhus-ridden, already jammed port. The twentieth century has witnessed many such scenes of refugee masses fleeing towards the sea to escape an oncoming army; the evacuation of Novorossiisk was one of the first and one of the most terrible.
>
> As in every such evacuation, there were innumerably more refugees than there were places on the ships, both foreign and Russian, in Novorossiisk harbor. That some semblance of order was preserved was due in large measure to the presence of the nearly 2,000 officers and men of the British military mission. Many of them had been stationed in Novorossiisk itself, which had been the port of entry for nearly all of the British military supplies sent to Denikin's forces. The greater number, however, including R.A.F. and tank contingents and liaison officers and instructors of every sort, had shared in the victories and defeats of the White armies throughout South Russia. As they converged upon Novorossiisk along the choked railway lines they joined in the rearguard fighting. Once in the town, they patrolled the streets around the waterfront.
>
> They also worked to destroy the vast quantities of British military supplies that had been discharged—some of it months previously—and left standing on the quays because of the chaos and lack of organization that prevailed in the rear of the White forces. New De Havilland 9 bombing aircraft, still in their packing cases, were pushed to the end of a pier to be pulverized by tanks. When their duties of destruction were completed the tanks were sent

* *On March 2, 1920, ninety-three officers and 291 other ranks of the Royal Air Force were still with Denikin's forces, along with 301 officers and 1,238 other ranks from the army and navy (Ullman, Anglo-Soviet Accord, p. 67, citing Churchill, 126 House of Commons Debates, col. 221).*

waddling off the docks into the bay, there to be joined by rows of field guns stripped of their breech-blocks. In all, something like £10,000,000 worth of supplies was either destroyed or left to the invading Bolsheviks. . . .

The evacuation was completed in the early hours of 27 March. During the previous month some 10,000 refugees and 3,000 ill and wounded soldiers had been removed, largely on British transports. In the forty-eight hours following 25 March Russian ships, using coal brought by the British from Constantinople, evacuated over 60,000 people, and on the night of 26-27 March another 10,000 troops of Denikin's army, together with the British military mission, were removed on British warships.[16]

From Djankoi in the Crimea Collishaw carried out one last reconnaissance flight on March 30, turned his aircraft over to the White Russians, and embarked with the remainder of his men, as ordered by the Air Ministry, for Constantinople and England. Their departure marked the end of the involvement of the R.A.F.—and Canadians—in the Russian civil war. Convinced that Denikin's government had failed to demonstrate any ability to win popular support, the British government ended its assistance to him. Although Denikin continued, indirectly, to receive small amounts of Allied aid, he was officially informed on April 2, 1920, of the termination of all British co-operation. Under Baron Peter Wrangel, who succeeded Denikin on April 4, the White Russians held on in the Crimea through the summer of 1920, despite repeated urgings by the British government to negotiate a settlement with Moscow (with which London itself was beginning the discussions that were soon to lead to an Anglo-Soviet trade agreement). By November 20, Wrangel's troops were finally overwhelmed, following an initial successful foray inland, and the last outpost of the Whites in southern Russia passed under Soviet control.

Collishaw's own fighting against the Bolsheviks was not, however, finished. Within eight months of escaping from southern Russia and after three months' home leave in Canada, he was appointed to command No. 30 Squadron, R.A.F., operating in Persia as part of the North Persian Force under the over-all direction of Major-General Sir Edmund Ironside.

Ironside, after his return to London from his mission to Archangel, and from other missions to Hungary and Turkey, had been assigned an equally difficult task when he had been given command of "Norper" Force in October 1920.

The British government, the government of India, and especially the Foreign Secretary, Lord Curzon (who had succeeded Balfour in October 1919), had always been nervous about any Russian move in the direction of India. The "First Congress of the Peoples of the East" in Baku in September 1920 and the activities of the Pan-Hindu Revolutionary Committee in Tashkent now seemed to give tangible form to Lenin's announced intention of stirring the Indian masses to revolt. In addition, Dunsterville's erstwhile antagonist, Kuchik Khan, had become convinced that he could achieve his nationalist goals by accepting, temporarily, Soviet assistance for his struggle to expel the British and other foreigners from Persia. More than a year before, the Anglo-Persian Treaty of August 9, 1919, had been intended to give Britain a special status in Persia. The treaty had not, however, been ratified by the Persian Assembly, which with reason regarded it as relegating Persia to the status of little more than a British protectorate.

Although Norper Force (consisting of one British and three Indian infantry battalions, a squadron of cavalry, and a field and mountain battery) had been in northern Persia since before Dunsterville's withdrawal from Baku in September 1918, its role had been largely a passive one, a safeguard against any attempt by the Bolsheviks to reassert pre-war Russian influence in northern Persia. In this role it was not entirely successful. In May 1920, Curzon's worst fears about what the Bolsheviks intended were deepened by the Red Army's sudden seizure of the port of Enzeli and its expulsion of the small British garrison there. The Red units soon moved inland toward Kasvin, along the same route Dunsterville had followed northward more than two years before. Ironside was hurriedly sent to Persia early in October, to do whatever he could to stem any further Red advance, hinder Soviet assistance to Kuchik Khan, and encourage the establishment of a viable pro-British government in Teheran. Ironside was provided with no resources additional to those already in Persia and in any case was aware that, given budgetary restraints at home and in India, and the need for troops elsewhere in the Empire, Norper Force would be withdrawn in the spring of 1921.

The winter of 1920-1 had already set in when Collishaw and part of No. 30 Squadron arrived in Kasvin to assist Ironside's limited ground forces. By using pack animals to tread down the snow on rough fields in the mountains, they were able to launch a few reconnaissance and bombing flights against the Red Army along the Caspian littoral, despite the severe winter weather. When the weather permitted them to move their advanced base towards the coast, they also flew their DH 9s and Camels against Bolshevik shipping in the Caspian.

> . . . our most valuable work [Collishaw wrote later] was reconnaissance. We were able to determine that the Bolsheviks, the counter-revolutionary movement by now crushed, had been able to move very strong forces into the area and that it was but a matter of time before a major onslaught would be launched against Ironside. It was a case of either being prepared to fight a major operation or withdraw and wisely the British government took the latter course. We withdrew as soon as snow conditions permitted, in the spring of 1921.[17]

Acutely conscious of budgetary pressures at home, and realizing that there was no further hope of the Assembly in Teheran ratifying the Anglo-Persian Treaty, the British government in the spring of 1921 took the calculated risk that, if British troops were withdrawn, the Red Army would also march out as envisaged in the terms of the Soviet-Persian Treaty of February 1921. In April, as part of the withdrawal, No. 30 Squadron was ordered to fly to an R.A.F. base in Mesopotamia. Direct British military confrontation with the Bolsheviks in Persia thus ended, as well as Raymond Collishaw's own long service against them.*

---

* Collishaw's subsequent career in the R.A.F. kept him in the Middle East for many of the years between the First and Second World Wars. After also serving in aircraft carriers, he distinguished himself in the Second World War in command of the R.A.F. units flying against the Italians in the Western Desert. He retired from the R.A.F. at the end of the War as an air vice-marshal.

In September 1921, Moscow also withdrew its troops from northern Persia, partly in the belief that there was more to be gained by carrying on world revolution by means less direct than the troublesome occupation of foreign territory.

Gregori Semenov

By the early spring of 1922, it was obvious to Gregori Semenov that neither he nor his mentors, the Japanese, had any future, at least in the short run, in Siberia. Semenov and his wife arrived in Vancouver on March 14, 1922, *en route* to the United States and France.

Semenov was not granted immediate permission to enter the United States, having to submit first to a Board of Special Inquiry of the United States Immigration Service in Vancouver. Possibly at Semenov's request, three former Canadian army officers came forward to vouch for his good character.

Major-General R. G. Leckie, the officer commanding the British Columbia and Yukon Military District when the Canadians sailed for Siberia (and a brother of Colonel J. E. Leckie of the Murmansk force), wrote to the inspector-in-charge of the United States Immigration Service in Vancouver that he felt from his "personal observations" that Semenov had never sanctioned any brutality towards either enemy or Allied troops or civilians. Considering that Leckie had not served in Russia, and given the abundant evidence of Semenov's complicity in acts of the greatest brutality (United States Army Intelligence estimated that Semenov was responsible for 30,000 executions in one year), this is a surprising statement.

Colonel John Warden, formerly of Dunsterforce and of the British Military Mission in Vladivostok, contended in a letter to the board that Semenov's subordinates were responsible for the atrocities. Lieutenant John Samuel Atkinson of Toronto (who had served with the British Red Cross in Siberia from the departure of the Canadian force until January 1921) urged that Semenov be allowed to enter the United States and, for good measure, also recommended to the Canadian immigration authorities that Semenov be allowed to remain in Canada if he so wished. The Canadian Superintendent of Immigration subsequently so ruled.

Ten days after Semenov had disembarked in Vancouver, the United States Immigration inquiry board granted him permission to enter the United States as a visitor. In explaining his decision, the inspector-in-charge noted: "He has been entertained while here by businessmen at the best clubs in the city." However, Semenov's presence in the United States was not welcome to certain Americans. Their protests resulted in an early hearing by the Committee on Education and Labor of the United States Senate. The efforts of this committee to determine how Semenov had been granted permission to enter the United States and, as background, to gather accurate information about his activities in Siberia resulted in Semenov's early departure for France and, incidentally, brought to light the curious intervention on his behalf by Leckie, Warden, and Atkinson.*

After spending much of the inter-war period in Europe, living on his plunder from Siberia, Semenov returned to Manchuria during the Second World War as a puppet ruler again under the Japanese. He was captured and executed by the Red Army in 1945.

* *This information is from "Deportation of Gregorie Semenoff–Hearings before the Committee on Education and Labor" (United States Senate, Sixty-seventh Congress, Second Session, April 12-18, 1922, Part I, Washington, Government Printing Office), which is a record of only the first hearings of the Committee. Unfortunately, neither the Senate nor the Library of Congress has been able to find any record of Part II of the proceedings–if it was ever published.*

Bibliography

Books

Ackerman, Carl W., *Trailing the Bolsheviki*. New York, Scribner's, 1919.

Albertson, R., *Fighting Without a War*. New York, Harcourt, Brace and Howe, 1920.

Allen, W. E. D., and Paul Muratoff, *Caucasian Battlefields. A History of the Wars on the Turco-Caucasian Border, 1828-1921*. Cambridge, at the University Press, 1953.

Anon., *N.R.E.F., 16th Brigade CFA*. Toronto, n.d.

Appleton, Thomas E., *Usque ad Mare*. Ottawa, Queen's Printer, Department of Transport, 1968.

Aten, Marion, and Arthur Orrmont, *Last Train over Rostov Bridge*. New York, Messner, 1961.

Balawyder, Aloysius, *Canadian-Soviet Relations between the World Wars*. Toronto, University of Toronto Press, 1972.

Barker, A. J., *The Neglected War: Mesopotamia, 1914-1918*. London, Faber and Faber, 1967.

Beckhofer, C. E., *In Denikin's Russia and the Caucasus, 1919-1920*. London, Collins, n.d.

Bell, James Mackintosh, *Side Lights on the Siberian Campaign*. Toronto, Ryerson, n.d.

Berger, Carl, *The Sense of Power*. Toronto, University of Toronto Press, 1970.

Borden, Robert Laird, *His Memoirs*, ed. Henry Borden. 2 vols. New York, Macmillan, 1938.

Bradley, John, *Allied Intervention in Russia*. London, Weidenfeld and Nicolson, 1968.

Brinkley, George A., *The Volunteer Army and Allied Intervention in South Russia, 1917-1921*. Notre Dame, Ind., University of Notre Dame Press, 1966.

Canada, *Report of the Canadian Economic Commission (Siberia)*. Ottawa, King's Printer, n.d. [c. 1920].

——, *Report of the Royal Northwest Mounted Police, 1919*. Ottawa, King's Printer, 1920.

——, Department of External Affairs, *Documents on Canadian External Relations*. Ottawa, Queen's Printer, vol. I, 1967, and vol. II, 1969.

Candler, Edmund, *The Long Road to Baghdad*. 2 vols. London, Cassell, 1919.

Chamberlin, William Henry, *The Russian Revolution, 1917-1921*, vol. 2. New York, Macmillan, 1935.

"Chronicler", *Archangel: The American War with Russia*. Chicago, McClung, 1924.

Churchill, Winston, *The World Crisis: The Aftermath*. London, Butterworth, 1929.

Coates, W. P., and Z. K. Coates, *Armed Intervention in Russia, 1918-1922*. London, Gollancz, 1935.

Collishaw, Raymond, *Air Command*. London, William Kimber, 1973.

Committee of Imperial Defence, Historical Section, *Operations in Persia, 1914-1919*. London, His Majesty's Stationery Office, n.d.

Donnell, Allan, "The Campaign in Northern Russia", in *Canada in the Great World War*, vol. IV. Toronto, United Publishers, 1921.

Donohoe, M. H., *With the Persian Expedition*. London, Arnold, 1919.

Doolen, Richard M., *Michigan's Polar Bears: The American Expedition to North Russia, 1918-1919*. Ann Arbor, Mich., University of Michigan Press, 1965.

Drew, George, *Canada's Fighting Airmen*, Toronto, Maclean, 1930.

Dunsterville, L. C., *The Adventures of Dunsterforce*. London, Arnold, 1920.
——, *Stalky's Reminiscences*. London, Cape, 1928.

Dupuy, R. E., *Perish by the Sword*. Harrisburg, Pa., Military Service Publishing, 1939.

Eayrs, James, *In Defence of Canada*. Toronto, University of Toronto Press, 1964.

Ellis, C. H., *The British Intervention in Transcaspia, 1918-1919*. Berkeley, Cal., University of California Press, 1963.

Fleming, Peter, *The Fate of Admiral Kolchak*. London, Rupert Hart-Davis, 1963.

Footman, David, *Civil War in Russia*. London, Faber and Faber, 1961.

French, F. J. E., *From Whitehall to the Caspian*. London, Odhams, n.d.

Gilbert, Martin, *Winston S. Churchill*, vol. IV. London, Heinemann, 1975.

Glazebrook, George P. de T., *Canada at the Paris Peace Conference*. Oxford, at the University Press, 1942.

Graves, W. S., *America's Siberian Adventure, 1918-1920*. New York, Cape, 1931.

Halliday, E. M., *The Ignorant Armies*. New York, Harper, 1960.

Hodges, Phelps, *Britmis: A Great Adventure of the War*. London, Cape, 1931.

Hodgson, John Ernest, *With Denikin's Armies*. London, Lincoln Williams, 1932.

Horrocks, Brian, *A Full Life*. London, Collins, 1960.

Hunt, Frazier, *This Bewildered World*. New York, Stokes, 1934.

——, *One American*. New York, Simon and Schuster, 1938.

Ironside, Edmund, *Archangel, 1918-1919*. London, Constable, 1953.

——, *High Road to Command*. London, Cooper, 1972.

Jackson, Robert, *At War with the Bolsheviks*. London, Stacey, 1972.

Jones, H. A., *Over the Balkans and South Russia: The History of the 47th Squadron, RAF*. London, Arnold, 1923.

——, *The War in the Air*, vol. VI. Oxford, Clarendon Press, 1937.

Kazemzadeh, Firuz, *The Struggle for Transcaucasia, 1917-1921*. New York, Philosophical Library, 1951.

Kenez, Peter, *Civil War in South Russia, 1918*. Berkeley, Cal., University of California Press, 1971.

Kennan, George F., *Soviet-American Relations, 1917-1920*, vol. I, *Russia Leaves the War*, 1956; and vol. II, *The Decision to Intervene*, 1958. Princeton, N.J., Princeton University Press.

——, *Russia and the West under Lenin and Stalin*. Boston, Little, Brown, 1960.

Kindall, Sylvian G., *American Soldiers in Siberia*. New York, Smith, 1945.

Lenczowski, George, *Russia and the West in Iran, 1918-1948*. Ithaca, N.Y., Cornell University Press, 1949.

Lloyd George, David, *War Memoirs*, vol. VI. London, Nicholson & Watson, 1936.

Luckett, Richard, *The White Generals*. New York, Viking Press, 1971.

MacDonell, Ranald, *And Nothing Long*. London, Constable, 1938.

Manning, Clarence A., *The Siberian Fiasco*. New York, Library Publishers, 1952.

Mayer, Arno J., *Politics and Diplomacy of Peacemaking: Containment and Counter-revolution at Versailles, 1918-1919*. New York, Knopf, 1967.

Maynard, C., *The Murmansk Venture*. London, Hodder and Stoughton, 1927.

Moore, Joel R., Harry M. Mead, and Lewis E. Jahns, *History of the American Expedition Fighting the Bolsheviki*. Detroit, Polar Bear, 1920.

Morley, J. W., *The Japanese Thrust into Siberia, 1918*. New York, Columbia University Press, 1957.

Nicholson, G. W. L., *Canadian Expeditionary Force, 1914-1919*. Ottawa, Queen's Printer, 1964.

——, *The Gunners of Canada*, vol. I. Toronto, McClelland and Stewart, 1967.

Pares, Bernard, *My Russian Memoirs*. London, Cape, 1931.

Prang, Margaret, *N.W. Rowell, Ontario Nationalist*. Toronto, University of Toronto Press, 1975.

Preston, Richard A., *Canada and "Imperial Defence"*. Durham, N.C., Duke University Press, 1967.

Rawlinson, A., *Adventures in the Near East, 1918-1922*. New York, Dodd, Mead, 1924.

Raymond, Ernest, *The Old Tree Blossomed: A Realistic Romance*. London, Cassell, 1928.

——, *The Story of My Days: An Autobiography, 1888-1922*. London, Cassell, 1968.

Rodney, William, *Soldiers of the International*. Toronto, University of Toronto Press, 1968.

——, *Joe Boyle, King of the Klondike*. Toronto, McGraw-Hill Ryerson, 1974.

Roskill, Stephen, *Hankey, Man of Secrets*. London, Collins, 1970.

Silverlight, John, *The Victors' Dilemma*. London, Barrie and Jenkins, 1970.

Singleton-Gates, G. R., *Bolos & Barishynas*. Aldershot, Gale and Polden, 1920.

Soutar, Andrew, *With Ironside in North Russia*. London, Hutchinson, 1940.

Stewart, George, *The White Armies of Russia*. New York, Macmillan, 1933.

Strakhovsky, Leonid, *Intervention at Archangel*. Princeton, N.J., Princeton University Press, 1944.

——, *The Origins of American Intervention in North Russia, 1918*. Princeton, N.J., Princeton University Press, 1937.

Suny, Ronald Grigor, *The Baku Commune, 1917-1918*. Princeton, N.J., Princeton University Press, 1972.

Swettenham, John, *Allied Intervention in Russia, 1918-1919*. Toronto, Ryerson, 1967.

Thompson, John M., *Russia, Bolshevism and the Versailles Peace*. Princeton, N.J., Princeton University Press, 1966.

——, "Allied and American Intervention in Russia, 1918-1921", in *Rewriting Russian History: Soviet Interpretations of Russia's Past*, ed. C.E. Black, New York, Praeger, 1956.

Ullman, R. H., *Anglo-Soviet Relations, 1917-1921*, vol. I, *Intervention and the War*, 1961; vol. II, *Britain and the Russian Civil War*, 1968; and vol. III, *The Anglo-Soviet Accord*, 1972. Princeton, N.J., Princeton University Press.

United States Senate, Sixty-Seventh Congress, Second Session. Committee on Education and Labor. "Deportation of Gregori Semenoff", Part I, April 12, 18, 1922. Washington, D.C., Government Printing Office, 1922.

Unterberger, Betty Miller, *America's Siberia Expedition, 1918-1920*. Durham, N.C., Duke University Press, 1956.

——, ed., *American Intervention in the Russian Civil War*. Lexington, Ky., Heath, 1969.

Vining, L. E., *Held by the Bolsheviks*. London, St. Catherine Press, 1924.

War Office, *The Evacuation of North Russia 1919* (Cmd. 818). London, His Majesty's Stationery Office, 1920.

——, *History of the Great War Based on Official Documents: The Campaign in Mesopotamia, 1914-1918*, vol. IV. London, His Majesty's Stationery Office, 1927.

Ward, John, *With the "Die-Hards" in Siberia*. London, Cassell, 1920.

Warth, Robert D., *The Allies and the Russian Revolution*. Durham, N.C., Duke University Press, 1954.

White, John Albert, *The Siberian Intervention*. Princeton, N.J., Princeton University Press, 1950.

Wilgress, Dana, *Memoirs*. Toronto, Ryerson, 1967.

Williamson, H. N. H., *Farewell to the Don*, ed. John Harris. London, Collins, 1970.

Wilson, Harold A., *The Imperial Policy of Sir Robert Borden*. Gainesville, Fla., University of Florida Press, 1966.

Articles

Abbott, A. W., "Lapland 1918-19. The British Army's Fartherest North". *The Army Quarterly*, London, vol. LXXXIV, no. 2, July 1962.

——, "Campaign by Rail: Murmansk to Lake Onega, 1918-19". *The Army Quarterly*, London, vol. LXXXVIII, no. 2, July 1964.

——, "Combined Operations—500 Miles in the Interior of Russia". *The Army Quarterly*, London, vol. LXXXIX, no. 2, January 1965.

Altham, E., "The Dwina Campaign". *Journal of the Royal United Service Institution*, London, vol. LXVIII, no. 470, May 1923, and *Canadian Defence Quarterly*, vol. I, no. 1, October 1923.

Anon., "Further Adventures of the Armoured Cars: Persia and Baku". *Blackwood's Magazine*, London, vol. CCV, no. MCCXLI, March 1919.

——, "Red or White?". *The Army Quarterly*, London, vol. XXI, no. 1, October 1930.

"An Army Officer", "Archangel Adventure". *American Mercury*, Torrance, Calif., vol. XIX, March 1930.

Balogh, Eva, "Hesitant Encounter: Episodes from Early Russo-Canadian Trade Relations". *Canadian Slavonic Papers*, VIII, University of Toronto Press, 1966.

Beattie, Steuart, "Canadian Intervention in Russia, 1918-1919". Unpublished M.A. thesis, McGill University, Montreal, 1957.

Boyle, J. W., "A Canadian Officer's Adventures among the Bolsheviks". *Canadian Defence Quarterly*, Ottawa, vol. IV, no. 2, January 1927.

Chaulkin, T. B., "Siberia, 1918-19". *R.C.M.P. Quarterly*, Ottawa, vol. 9, no. 2, October 1941.

Chenevix Trench, R., "A Signal Officer in North Russia, 1918-1919". *Journal of the Royal United Service Institution*, London, vol. 104, nos. 613-16, February-November 1959.

Chown, J. D., "Sleighs and Skis". *The Canadian Gunner 1965*, Shilo, Man., 1965.

Clingan, George F., "Siberian Sideshow". *The Legionary*, Ottawa, vol. XXX, no. 1, June 1955.

Collishaw, Raymond, "Memories of a Canadian Airman". *Roundel*, Ottawa, vol. 16, nos. 4, 5, 6 and 7, May-September 1964.

Dodds, R. V., "The Cossack Killers". *Air Classics*, Canoga Park, Calif., vol. 5, no. 2, December 1968.

Dunham, W. E., "The Canadians in Siberia". *Maclean's*, Toronto, vol. XXXII, no. 5, May 1919.

Ellis, C. H., "The Revolt in Transcaspia, 1918-1919". *Central Asian Review*, London, vol. VII, no. 2, 1959.

"Eloper", "Among the Eskimos: with 'Elope' and 'Syren' ", "A Series of Mutinies: Elope Diversions", and "Reds Become White". *Reveille*, Sydney, vol. 6, nos. 10 and 12, and vol. 7, no. 2, June, August, and October 1933.

Evans, Frederic, "Campaigning in Arctic Russia". *Journal of the Royal United Service Institution*, London, vol. LXXXVI, no. 542, May 1941.

Faulstich, Edith M., "The Canadian Expeditionary Force in Siberia, 1918-1919". *The Postal History Journal*, Yonkers, N.Y., January 1968.

Fraser, R. J., "Early Canadian Icebreakers". *Arctic*, Montreal, vol. 16, no. 1, March 1963.

Goldstein, Leo, "More Adventures with 'Elope' in North Russia". *The Queensland Digger*, Brisbane, vols. X and XI, November 1934—March 1935.

Horrall, S. W., "The Force's Siberian Patrol". *R.C.M.P. Quarterly*, Ottawa, vol. 36, no. 5, July 1971.

Hudson, C. E., "Back to the Front". *The Army Quarterly*, London, vol. XXVIII, no. 1, April 1934.

Hundevad, John, "A Saga of the North". *The Legionary*, Ottawa, March 1936—March 1937.

Hyde, Walter C., "With the Canadian Guns in North Russia". *The McGill News*, Montreal, vol. 14, no. 3, June 1933.

Ireland, Erskine, unpublished diary, 1919, in the possession of Mrs. E. Ireland, Toronto.

Ironside, Edmund, "Snow Campaigns". *The Journal of the Royal Artillery*, Woolwich, vol. LI, no. 6, 1925.

——, "The North Russian Campaign". *The Journal of the Royal Artillery*, Woolwich, vol. LIII, no. 3, 1926.

Jamieson, F. C., "The Siberian Expeditionary Force". *Edmonton Military Institute Annual Journal*, Edmonton, 1938.

Jones, Roy, "The Canadians Who Got Home Too Late for the Celebrations". *Weekend Magazine*, Montreal, February 23, 1974.

Kelsey, Tom, "The Road to Bijar: Dunsterforce Sidelights". *Reveille*, Sydney, vol. 6, nos. 8-10, April, May, June 1933.

Kennan, George, "American Troops in Russia". *Atlantic Monthly*, Boston, January 1959.

Kettle, John, "Colonel Sharman and the Canadians Who Fought the Red Army". *Canada Month*, Montreal, March 1966.

Kingsley, H., "The Baku Episode". *Canadian Defence Quarterly*, Ottawa, vol. VII, no. 1, October 1929.

Knollys, D. E., "Military Operations in Transcaspia, 1918-19". *Journal of the Central Asian Society*, London, vol. XIII, part II, 1926.

Latchford, E. W., "With the White Russians", *Reveille*, Sydney, vol. 6, no. 12, to vol. 7, no. 8, August 1933—April 1934.

——, "With the Dunsterforce Irregulars". *Reveille*, Sydney, vol. 5, no. 12, to vol. 6, no. 2, August-October 1932.

Lawson, H., "Soldiering in the Arctic: Some Memories of the Elope Expedition". *Scots Magazine*, Dundee, vol. XXXII, 1940.

MacMosland, E. E., "Our First War with the Russians". *Collier's*, New York, vol. CXXVIII, October 13, 1951.

Martin, J. H., "North Russian Expedition". *Fortnightly Review*, London, vol. CVII, 1920.

Moore, Joel R., "North Russia Expedition". *United States Infantry Journal*, Washington, vol. XXIX, July 1926.

Murray, W. W., "Canadians in Dunsterforce". *Canadian Defence Quarterly*, Ottawa, vols. VIII and IX, January 1931—January 1932.

Nielsen, Robert F., "Combatting the Cold in Siberia". *Maclean's*, Toronto, October 1972.

Norris, David, "Caspian Naval Expedition". *Journal of the Central Asian Society*, London, vol. X, part III, 1923.

O'Brien, R. Barry, "Icebreaking Operations in the White Sea, 1918-19". *Journal of the Royal United Service Institution*, London, vol. LXXVI, no. 503, August 1931, and no. 504, November 1931.

Pantazzi, Ethel Greening, "In the Days of Anarchy", *Maclean's*, Toronto, February 1920.

Paterson, W. L., "The Story of Dunsterforce". *Reveille*, Sydney, vol. 6, no. 3, March 1933.

Prinsep, E. S. MacLeod, "Knox's Mission, Siberia, 1919-1920: The Personal Reminiscences of One of Its Members". *The Army Quarterly*, London, vol. LXXXI, no. 1, October 1960.

Reed, Ernest, and Gordon Smith, "Story of the American Expeditionary Force in North Russia". *Current History*, New York, vol. 32, 1930.

Richardson, Wiles, "America's War in North Russia". *Current History*, New York, vol. 13, February 1921.

Rodney, William, "Siberia in 1919: A Canadian Banker's Impressions", *Queen's Quarterly*, Kingston, Ont., vol. LXXIX, no. 3, Autumn 1972.

——, "Russian Revolutionaries in the Port of Vancouver, 1917". *B.C. Studies*, Vancouver, no. 16, Winter 1972-3.

Sellen, R.W., "The British Intervention in Russia, 1917-1920". *Dalhousie Review*, Halifax, vol. XL, Autumn-Winter 1960-61.

Smith, Gaddis, "Canada and the Siberian Intervention, 1918-1919". *American Historical Review*, New York, vol. LXIV, no. 4, July 1959.

Soward, F. W., "Sir Robert Borden and Canada's External Policy 1911-20". *Canadian Historical Association*, Toronto, 1941.

Steele, D., "Armistice? Never Heard of It", *American Legion Magazine*, New York, October 1938.

——, "Defence of Ust Padenga". *American Legion Weekly*, New York, October 20, 1922.

Strakhovsky, Leonid, "The Canadian Artillery Brigade in North Russia, 1918-1919". *Canadian Historical Review*, Toronto, June 1958.

Sutherland, J. Bruce, "How Canadians Fought the Bolsheviki in North Russia". *Toronto Star Weekly*, July 12, 19, 26, and August 2, 9, 1919.

Tod, J. K., "Operations in Trans-Caspia, 1918-1919". *The Army Quarterly*, London, vol. XVI, no. 2, July 1928.

Wilgress, L. Dana, "From Siberia to Kuibyshev". *International Journal*, Toronto, vol. XXII, no. 3, Summer 1967.

Wood, Henry Fairley, "Adventure in North Russia". *Canadian Army Journal*, Ottawa, vol. XI, October 1957.

———, "The Fartherest North Campaign". *The Legionary*, Ottawa, September 1962.

Source Notes

Introduction

1. Churchill, *The Aftermath*, p. 89.
2. Lloyd George, *War Memoirs*, vol. VI, p. 3157.
3. Borden, *Memoirs*, vol. II, p. 697.
4. Kennan, *Russia and the West*, p. 79.
5. Ullman, vol. II, *Britain and the Russian Civil War*, p. 349.
6. Public Archives of Canada (P.A.C.), Borden Papers, OC-628.

Part One

1. Murray, "Canadians in Dunsterforce", p. 213.
2. *Ibid.*, p. 213.
3. *Ibid.*, pp. 211 and 213.
4. P.A.C., Borden Papers, OC-628.
5. Ullman, vol. I, *Intervention and the War*, p. 305.
6. Dunsterville, *Dunsterforce*, p. 3.
7. *Ibid.*, p. 29.
8. *Ibid.*, p. 57.
9. P.A.C., Borden Papers, Memoir Notes, vol. V, 1917-18.
10. Suny, *Baku Commune*, p. 115.
11. Murray, "Canadians in Dunsterforce", p. 487.
12. Dunsterville, *Dunsterforce*, pp. 236-7.

13. Lieutenant-Colonel A. Rawlinson described his efforts to bring some order to the chaotic ordnance situation in Baku on pp. 71-101 of his *Adventures in the Near East*.

14. "Narrative about Dunsterforce by Captain Harrison", April 16, 1919; P.A.C., RG 9, B-1-36, file O-11-36.

15. Donohoe, *With the Persian Expedition*, p. 215.

16. P.A.C., Warden's diary, MG 30, G 152.

17. Murray, "Canadians in Dunsterforce", p. 491.

18. *Ibid.*, p. 495; an article by Murray about the welfare work of Dunsterforce among the Assyrian Christians is in the Toronto *Evening Telegram* of August 26, 1933.

19. *Ibid.*, p. 496.

20. *Ibid.*, p. 240.

21. P.A.C., Warden's diary, MG 30, G 152.

22. Anon., "Further Adventures of the Armoured Cars", p. 297.

Part Two

1. Chenevix Trench, "A Signal Officer in North Russia", p. 71.

2. Lloyd George, *War Memoirs*, vol. VI, p. 3168.

3. P.A.C., RG 9, III, OMFC 0-10-36, vol. I.

4. Maynard, *Murmansk Venture*, p. 30.

5. Hyde, "With the Canadian Guns in North Russia", pp. 38-9.

6. "Eloper", "Among the Eskimos", p. 40.

7. Donnell, "The Campaign in Northern Russia", p. 222.

8. P.A.C., RG 9, III; PARC Box 203336; H.S. file 37-8-1(a), folder 163.

9. Ironside, *Archangel*, London, Constable, 1953.

10. *Ibid.*, p. 22.

11. Strakhovsky, "Canadian Artillery Brigade", p. 129.

12. Chenevix Trench, "A Signal Officer in North Russia", p. 76.

13. Ironside, *Archangel*, pp. 65-6.

14. P.A.C., RG 9, III; PARC Box 203336; H.S. file 37-8-1(a), folder 163.

15. Letter of March 20, 1968, from Frank Shrive to the Director of History, Canadian Forces Headquarters, Ottawa.

16. Hyde, "With the Canadian Guns in North Russia", p. 40.

17. *Ibid.*, p. 40.

18. Soutar, *With Ironside in North Russia*, p. 104.

19. Moore, Mead, and Jahns, *American Expedition*, p. 59.

20. Letter of March 20, 1968, from Frank Shrive, *op. cit.*

21. War Office, *Evacuation of North Russia*, p. 5.

22. P.A.C., MG 27, II, D-13, vol. 17, and Rowell Papers, file 17.

23. *Ibid.*

24. *N.R.E.F. [North Russian Expeditionary Force], 16th Brigade CFA*, p. 19.
25. Donnell, "The Campaign in Northern Russia", pp. 229-30.
26. Ironside, *Archangel*, pp. 66-7.
27. *N.R.E.F., 16th Brigade CFA*, p. 21.
28. P.A.C., RG 9, III; PARC Box 203336; OMFC 0-10-36, vol. I.
29. *Ibid.*
30. Halliday, *The Ignorant Armies*, p. 134.
31. *Ibid.*, p. 138.
32. *N.R.E.F., 16th Brigade CFA*, p. 40.
33. Steele, "Armistice? Never Heard of It", p. 48.
34. Sharman's diary account of his role in the evacuation is in P.A.C., MG 30, G 78.
35. Sharman's final report is in P.A.C., RG 9, III; H.S. file 37-8-1(a).
36. *N.R.E.F., 16th Brigade CFA*, p. 44.
37. Ironside, *Archangel*, p. 43.
38. Abbott, "Lapland 1918-1919 . . . ", p. 239.
39. *Ibid.*, p. 240.
40. Maynard, *Murmansk Venture*, p. 146.
41. Sutherland, "How Canadians . . . ", July 19, 1919, p. 11.
42. P.A.C., RG 9, III, OMFC file 0-10-36, vol. I.
43. *Ibid.*
44. Soutar, *With Ironside in North Russia*, p. 213.
45. P.A.C., RG 24, vol. 1840, GAQ file 10-28. A note by Kelly about the service of the dog teams is in P.A.C. MG 30-G 76.
46. Hundevad, private letter.
47. P.A.C., MG 30, G 56.
48. War Office, *Evacuation of North Russia*, p. 9.
49. *Ibid.*, p. 9.
50. "Eloper", "A Series of Mutinies: Elope Diversions", p. 29.
51. P.A.C., RG 9, III; OMFC 10-9-91.
52. *Ibid.*
53. *Ibid.*
54. *N.R.E.F., 16th Brigade CFA*, p. 48.
55. Sutherland, "How Canadians fought the Bolsheviki . . . ".
56. *N.R.E.F., 16th Brigade CFA*, p. 29.
57. P.A.C., RG 9, III; PARC Box 203336; H.S. file 37-8-1(a).
58. *Ibid.*
59. *Ibid.*
60. P.A.C., RG 24, vol. 1840, OMFC 10-9-91.
61. P.A.C., RG 9, III, GAQ 10-28, and Borden Papers, OC-518(2).
62. P.A.C., RG 9, III, OMFC 10-9-91.
63. P.A.C., MG 30, G 56, and Leckie Papers: GHQ Syren Diary.
64. P.A.C., Borden Papers, OC-518(2).
65. P.A.C., RG 24, vol. 1840, GAQ 10-28.

66. "Eloper", "Among the Eskimos", p. 31.
67. P.A.C., MG 30, G 56.
68. War Office, *Evacuation of North Russia*, pp. 7-8.

Part Three

1. Kennan, *Russia and the West*, p. 91.
2. P.A.C., Borden Papers, OC-515.
3. Kennan, *Decision to Intervene*, pp. 61-4.
4. Ackerman, *Trailing the Bolsheviki*, p. 42.
5. Kennan, *Decision to Intervene*, p. 294.
6. *Ibid.*, p. 152.
7. Memorandum by Knox, June 7, 1918, P.A.C., Borden Papers, OC-515. Sent by Leopold Amery to Borden June 11, 1918.
8. P.A.C., MG 27, II, D 13, vol. 17, and Rowell Papers, file 71.
9. P.A.C., Borden Papers, OC-518(1).
10. *Ibid.*
11. P.A.C., MG 27, II, DB, vol. 17, and Rowell Papers, 71.
12. P.A.C., Rowell Papers, speech at Port Hope, August 15, 1918.
13. P.A.C., RG 24, vols. 2554-9.
14. P.A.C., Borden Papers, OC-518(1).
15. *Ibid.*
16. P.A.C., RG 9, III, vols. 361-2.
17. P.A.C., Borden Papers, OC-518(1).
18. *Ibid.*
19. Clingan, "Siberian Sideshow", p. 10.
20. P.A.C., RG 9, III, vols. 361-2.
21. *Ibid.*
22. P.A.C., MG 27, II, D 13, vol. 17, and Rowell Papers, vol. 71.
23. P.A.C., RG 24, A, box 366.
24. P.A.C., Borden Papers, OC-518(1).
25. P.A.C., Borden Papers, Memoir Notes, vol. V, 2910, 32-6.
26. *Ibid.*
27. *Ibid.*
28. Quoted in Ullman, vol. II, *Britain and the Russian Civil War*, p. 30.
29. War Office telegram to Knox, repeated to Elmsley, November 23, 1918; P.A.C., RG 9, III, vols. 361-2.
30. P.A.C., Borden Papers, OC-518(1).
31. P.A.C., RG 9, III, vols. 361-2.
32. P.A.C., RG 24, vols. 2554-9.
33. Private diary of T. S. Morrisey.
34. P.A.C., Borden Papers, OC-518(1).
35. *Ibid.*

36. P.A.C., RG 24, A, box 366.
37. P.A.C., RG 9, II, War Diaries, folder 959.
38. P.A.C., Borden Papers, OC-518(2).
39. P.A.C., RG 24, A, box 366.
40. *Ibid.*
41. *Ibid.*
42. C. E. Callwell, *Field-Marshal Sir Henry Wilson*, London, Cassell, 1927, vol. II, pp. 158-9.
43. Ireland, diary, pp. 49-61.
44. Vining, *Held by the Bolsheviks*, p. 38.
45. P.A.C., Warden's Diary, MG 30, G 152.
46. Graves, *America's Siberian Adventure*, p. 83.
47. Ward, *With the "Die-Hards" in Siberia*, pp. 162-3.
48. P.A.C., RG 9, War Diaries, folder 964.
49. *Ibid.*
50. P.A.C., Rowell Papers.
51. P.A.C., RG 24, vols. 2554-9.
52. P.A.C., RG 9, III, vols. 376-8.
53. *Ibid.*
54. P.A.C., RG 24, vols. 2554-9.
55. *Ibid.*
56. P.A.C., Borden Papers, OC-518(2).
57. *Ibid.*
58. *Ibid.*
59. *Ibid.*
60. P.A.C., RG 9, III, War Diaries, folder 964.
61. P.A.C., RG 9, III, War Diaries, folder 959.
62. *Ibid.*
63. *Ibid.*
64. P.A.C., RG 9, III, vols. 376-8.
65. Telegram of April 27, 1919; P.A.C., Borden Papers, OC-518(2).
66. Ireland diary, p. 80.
67. P.A.C., Borden Papers, file OC-518(2).
68. *Ibid.*
69. Horrall, "The Force's Siberian Patrol", p. 5.
70. *Report of the R.N.W.M.P., 1919*, p. 20.
71. Vining, *Held by the Bolsheviks*, p. 69.

Part Four

1. P.A.C., Borden Papers, OC-518(1).
2. Quoted in A. Gorden Dewey, *The Dominions and Diplomacy; The Canadian Contribution*, New York, Longmans Green, 1929, vol. I, p. 293.

3. Borden, *Memoirs*, vol. II, p. 667.

4. P.A.C., Borden Papers, OC-559.

5. P.A.C., Foster Papers, "Canadian Economic Commission to Siberia", Memorandum by Conradin Just, August 29, 1918.

6. P.A.C., Borden Papers, OC-518.

7. P.A.C., MG 27, II, D 7, vol. 44, and Foster Papers, 73.

8. P.A.C., RG 20, vol. 1369, Department of Trade and Commerce, file 21916, vol. I.

9. *Report of the Canadian Economic Commission (Siberia)*.

10. P.A.C., RG 20, vol. 1369, Department of Trade and Commerce, file 22804, vol. I.

11. *Ibid.*

12. Toronto *Daily Mail and Empire*, April 4, 1919. The article also appeared in the Toronto *Globe* of April 3, and the Montreal *Gazette* of April 4, 1919.

13. Wilgress, "From Siberia to Kuibyshev", pp. 366-7.

14. White, *Siberian Intervention*, p. 160.

15. P.A.C., RG 20, vol. 98, Department of Trade and Commerce, file 22804, vol. I.

16. *Ibid.*

17. Wilgress, "From Siberia to Kuibyshev", pp. 368-9.

18. Quoted in Ray Stannard Baker, *Woodrow Wilson and World Settlement*, New York, Doubleday, Page, 1923, vol. II, p. 38.

19. Silverlight, *Victors' Dilemma*, p. 146.

20. *Diary of Lord Bertie of Thame*, ed. Lady Algernon Gordon Lennox, London, Hodder and Stoughton, 1924, vol. II, pp 314-5.

21. Berger, *The Sense of Power*, p. 264.

Appendix "A"

1. Silverlight, *Victors' Dilemma*, p. 271.

2. Letter to Headquarters, R.A.F. Middle East, Cairo, from Lieutenant-Colonel A. C. Maund, June 29, 1919; Public Records Office, London, Air 1, box 1958.

3. Collishaw, *Air Command*, p. 179.

4. Jones, *Over the Balkans*, p. 139.

5. Quoted in Drew, *Canada's Fighting Airmen*, p. 97.

6. Quoted in Jones, *Over the Balkans*, p. 156.

7. Public Records Office, London, Air 1, box 1958.

8. Collishaw, "Memories of a Canadian Airman", *Roundel*, vol. 16, no. 6, p. 22.

9. Collishaw, *Air Command*, p. 200.

10. Quoted in Dodds, "The Cossack Killers", p. 46.

11. Collishaw, *Air Command*, pp. 189-91.

12. Churchill, *The Aftermath*, pp. 256.
13. Quoted in Dodds, "The Cossack Killers", p. 46.
14. Collishaw, "Memories of a Canadian Airman", *Roundel*, vol. 16, no. 6, p. 23.
15. Quoted in Dodds, "The Cossack Killers", p. 48.
16. Ullman, vol. III, *The Anglo-Soviet Accord*, pp. 66-8.
17. Collishaw, *Air Command*, pp. 216-7.

Index